Lecture Notes in Computer Science 14626

The series Lecture Notes in Computer Science (LNCS), including its subseries Lecture Notes in Artificial Intelligence (LNAI) and Lecture Notes in Bioinformatics (LNBI), has established itself as a medium for the publication of new developments in computer science and information technology research, teaching, and education.

LNCS enjoys close cooperation with the computer science R & D community, the series counts many renowned academics among its volume editors and paper authors, and collaborates with prestigious societies. Its mission is to serve this international community by providing an invaluable service, mainly focused on the publication of conference and workshop proceedings and postproceedings. LNCS commenced publication in 1973.

Patrick Diehl · Joseph Schuchart ·
Pedro Valero-Lara · George Bosilca

Editors

Asynchronous Many-Task Systems and Applications

Second International Workshop, WAMTA 2024
Knoxville, TN, USA, February 14–16, 2024
Proceedings

 Springer

Editors
Patrick Diehl ⓘ
Louisiana State University
Baton Rouge, LA, USA

Joseph Schuchart
University of Tennessee
Knoxville, TN, USA

Pedro Valero-Lara
Oak Ridge National Laboratory
Oak Ridge, TN, USA

George Bosilca
NVIDIA Corporation
Santa Clara, CA, USA

ISSN 0302-9743   ISSN 1611-3349 (electronic)
Lecture Notes in Computer Science
ISBN 978-3-031-61762-1   ISBN 978-3-031-61763-8 (eBook)
https://doi.org/10.1007/978-3-031-61763-8

Preface

This volume contains sixteen papers presented at WAMTA 2024, the second edition of the Workshop on Asynchronous Many-Task Systems and Applications, hosted by the Innovative Computing Laboratory at the University of Tennessee, Knoxville campus in Knoxville, TN, USA, from February 14–16, 2024. The workshop was a hybrid event, with the options for authors and attendees to present, attend, and interact both in-person and online.

WAMTA was created in response to the ever-growing scale of high performance computing, and in recognition of the increasing strain this growth puts on software systems at all levels. Core challenges in this context include load-balancing, fast data transfers, and efficient resource utilization. Task-based models and runtime systems have shown that it is possible to address these challenges by providing mechanisms such as oversubscription, task/data locality, shared memory, and data-dependence-driven execution.

The objective of WAMTA is to provide a forum for exploring the advantages and challenges of task-based programming on modern and future HPC systems. It allows developers, users, and proponents of these models and systems to share experiences, discuss how they meet the challenges posed by Exascale system architectures, and explore opportunities for increased performance, robustness, productivity, and full-system utilization.

More than twenty short and full papers were submitted to WAMTA 2024, and the 26 members of the Program Committee (PC) assessed the quality, relevance, and presentation of these contributions. Each paper received at least two reviews by PC members. If the two reviews did not agree, a third reviewer was consulted. In the end, a total of sixteen papers were accepted. For each paper, one author in the author list was chosen to present the work. The result is sixteen papers of very high quality.

In addition to the presentations of these technical papers, the two and a half day workshop program included three keynote talks, an industrial talk, and 15 technical talks, as well as a poster session.

We would like to thank all authors, speakers, chairs, organizers, PC members and attendees for their contributions towards the success of WAMTA 2024.

Furthermore, we would like to thank our sponsors, the Tactical Computing Lab, the Innovative Computing Laboratory at the University of Tennessee, Knoxville, and Louisiana State University, which all helped make WAMTA 2024 a success.

April 2024

Patrick Diehl
Joseph Schuchart
Pedro Valero-Lara
George Bosilca

Organization

Program Committee Chairs

Patrick Diehl   Louisiana State University, USA
Joseph Schuchart   University of Tennessee, Knoxville, USA
Pedro Valero-Lara   Oak Ridge National Laboratory, USA
George Bosilca   NVIDIA, USA

Steering Committee

Alex Aiken   Stanford, USA
Bryce Adelstein Lelbach   NVIDIA, USA
Brad Chamberlain   HPE and University of Washington, USA
Laxmikant V. Kale   University of Illinois at Urbana-Champaign, USA
Erwin Laure   Max Planck Computing & Data Facility, Germany

Program Committee

Brad Richardson   Sourcery Institute, USA
Kevin Huck   University of Oregon, USA
Dirk Pflüger   University of Stuttgart, Germany
Metin H. Aktulga   Michigan State University, USA
Huda Ibeid   Intel, USA
Dirk Pleiter   KTH Royal Institute of Technology, Sweden
Didem Unat   Koç University, Turkey
Keita Teranishi   Sandia National Laboratories, USA
Gregor Daiß   University of Stuttgart, Germany
Najoude Nader   Louisiana State University, USA
Weile Wei   Google, USA
Jeff Hammond   NVIDIA, Finland
Hartmut Kaiser   Louisiana State University, USA
J. Ram Ramanujam   Louisiana State University, USA
Steven R. Brandt   Louisiana State University, USA
Narasinga Rao Miniskar   Oak Ridge National Laboratory, USA
Markus Rampp   Max Planck Computing and Data Facility,
              Germany

Sumathi Lakshmiranganatha	Los Alamos National Laboratory, USA
Nikunj Gupta	Amazon, USA
Jonas Posner	University of Kassel, Germany

Sponsors

Innovative Computing Laboratory, University of Tennessee, Knoxville
LSU Center for Computation & Technology
Tactical Computing Lab

Contents

Speaking Pygion: Experiences Writing an Exascale Single Particle Imaging Code

Seema Mirchandaney[1(✉)], Alex Aiken[1,2], and Elliott Slaughter[1]

[1] SLAC National Accelerator Laboratory, Menlo Park, USA
seema@slac.stanford.edu
[2] Stanford University, Stanford, USA

Abstract. The goal of the SpiniFEL project was to write, from scratch, a single particle imaging code for exascale supercomputers. The original vision was to have two versions of the code, one in MPI and one in Pygion, a Python-based interface to the Legion task-based runtime. We describe the motivation for the project, some of the programming challenges we encountered along the way, what worked and what didn't, and why only the Pygion code eventually succeeded in running at scale.

Keywords: task-based programming · exascale computing · single particle imaging

1 Introduction

The ExaFEL project had as its goal to develop scalable and rapid approaches to the analysis of images produced by LCLS-II, the second generation free electron laser at the SLAC National Accelerator Laboratory. One component of the project was to develop a single particle imaging (SPI) code that could make use of the DOE's exascale supercomputers to perform reconstruction of 3D conformations of molecules from the 2D diffraction patterns generated by SPI experiments. By exploiting large numbers of GPU's, reconstructions that would normally take hours or days could be computed in minutes, allowing scientists to adjust their experiments based on near real-time feedback from shots of the laser.

From the start of the development of SpiniFEL, the plan was to implement a version targeting the Legion task-based runtime [2], but to mitigate risk it was decided that an equivalent MPI version should also be written since most of the team had experience with MPI, no experience with Legion, and Legion had not been previously demonstrated on any similar application. The decision to develop two versions led, in retrospect, to some predictable difficulties for the project. The MPI code received more attention and development effort, and as a result the Legion version was perpetually behind: features would first appear in the MPI code and only later be ported to Legion. Second, because developing two completely independent implementations was impractical, the two versions shared as much code as possible. Because features were supported

© The Author(s), under exclusive license to Springer Nature Switzerland AG 2024
P. Diehl et al. (Eds.): WAMTA 2024, LNCS 14626, pp. 1–8, 2024.
https://doi.org/10.1007/978-3-031-61763-8_1

in MPI first, the realization of features tended to be idiomatic for MPI, making it more difficult than necessary to take advantage of Legion's task-based features.

Another issue, however, proved to be the most important: SpiniFEL would be developed in Python, and when the project started Legion support for Python was minimal. At the time (2017), Legion had two well-supported programming interfaces, the API for Legion's C++ runtime system [2], and Regent, a programming language for the Legion programming model [10]. Regent had a number of advantages over programming directly to the C++ API, including compiler support for statically checking that the programming model is used correctly and a number of important optimizations. However, like Legion's C++ API, Regent's support for inter-operation with Python was primitive. Motivated by SpiniFEL, we developed Pygion, a native Python interface to Legion based on Regent [9].

Initially development of SpiniFEL focused on a batch computation that took a set of 2D diffraction patterns and reconstructed a single conformation. Once that essential functionality was implemented, the focus shifted to adding two significant extensions. The first was real-time processing of diffraction images using Psana2 [6], an infrastructure for managing images arriving directly from the X-ray laser, and the second was reconstructing multiple conformations from a single experiment—a single LCLS-II experiment consists of images of many different molecules, and so it is natural to identify multiple conformations.

Implementing these extensions was a turning point in the project: It was more difficult and time-consuming to modify the MPI code to support these features than it was to modify the Pygion version, in part because the extensions were less friendly to an SPMD-style program, but mainly because Pygion's flexibility, automatic discovery of dependencies and support for data partitioning proved to be significantly more productive to use when restructuring existing code. Eventually the Pygion version scaled and performed well with these additional features, while neither feature was fully implemented in MPI at the end of the project.

In this paper we give additional details of the development of SpiniFEL, focusing on the Pygion/Legion features used to support computing multiple conformations. After discussing related work in Sect. 2, we briefly describe the initial SPI parallel algorithm for single conformations and its extension to multiple conformations in Sect. 3. We then elaborate on the features of Pygion that simplified the restructuring of the code to go from computing single to computing multiple conformations in Sect. 4. Results from and the scaling performance of the Pygion version of SpiniFEL are in Sect. 5.

2   Related Work

The productivity benefits described in this paper were sufficiently significant that, while the details might be quite different, we would not be surprised if other task-based systems could provide similar benefits when developing a code in both MPI and the task-based framework. We briefly discuss five systems, two where we expect that the experience could be similar and three where we speculate that the experience could be very different.

StarPU [1] provides asynchronous tasking, automatic discovery of dependencies, and data partitioning built into the task programming model, three features that we highlight as having been particularly important in this work. StarPU has also recently added a Python interface. We note that the Pygion interface is at a somewhat higher level than StarPU's, as the Pygion implementation (dynamically) performs many of the optimizations done by the Regent (statically compiled) language for Legion, but we expect that any reasonable Python interface would be sufficient to realize an application such as SpiniFEL in StarPU.

PaRSEC [4] is another tasking system with asynchronous tasks, automatic discovery of dependencies, and a data partitioning subsystem, and so is another system that we would expect to experience similar benefits in relationship to MPI for a project of the scale of SpiniFEL. To the best of our knowledge, PaRSEC does not currently have a Python interface.

DASK is a native Python-based tasking system, built from the start to seamlessly integrate distributed tasking into Python and its ecosystem. DASK's main drawback is performance; the runtime system is centralized and also implemented in Python. The resulting high overheads per task [11] and inefficiencies in distributing work on a very large cluster would likely make implementing SpiniFEL efficiently in DASK challenging.

Charm++ [7] is an actor-based programming model; instead of having stateless tasks Charm++ relies on stateful actors called *chares* as its core building block. Chares execute methods in response to messages sent from other chares. In general the order of execution of the methods of a chare is non-deterministic which, combined with chares' internal updateable state, means that Charm++ programs are potentially non-deterministic in their visible behavior. The task-based systems, on the other hand, provide parallel execution with deterministic sequential semantics. Thus, it is not clear what lessons from the experience described in this paper would apply to Charm++. At the least, in our view the difficulty of debugging significant changes to explicitly parallel MPI code compared to debugging the more straightforward deterministic semantics of Pygion programs contributed to Pygion's greater productivity in writing SpiniFEL. Charm++ has extensive Python support through its charm4py library.

Ray, like DASK, is a native Python tasking library. Ray provides both pure tasks and actors [8]. Ray's overheads are similar to DASK, and so we would expect similar issues in supporting fine-grain tasks, and exploiting Ray's actors would likely be comparable to the experience of using Charm++.

3   SpiniFEL

The parallel algorithm for computing a single conformation is described in [3,5] and was implemented in both MPI and Pygion. A number of phases are performed iteratively until either convergence or the maximum number of iterations is reached. Throughout the computation a current estimate of the 3D electron density is maintained and improved by the algorithm. The phases are:

- *Slicing* computes 2D images (slices) through the current electron density estimate.
- *Orientation matching* compares the actual 2D diffraction patterns from an SPI experiment to the slices, which is used to compute the orientation of the images using a closest Euclidean distance metric.
- *Merging* computes a non-uniform fast Fourier transform (NUFFT) of the autocorrelation of the electron density. This step produces a new estimate of the electron density.
- *Phasing* converts the 3D diffraction volume into a molecular structure, which is used to refine the electron density computed in the merging phase.

The parallel algorithm that supports multiple conformations reuses the components of the single conformation algorithm but rearranges them in ways that result in a very different overall structure. There is an additional level of parallelism, as each of the phases is now carried out for each of several conformations, and there are two additional phases, one to cluster the diffraction patterns by conformation and one to detect when a conformation has converged. The changes also result in new communication patterns between and within some of the phases. Specifically:

- *Slicing* is done per conformation.
- *Orientation matching* compares each of the 2D diffraction patterns from SPI to the model slices for every conformation and the closest Euclidean distance is computed.
- *Conformation* assigns each 2D diffraction pattern to a conformation based on the minimum Euclidean distance obtained across all conformations.
- *Merging* and *Phasing* compute and refine a new electron density estimate for each conformation.
- If enabled, *Convergence* determines whether each conformation has converged and its resolution. The results are used to determine which conformations should continue to the next iteration—converged conformations are removed from the computation.

4 Pygion Implementation

Once the single conformation algorithm was implemented in MPI and Pygion the project began working towards the multiple conformation algorithm. The multiple conformation algorithm described in Sect. 3 is the end result of an iterative process in which many variations were explored, each of which required time to code and test. This iterative process progressed much more quickly with the Pygion version than with the MPI version for two primary reasons.

First, many changes to the code involved adding or removing *tasks*, which are just distinguished functions that can be executed asynchronously. In Pygion, calling a new task simply meant writing that task and adding it in the appropriate place in the sequential execution order. The Legion runtime that underlies Pygion performs a dependence analysis that automatically preserves sequential execution semantics while extracting parallelism and also inserts all needed communication and synchronization between tasks. Thus adding (or removing) a task is a *local* program change in Pygion—even though a task addition (or removal) can have global effects on the dependence graph of tasks, the dependency information is computed by Pygion and is not the responsibility of the programmer. In the MPI version, however, adding (or removing) a task involves more than the task call itself. Because the programmer is responsible for synchronization and communication in MPI, the programmer must manually determine how the synchronization and communication by other parts of the code must be modified to ensure correctness in light of the insertion or removal of a task, which in general can require *global* changes to the program.

Second, code changes often required creating new data structures, partitioning data in new ways, or both. Pygion has first-class support for *regions* (data collections) and for partitioning and distributing regions across the machine. In SpiniFEL a region of all the 2D diffraction patterns is partitioned into n subregions, where n is the number of *ranks* (the number of GPUs used in the computation). Pygion/Legion also allows multiple different partitions of the same region to exist and be used simultaneously. Another partitioning of the 2D diffraction patterns, for example, keeps track of which conformation each image belongs to. The conformation phase may update an image's assigned conformation each iteration; any updates are tracked automatically by Legion and when a merging task needs the images associated with a particular conformation the correct set of images is delivered to the task by the runtime system, reflecting all of the changes up to that point in the computation.

Pygion/Legion's built-in support for regions and partitioning means that adding a new kind of data collection or a new partitioning of an existing collection is also always a local change to the program, even though the communication pattern of the program may change globally through the new dependencies implied by changing or adding partitions. As with adding tasks, adding new regions or partitions in the MPI version requires that explicit synchronization and communication be added for each of those new dependencies, as it is the programmer's job, not MPI's, to communicate changes to data structures.

Note that partitioning in Legion is a dynamic operation: partitions are computed at runtime, and regions can be re-partitioned on the fly. In SpiniFEL dynamically creating new regions and partitions was important for integrating with Psana2, because Psana2 delivers the diffraction images periodically as the images arrive from the laser's data-gathering detectors. We use the ability to define regions and partitions dynamically to add new 2D diffraction patterns during each iteration—specifically a new region is created by taking the union of a region of the new images with the existing image region.

Figure 1 gives an excerpt from the merging phase of SpiniFEL. Shown are two *index launches*, loops that launch sets of tasks distinguished by an index i. The `solve_simple_adjoint` tasks each take three regions (among others that are elided): `slices_p[i]`, `ugrid`, and `uvect`; for each `solve_simple_adjoint` task there is a corresponding `solve_simple_linear` task in the second index

```
...
for  i  in  IndexLaunch(N_procs):
    solve_simple_adjoint(..., slices_p[i],ugrid,uvect,...)
for  i  in  IndexLaunch(N_procs):
    solve_simple_linear(..., slices_p[i],ugrid,uvect,...)
...
```

Fig. 1. An excerpt from SpiniFEL's merging phase.

launch that takes the same arguments. Not shown are how the tasks use these regions: the `solve_simple_adjoint` tasks read their set of slices and perform reductions into the `ugrid` and `uvect` regions, while the `solve_simple_linear` tasks only read form these regions. Note that there is no explicit parallelism or communication—Legion automatically discovers which tasks can run in parallel and where communication is needed. Adding, removing, or modifying a task to take different arguments are always local changes, regardless of the (potentially large) effect on the program's communication pattern.

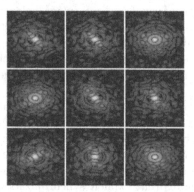
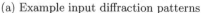
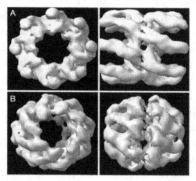

(a) Example input diffraction patterns   (b) Open and closed conformations

Fig. 2. Input and output of SpiniFEL

5   Results

We obtained results for 4096 ranks (GPUs) on the Frontier supercomputer at Oak Ridge National Laboratory. This experiment computed two conformations of Mm-cpn (the molecule methanococcus maripaludis chaperonin): 3IYF (open) and 3J03 (closed). Figure 2(a) shows examples of some of the input diffraction patterns, while Fig. 2(b) shows the output conformations; the images labeled (A) are two views of the 3D electron density structure in the open state, while (B) shows the closed state after 20 iterations.

Weak scaling results for 256 images per rank and 20 iterations on Frontier are shown in Fig. 3. SpiniFEL achieves almost perfect weak scaling to 2000 ranks, after which the communication between some of the phases begins to be exposed, resulting in about 70% parallel efficiency at 4000 ranks.

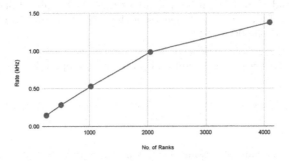

Fig. 3. Weak scaling results

We also tested convergence for both conformations. The table below gives the results for 16,384 images for 30 iterations. In the table gen refers to the number of generations (iterations) until convergence, resolution is in angstroms, and corr. coeff. is the final correlation coefficient of the electron density map.

ranks	images/rank	3iyf			3j03		
		gen	resolution	corr. coeff.	gen	resolution	corr. coeff.
128	128	18	16.4	0.837	13	13.3	0.835
256	64	14	18.09	0.806	17	13.0	0.834

We cannot compare the Pygion code with MPI on multiple conformations because there is no MPI implementation. The single conformation MPI code is 50% slower than the corresponding Pygion code, primarily because Pygion handles the merging phase better [5]. In principle the MPI version could reproduce the performance of Pygion, but as discussed it would require more effort due to the need to make all communication and synchronization explicit.

6   Conclusion

Using Pygion we implemented SpiniFEL, a scalable, parallel code to reconstruct multiple molecular conformations from single particle imaging experiments. When the code reached sufficient complexity, the time and effort to add new features to a task-based code turned out to be much less than modifying an MPI code, primarily because the implicit parallelism of the task-based system made most changes local (only a small part of the program needed to be changed) in contrast to the MPI version, where often considerable effort was needed to express changes in the communication/dependency structure with numerous, non-local additions of MPI communications and synchronization.

Acknowledgments. This research was supported by the Exascale Computing Project (17- SC-20-SC), a collaborative effort of the U.S. Department of Energy Office of Science and the National Nuclear Security Administration. This research used resources of the Oak Ridge Leadership Computing Facility at the Oak Ridge National Laboratory, which is supported by the Office of Science of the U.S. Department of Energy under Contract No. DE-AC05-00OR22725.

Disclosure of Interests. The authors have no competing interests for this publication.

References

1. Augonnet, C., Thibault, S., Namyst, R., Wacrenier, P.A.: STARPU: a unified platform for task scheduling on heterogeneous multicore architectures. Concurr. Comput. Pract. Exp. **23**, 187–198 (2011)
2. Bauer, M., Treichler, S., Slaughter, E., Aiken, A.: Legion: expressing locality and independence with logical regions. In: High Performance Computing, Networking, Storage and Analysis (SC) (2012)
3. Blaschke, J., et al.: MTIP single particle imaging (SpiniFEL) (2021). https://www.osti.gov//servlets/purl/1834376
4. Bosilca, G., Bouteiller, A., Danalis, A., Faverge, M., Hérault, T., Dongarra, J.J.: PaRSEC: exploiting heterogeneity to enhance scalability. Comput. Sci. Eng. **15**(6), 36–45 (2013)
5. Chang, H.Y., Slaughter, E., Mirchandaney, S., Donatelli, J., Yoon, C.H.: Scaling and acceleration of three-dimensional structure determination for single-particle imaging experiments with SpiniFEL. arXiv preprint arXiv:2109.05339 (2021)
6. Damiani, D., et al.: Linac coherent light source data analysis using Psana. J. Appl. Crystallogr. **49**(2), 672–679 (2016)
7. Kalé, L.V., Krishnan, S.: CHARM++: a portable concurrent object oriented system based on C++. In: OOPSLA, pp. 91–108 (1993)
8. Moritz, P., et al.: Ray: a distributed framework for emerging AI applications. In: 13th USENIX Symposium on Operating Systems Design and Implementation (OSDI 2018), pp. 561–577 (2018)
9. Slaughter, E., Aiken, A.: Pygion: flexible, scalable task-based parallelism with Python. In: Proceedings of the Parallel Applications Workshop, Alternatives To MPI, pp. 58–72. IEEE (2019)
10. Slaughter, E., Lee, W., Treichler, S., Bauer, M., Aiken, A.: Regent: a high-productivity programming language for HPC with logical regions. In: High Performance Computing, Networking, Storage and Analysis (SC) (2015)
11. Slaughter, E., et al.: Task bench: a parameterized benchmark for evaluating parallel runtime performance. In: Supercomputing (SC), pp. 1–15. IEEE (2020)

Futures for Dynamic Dependencies – Parallelizing the $\mathcal{H}$-LU Factorization

Rüdiger Nather[✉] and Claudia Fohry

Department of Electrical Engineering and Computer Science, University of Kassel, Kassel, Hessen, Germany
{r.nather,fohry}@uni-kassel.com

Abstract. The LU factorization of hierarchical matrices ($\mathcal{H}$-matrices) is a challenging problem for efficient parallelization, due to complex dependency patterns. Previous research suggested the usage of tasks, but existing task-based algorithms still need a preprocessing step to prepare information about the matrix structure. In consequence, this structure must not change afterwards.

This paper proposes a novel algorithm that eliminates the need for preprocessing. Its core idea is usage of the future construct. A particularly expressive type of future is needed that is not yet supported by current AMT runtime systems. This paper defines the type and shows that it promotes a clear and concise way to program parallel $\mathcal{H}$-LU factorization.

Keywords: Futures · Task-Parallel Programming · Dynamic Task-level Dependencies · Hierarchical Linear Algebra · LU Factorization

1   Introduction

Hierarchical matrices ($\mathcal{H}$-matrices) are a well-known numerical tool to store matrices in a compressed form [12]. As depicted in Fig. 1A, these matrices are recursively subdivided into blocks. The partitioning ends at different nesting levels for different blocks, for instance when the contents of a particular block can be approximated by a pair of matrices. Only leaf blocks of the partitioning have a contiguous memory layout; whereas the sub-blocks of higher-level blocks are stored in different locations and are addressed by pointers.

Common linear algebra operations on matrices have been adapted to directly work with $\mathcal{H}$-matrices [12], but their efficient parallelization is challenging. Particularly hard to parallelize is the $\mathcal{H}$-LU factorization, in which data dependencies extend across matrix regions and recursion levels.

Kriemann [16] was the first to propose a task-based approach. His algorithm performs a preprocessing step to construct a dag of tasks and their dependencies. Then, each task is started when its dependencies are met. Building on this work,

P. Diehl et al. (Eds.): WAMTA 2024, LNCS 14626, pp. 9–21, 2024.
https://doi.org/10.1007/978-3-031-61763-8_2

Sáez et al. [2,8] later introduced recursive task-based algorithms that dynamically spawn nested tasks. They implemented the algorithms on the OpenMP-like OmpSs-2 [10] platform, and specify dependencies with in/out parameter qualifiers. Thereby they had to overcome two problems: 1) A single task may depend on an unknown number of fine-grained blocks, which are stored non-consecutively in memory, and 2) dependencies between non-sibling tasks can not be expressed with in/out qualifiers. The authors solved the first problem with a preprocessing step, in which they collect representatives of all leaf blocks into a suitably arranged skeleton array. Their solution to the second problem uses weak dependencies, which exist in OmpSs-2, but not in OpenMP.

In consequence, both the algorithms by Kriemann and Sáez et al. involve a preprocessing step. This step generates overhead and precludes later changes of the matrix structure. However, such changes are required by some numerical techniques such as recompression [11].

Therefore, this paper proposes a novel task-based $\mathcal{H}$-LU factorization algorithm. It does not require preprocessing, and so the matrix structure is allowed to change during the computation. The core idea of the algorithm is usage of the future construct to express task dependencies. Futures are placeholders for values to be computed asynchronously. The concept of futures is well known, and systems such as HPX [15] and Cilk-F [17] provide futures. However, our algorithm needs a particularly powerful type of future, which is not yet supported by current AMT runtime systems. For instance, it must be able to express futures of futures. Overall, we make the following contributions:

- We define the new future type.
- We present a novel $\mathcal{H}$-LU factorization algorithm that uses this future type.
- We discuss the advantages of futures over in/out qualifiers within the algorithm.

The rest of the paper is structured as follows. In Sect. 2, we provide background on $\mathcal{H}$-LU factorization, and describe the existing algorithms. Section 3 outlines our new future-based algorithm, with focus on the usage of the future construct. Afterwards, in Sect. 4, we define the required future type. Then, Sect. 5 presents the resulting $\mathcal{H}$-LU factorization algorithm and discusses its advantages over the previous ones. The paper finishes with related work and conclusions, in Sects. 6 and 7, respectively.

2 Background

Hierarchical Matrices ($\mathcal{H}$-matrices) are square matrices from $\mathbb{R}^{n \times n}$ that are recursively subdivided into blocks. The partitioning ends at different nesting levels for different blocks. For simplicity of presentation, we assume that each block is either not partitioned, or partitioned into $m \times m$ equal-sized sub-blocks, for some constant m (thereby implicitly imposing a restriction on n). An example of an $\mathcal{H}$-matrix with $m = 3$ is given in Fig. 1A.

We use two different notations for blocks: In colon-style notation, coordinates denote the rows and columns of the matrix to which the block extends. For instance, in Fig. 1A, block $A[0\!:\!8, 18\!:\!26]$ denotes the upper-right 9×9-block. In comma-style notation, coordinates refer to an indexing of sub-blocks inside their parent block. For instance, block $A[0, 2]$ inside A is block $A[0\!:\!8, 18\!:\!26]$.

The structure of an $\mathcal{H}$-matrix can be represented by a tree, where the root corresponds to the matrix itself and each other node corresponds to a block of the matrix. Figure 1B depicts part of the tree for the example in Fig. 1A. As can be seen, internal tree nodes correspond to blocks with an internal partitioning, and tree leaves correspond to elementary blocks. These can be dense matrices (as in the figure), or low-rank approximations (not shown). A low-rank approximation is a pair of matrices, which can change their size during the computation [8, 12].

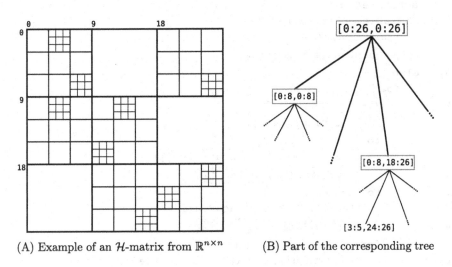

(A) Example of an $\mathcal{H}$-matrix from $\mathbb{R}^{n \times n}$ (B) Part of the corresponding tree

Fig. 1. (A) Example of an $\mathcal{H}$-matrix from $\mathbb{R}^{n \times n}$ (B) Part of the corresponding tree

Operations on leaf nodes are performed sequentially. Their internal functioning is not relevant for this paper, and neither is the difference between the two types of leaves. In our later presentations of $\mathcal{H}$-matrix algorithms, we will assume a one-to-one correspondence between tasks and tree nodes. In contrast, efficient implementations may incorporate granularity control by running small subcomputations sequentially within their parent task to avoid tasking overhead [8]. We ignore this optimization for simplicity, but all algorithms discussed in this paper could be easily adjusted.

An important computational problem on $\mathcal{H}$-matrices is the $\mathcal{H}$-LU factorization. Most of the existing parallel algorithms are based on Algorithm 1 (see listing), which was adapted from Kriemann [16].

The algorithm is recursive and starts with the original $\mathcal{H}$-matrix from $\mathbb{R}^{n \times n}$. At each recursion level, function h_factorize takes as input a block a from this matrix. If a is elementary, some sequential computation is performed (marked in grey). Otherwise, lines 6 to 17 are executed, whose functionality is visualized in Fig. 2. Ignoring the tasking constructs for a moment, the algorithm loops through indices $k = 0 \ldots m - 1$. For each k, it first updates block a[k,k] on the diagonal of a by recursively calling h_factorize (marked in orange). Then it uses the updated a[k,k] to update all blocks to the right and below a[k,k] by calling solve_x or solve_y (marked in blue). Finally, it uses the results to update all blocks in the trailing lower-right part of a by calling update (marked in green). To ease presentation, we write solve when the difference between solve_x and solve_y does not matter.

Algorithm 1: parallel, recursive $\mathcal{H}$-LU factorization (adapted from [16])

```
1  h_factorize(a):
2      if (isElementary(a))
3          #task inout(a)
4          sequential_factorize(a)
5      else
6          for (k=0, ...,m-1)
7              #task inout(a[k,k])
8              h_factorize(a[k,k])
9              for (j=k+1, ...,m-1)
10                 #task in(a[k,k]) inout(a[k,j])
11                 solve_x(a[k,j], a[k,k])
12             for (i=k+1, ...,m-1)
13                 #task in(a[k,k]) inout(a[i,k])
14                 solve_y(a[i,k], a[k,k])
15             for (i,j = k+1, ...,m-1)
16                 #task in(a[i,k], a[k,j]) inout(a[i,j])
17                 update(a[i,j], a[i,k], a[k,j])
18     #taskwait
```

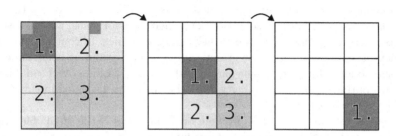

Fig. 2. Data dependencies on a fixed recursion level in Algorithm 1. (Color figure online)

The algorithm has obvious potential for parallelization: All `solve` calls can be run in parallel, as can all `update` calls. Additionally, each `update` call on block `a[i,j]` can be executed after the `solve` calls in row i and column j have finished. Regarding the outermost loop, the `h_factorize` call on `a[k+1,k+1]` can be run when the previous call of `update` on `a[k+1,k+1]` has finished.

Algorithm 1 expresses this parallelism with the tasking constructs, using one task for each function call. The tasks are spawned in program order, which is often called Sequential Task Flow (STF). To express the above data dependencies, we have added `in`/`out` qualifiers to all spawns. These qualifiers are available in OpenMP and OmpSs-2. They specify the set of memory locations that a task reads (`in`), writes (`out`), or reads and writes (`inout`). On this basis, the runtime system detects and enforces task dependencies. For instance, it ensures that `solve` is run after `h_factorize`, because `h_factorize` writes to block `a[k,k]`, and `solve` reads from it. The `taskwait` construct in line 18 ensures that `h_factorize` has updated all of a before the function returns, in accordance with the `out` qualifier for `h_factorize` in line 7.

Still, Algorithm 1 does not exploit the full parallelization potential of the $\mathcal{H}$-LU factorization. Additional potential comes from the recursive structure of the algorithm. It is only partly visible in the listing, because functions `solve` and `update` have been omitted for brevity. These functions resemble `h_factorize`, likewise performing recursive calls to `solve` and `update` on smaller matrix blocks. Details of the recursions are not important, but here are some general properties:

– An operation on a block depends only on data in the block itself and in at most two equal-sized other blocks from the same row(s) and/or column(s) of the matrix. In particular, `h_factorize` only depends on the block itself, `solve` depends on one other block, and `update` on two.
– When `solve` updates one block using another, one and/or both of the blocks may be partitioned inside. If both are partitioned, recursive function calls are performed on the sub-blocks. Otherwise, an elementary operation is performed, even if only one of the blocks is elementary.
– Thus, it may happen that an operation has been performed on sub-blocks, but its result is needed at the granularity of the full block. This is no problem: When all subcomputations have finished, the larger block immediately holds the correct data, as well.

Unfolding the recursion in Algorithm 1 reveals parallelism potential that is not exploited by Algorithm 1. Let us consider Fig. 2. Therein Algorithm 1 suspends the `solve` call on `a[0,2]` until `h_factorize` on `a[0,0]` has finished, even though `solve` just spawns operations on sub-blocks, for which it does not need access to the `a[0,0]` data. From a correctness point of view, the dark blue `solve` call could be started as soon as the dark orange `h_factorize` call has finished, but the `#taskwait` on the parent task prohibits that.

Previous research came up with two main ideas to exploit the recursive parallelism potential. First, Kriemann [16] proposed a preprocessing step, in which the recursion of Algorithm 1 is unrolled and a directed acyclic graph (dag) of tasks and their dependencies is built. Only elementary tasks are included in the dag. For an example, consider the `solve` task on `a[0,1]` in Fig. 2, assuming that `a[0,0]` is partitioned and `a[0,1]` is not. Then the dag includes dependencies from multiple subcomputations on `a[0,0]` (such as the dark orange one) to `a[0,1]`, but not from `a[0,0]` itself. After the preprocessing step, the tasks are scheduled so as to meet the dag dependencies.

Later, Sáez et al. [8] improved the algorithm by directly exploiting the recursive parallelism potential of Algorithm 1, without unrolling it. Their main idea is the usage of `in/out` qualifiers to specify the same fine-grained dependencies as in the dag of [16]. Thereby they had to overcome two problems, both originating from limitations of `in/out` qualifiers:

1) Each `in/out` qualifier must refer to a single memory block, but a task may have an unlimited number of dependencies (see above example, which gets worse if the partitioned block is deeply nested). The dependencies cannot be combined into one, since the corresponding memory blocks are stored non-consecutively. The authors solved the problem with a preprocessing step, in which they capture the matrix structure in a skeleton array. It has one entry per elementary block, and stores entries from the same parent block besides each other. This way, a single qualifier is sufficient to specify multiple dependencies.

2) Dependencies between non-sibling tasks of a nested parallel program, such as the dependence from the dark orange to the dark blue task in Fig. 2, cannot be expressed with `in/out` qualifiers. The authors solved the problem with weak dependencies and early release, which are OmpSs-2 [10] concepts not supported by OpenMP. Briefly stated, weak dependencies are annotations for parent tasks and early release refines their functionality.

Both of the above approaches exploit the recursive parallelism potential of $\mathcal{H}$-matrix factorization at the price of an additional preprocessing step. However, this step adds overhead and requires the $\mathcal{H}$-matrix structure to remain constant in subsequent computations. Although this constraint is often inconsequential, there exist cases in which the structure is not known in advance (as discussed in [9]). Also, requiring a constant structure prohibits the application of certain numerical techniques, such as pivoting [6] or recompression [11].

3   Future-Based Algorithm

To avoid the drawbacks of the previous algorithms, we propose to use futures. As noted in the introduction, a *future* is a placeholder for a value to be computed eventually by a task. Other tasks can access the value by *touching* the future, and then are suspended until the future becomes *ready*.

We started from Algorithm 1, like Sáez et al. [2] did. Our algorithm runs the same tasks and observes the same dependencies as theirs, but instead of in/out qualifiers, we use futures to specify the dependencies.

Recall that a core problem in $\mathcal{H}$-LU factorization is the synchronization of dependent non-sibling tasks. Figure 3 depicts a dependency from an h_factorize task (marked in orange) to a solve task (marked in blue). Thereby h_factorize writes to a matrix block, and solve reads from it. We concentrate on the handling of dependencies from h_factorize to solve, but other cases are similar.

Algorithm 1 enforces the dependency on all levels of the task tree, such as from the light orange to the light blue task in Fig. 3. Our algorithm, in contrast, only enforces it from the orange to the blue task, where it is required for correctness. The enforcement is marked by a solid straight red arrow. Generally speaking, a data dependency is enforced before performing "real" computation, i.e., when one or both of the connected tasks refer to an elementary block.

To cleanly distinguish the writer and reader sides of a dependency, we adopt the concepts of promises and futures from C++. Thereby, the same placeholder memory location is addressed by one *promise*, and by one or multiple associated *futures*. The promise is written to once, and then all associated futures become ready immediately and can be read from. Promises and futures are generated together. Futures can be passed as function/task parameters, and they can be duplicated during program execution.

A promise and its associated future are generated by a common ancestor of the dependent tasks in the task tree. In Fig. 3, the ancestor is marked in yellow. Such an ancestor always exists (at least the root).

Figure 5 illustrates the dependency specifically for $\mathcal{H}$-LU factorization. In part A, the (yellow) ancestor task spawns h_factorize and solve tasks to update the large orange and blue blocks, respectively. We call the tasks/blocks orangeA etc., indicating their type (h_factorize or solve), and size (A for large, etc.) Alongside spawning the tasks, the ancestor also generates promises/futures, which we name analogously. Then it passes the orangeA future as a parameter to the blueA task.

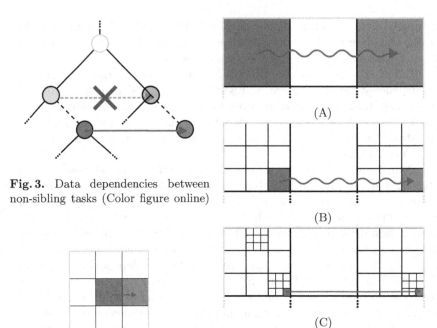

Fig. 3. Data dependencies between non-sibling tasks (Color figure online)

(A)

(B)

(C)

Fig. 4. Example of data dependency (Color figure online)

Fig. 5. Data and control dependencies in $\mathcal{H}$-LU factorization (Color figure online)

Promises and futures are propagated downwards in the task tree, as will be explained next. During propagation, such as in the transition from Subfigure 5A to 5B, the writer and reader sides do not have a data dependency, since there are no read/write accesses to the matrix at this point. However, task blueA must pass the orangeB future to task blueB. Therefore, the orangeB promise must have been generated before. We capture this as a *control* dependency. In Fig. 5, control dependencies are represented by wavy lines, and data dependencies by straight ones. Due to the control dependency, e.g., task blueA can start only when task orangeA has finished task spawning. Since task spawning (and the accompanying generation of promises) is all that a non-elementary task such as orangeA has to do, blueA in fact waits for the completion of orangeA. Note the difference: Task blueA waits for the end of task spawning (control dependency), but not for the update of the orangeA matrix block (*no* data dependency).

The propagation ends at an elementary block on the blue and/or orange side. Let us first consider the case that the blue block is elementary, such as blueC in the figure. Since blueC needs to access block orangeC, the *data* dependency from orangeC to blueC must be enforced. Thus, blueC must wait for the orangeC future, before it can start.

If only the orange block is elementary, the blue task is not aware of the situation. Thus, it acts as if in propagation, waiting for the orange future. Normally, during propagation, this future would become ready after subtask spawning.

Now, however, it becomes ready after the orange block has been updated. Nevertheless, readiness of the orange future is the right entrance condition for the blue task. In consequence, the two cases can be handled together.

Let us now look at the writer side propagation starting from orangeA. According to Fig. 2, each orange task spawns some fixed number of child tasks, which have pairwise dependencies. The parent task generates promises during spawning, and passes their futures to the dependent children. In Fig. 4, for instance, it passes a future for orangeA to blueA.

Like on the reader side, the propagation continues downwards until reaching an elementary task, such as orangeC. On the writer side, it always runs down to the elementary level, since a writer does not know its readers.

Readers for different nesting levels of a block may exist. In Fig. 5A, for instance, (non-marked) block A[0,1] is elementary and thus has a data dependency from orangeA; whereas the depicted dependency refers to orangeC. Thus, futures are needed for *all* nesting levels to signal the completion of blocks orangeA, orangeB, *and* orangeC. The following description of our approach is specific to the depicted case; other cases are either simpler or similar:

Since all of orangeA, orangeB, and orangeC are bottom-right blocks, they are the last blocks to be updated within their respective parent functions (see Fig. 2). Thus, we can use a single promise to signal completion of all of these blocks. To realize this, task orangeA does *not* generate a promise for task orangeB, but reuses its own promise and forwards it to task orangeB, which further forwards it to orangeC. So, once orangeC has finished, it fills the promise received and thereby signals completion of *all* nested blocks at once.

In summary, the propagation involves different operations on futures/promises, which are performed after receipt of a parent future/promise:

- generating child promises, and passing their associated futures as parameters to dependent other children
- thereby duplicating the future so that it can be passed to multiple children
- making a child task be the owner of a promise, who is responsible for filling it
- forwarding an owned promise to a child, thereby transferring ownership to it.

4   Definition of Futures

In summary, in our algorithm, a dependent `solve` task requires the following information about an `h_factorize` task at some point:

(i1) Has the task been completed? This question applies to both non-elementary tasks, for which a 'yes' means that all child tasks have been spawned; and to elementary tasks, for which it means that the associated matrix block has been updated. The cases are combined, since a (non-elementary) `solve` task does not know whether the `h_factorize` task is elementary or not.

(i2) Has the update of the associated matrix block been completed? (This question is only relevant for non-elementary tasks, where (i2) differs from (i1)) (i3) Contents of updated matrix block.

(i4) Futures of all child tasks (This is only relevant for non-elementary tasks).

Since (i1) takes precedence over (i2) to (i4), the most natural way to structure the information is to use one future for (i1) that *contains* (i2) to (i4) when ready. This requires futures being able to hold other futures. Moreover, (i4) requires futures to be storable in data structures such as arrays.

Information (i2) and (i3) could be combined into a future being ready at (i2) and wrapping (i3). However, block operations are often performed by BLAS libraries that work in-place. Therefore, we keep the matrix data in memory and let an (i2) future signal the availability of this data. Altogether, for the above information, we define type future<fnode> (for (i1)) with

```
1 struct fnode:
2   fut<void> full // for (i2)
3   hmatrix_block* this_block // for (i3)
4   fut<fnode>[][] part // for (i4)
```

Moreover, our algorithm needs support for the forwarding of promises to other tasks. Thus, promises must have their own identity (name, type), separate from that of their futures. We call these promises *free* and propose four constructs:

– promise<element_type> – type of promise
– make_promise<element_type>() – constructor for free promises
– into(name_of_promise) – parameter of spawn keyword, indicating that the spawned task should write its result into the given promise
– get_future(name_of_promise) – returns associated future of promise

Only part of the promises in our $\mathcal{H}$-LU algorithm need to be free; for instance, the orange promise in Fig. 4 is not forwarded because the orange block is not the last one to be computed inside the parent function. To avoid the higher programming expense of free promises in such cases, we propose to additionally support a more traditional type of futures. We call them *bound*. Bound promises are generated when a function is spawned as a task, and they are filled with the return value of the function. Bound promises are not visible to a programmer, but their futures are.

Finally, outside the specific case from Sect. 3, our algorithm can profit from the ability to touch multiple futures at once (*parallel touch*). Since the futures may become ready in any order, this corresponds to a "parallel wait".

In summary, a suitable future construct for the support of $\mathcal{H}$-LU factorization should have the following properties:

– allows to wrap any placeholder type, enabling, e.g., futures of futures,
– allows futures to be stored in data structures such as arrays,
– supports the duplicating of futures,
– supports the parallel touching of futures,
– allows (but does not enforce) the explicit naming of promises, and
– supports the forwarding of promises to new filling tasks.

5   Pseudocode and Discussion

Algorithm 2 presents pseudocode for the algorithm from Sect. 3, using our new future type. As before, only h_factorize is depicted, but update and solve are similar. The function has two parameters. If not needed, they are set to a ready future, or to a null promise, respectively.

Algorithm 2 has the same structure as Algorithm 1. The most significant changes have been replacing the tasking constructs by the spawn keyword and unrolling the last iteration of the k-loop. Additionally, future handling has been inserted. We use a temporary array of futures fAll for the contained child blocks. According to Fig. 2, the array elements are assigned different futures over time.

Algorithm 2: Future-based $\mathcal{H}$-LU factorization

```
1   fnode h_factorize(future<fnode> fIn, promise<void> pDone):
2     touch fIn
3     if (isElementary(fIn.this_block))
4       fAll[0..n][0..n] = fIn.part[0..n][0..n]
5       for (k = 0,...,n-2)
6         fAll[k][k] = spawn h_factorize(fAll[k][k], make_promise<void>())
7         for (j = k+1,...,n-1)
8           fAll[k][j] = spawn h_solve_x(fAll[k][j], fAll[k][k])
9         for (i = k+1,...,n-1)
10          fAll[i][k] = spawn h_solve_y(fAll[i][k], fAll[k][k])
11        for (i,j = k+1,...,n-1)
12          fAll[i][j] = spawn h_update(fAll[i][j], fAll[i][k], fAll[k][j])
13      fAll[n-1][n-1] = spawn h_factorize(fAll[n-1][n-1], pDone)
14      return (get_future(pDone), fIn.this_block, fAll)
15    else
16      touch fIn.full
17      spawn into(pDone) factorize(fIn.this_block)
18      return (get_future(pDone), fIn.this_block, {})
```

Partly due to the elimination of preprocessing, Algorithm 2 is more concise than the algorithms from Kriemann and Sáez et al. (see Sect. 2). Altogether, we feel it to be clean and easy to understand.

Comparing futures to in/out qualifiers, futures have the advantage of living entirely at runtime. This allows for a *dynamic* discovery of dependencies, which enabled us to eliminate the preprocessing step. In particular, the dynamic dependencies helped us to solve the problem of tasks depending on an unknown number of memory blocks. While Sáez et al. [8] deploy a skeleton array, our usage of a single future wrapping references to all blocks seems more natural.

Finally, futures can express data and control dependencies by the same means, whereas in/out qualifiers must be complemented by weak dependencies/early release to express dependencies between non-sibling tasks.

6   Related Work

In addition to the already discussed task-based $\mathcal{H}$-LU factorization algorithms from Kriemann [16] and Sáez et al. [8], there other parallel $\mathcal{H}$-LU factorization algorithms that exploit parallelism within elementary operations (e.g. [7]), or refine in/out qualifiers to introduce hierarchical dependencies [3].

The concept of futures originates from the 1970s [4,13], and has been shown to be suitable for the expression of nontrivial dependency patterns such as pipeline parallelism [5]. Several AMT programming systems offer future constructs, e.g. [1,15,17], but in less powerful forms than proposed in this paper. For instance, Cilk-F [17] does not clearly differentiate between futures and promises, and does not allow to express futures of futures. The futures of HPX resemble those in C++11 [14], and they inherit their drawback of disallowing futures of incomplete types (required for the part component of fnode). None of the systems cited incorporate a mechanism for parallel waiting on multiple futures.

7   Conclusion

This paper has presented a novel algorithm for the LU factorization of $\mathcal{H}$-matrices. Unlike previous approaches, it uses the future construct to express dependencies between parallel tasks. This required a particularly powerful type of future, which was defined in the paper. Our algorithm improves upon previous ones by eliminating the need for preprocessing. Thus it allows changes of the matrix structure during the computation. The algorithm can be formulated in a clean and concise way.

Unfortunately, the proposed future type is not yet supported by current AMTs. Therefore, the main open issue is its implementation in an experimental runtime system. Only then the algorithm itself can be evaluated experimentally.

Acknowledgments. This research was partially funded by the Deutsche Forschungs-gemeinschaft (DFG, German Research Foundation) under project number 512078735.

References

1. Aiken, A., Bauer, M.: Programming with Legion (2023). https://legion.stanford.edu/pdfs/legion-manual.pdf. Accessed 27 Feb 2024
2. Aliaga, J.I., Carratalá-Sáez, R., Kriemann, R., Quintana-Ortí, E.S.: Task-parallel LU factorization of hierarchical matrices using OmpSs. In: IEEE International Parallel and Distributed Processing Symposium Workshops (IPDPSW), pp. 1148–1157 (2017). https://doi.org/10.1109/IPDPSW.2017.124
3. Augonnet, C., Goudin, D., Kuhn, M., Lacoste, X., Namyst, R., Ramet, P.: A hierarchical fast direct solver for distributed memory machines with manycore nodes. Technical report, CEA/DAM, Total E&P, Université de Bordeaux (2019). https://cea.hal.science/cea-02304706
4. Baker, H.C., Hewitt, C.: The incremental garbage collection of processes. ACM SIGART Bull. **64**, 55–59 (1977). https://doi.org/10.1145/872736.806932

5. Blelloch, G.E., Reid-Miller, M.: Pipelining with futures. In: Proceedings of the ACM Symposium on Parallel Algorithms and Architectures (SPAA) (1997). https://doi.org/10.1145/258492.258517
6. Buoni, J.J.: A stable method for the incomplete factorization of H-matrices. Linear Algebra Appl. **129**, 143–154 (1990). https://doi.org/10.1016/0024-3795(90)90302-S
7. Börm, S.: $\mathcal{H}$2-lib (2023). https://www.h2lib.org/. Accessed 28 Feb 2024
8. Carratalá-Sáez, R., Christophersen, S., Aliaga, J.I., Beltran, V., Börm, S., Quintana-Ortí, E.S.: Exploiting nested task-parallelism in the H-LU factorization. J. Comput. Sci. **33**, 20–33 (2019). https://doi.org/10.1016/j.jocs.2019.02.004
9. Carratalá-Sáez, R., Faverge, M., Pichon, G., Sylvand, G., Quintana-Ortí, E.S.: Tiled algorithms for efficient task-parallel H-matrix solvers. In: IEEE International Parallel and Distributed Processing Symposium Workshops (IPDPSW), pp. 757–766 (2020). https://doi.org/10.1109/IPDPSW50202.2020.00131
10. Barcelona Supercomputing Center: OmpSs-2 Specification (2023). https://pm.bsc.es/ftp/ompss-2/doc/spec/. Accessed 06 Feb 2024
11. Grasedyck, L.: Adaptive recompression of H-matrices for BEM. Computing **74**, 205–223 (2005)
12. Grasedyck, L., Hackbusch, W.: Construction and arithmetics of H-matrices. Computing **70**, 295–334 (2003)
13. Halstead, R.H.: MULTILISP: a language for concurrent symbolic computation. ACM Trans. Program. Lang. Syst. **7**(4), 501–538 (1985). https://doi.org/10.1145/4472.4478
14. ISO: ISO/IEC 14882:2011 Information Technology – Programming Languages – C++. International Organization for Standardization, Geneva, Switzerland (2011)
15. Kaiser, H., Heller, T., Adelstein-Lelbach, B., Serio, A., Fey, D.: HPX: a task based programming model in a global address space. In: Proceedings of the 8th International Conference on Partitioned Global Address Space Programming Models (2014). https://doi.org/10.1145/2676870.2676883
16. Kriemann, R.: H-LU factorization on many-core systems. Comput. Vis. Sci. **16**(3), 105–117 (2013). https://doi.org/10.1007/s00791-014-0226-7
17. Singer, K., Xu, Y., Lee, I.T.A.: Proactive work stealing for futures. In: Proceedings of the 24th Symposium on Principles and Practice of Parallel Programming (2019). https://doi.org/10.1145/3293883.3295735

Evaluating PaRSEC Through Matrix Computations in Scientific Applications

Qinglei Cao[1]($\boxtimes$), Thomas Herault[2], Aurelien Bouteiller[2], Joseph Schuchart[2], and George Bosilca[2,3]

[1] Saint Louis University, St. Louis, USA
qinglei.cao@slu.edu
[2] University of Tennessee, Knoxville, USA
[3] NVIDIA, Knoxville, USA

Abstract. Task-based runtime systems, characterized by their dynamic execution models and optimized resource management, contribute significantly to the computational revolution. They enable the development of more intricate and adaptable algorithms, essential in the field of computational science. This paper provides an in-depth exploration of the PaRSEC task-based runtime system, particularly focusing on its versatility in managing a variety of matrix computations. More specifically, we examine PaRSEC's role in enhancing efficiency when solving linear systems and processing dense, low-rank, mixed-precision, and sparse matrix operations, which are crucial in scientific applications, e.g., climate/weather prediction and 3D unstructured mesh deformation-the primary focus of this study. Through experimentation and analysis, we showcase PaRSEC's ability to significantly boost computational efficiency and scalability across a range of computationally intensive and less intensive tasks on various hardware architectures. Our findings not only underscore the potential of PaRSEC in advancing sustainable, efficient, and accurate domain modeling and simulation but also emphasize the growing necessity of task-based runtime systems in supporting the next generation of matrix computations.

Keywords: Task-based runtime · Matrix computations · Cholesky factorization · Low rank approximation · Mixed precision · Sparse operation

1 Introduction

The world of High-Performance Computing (HPC) has undergone a remarkable evolution, transitioning from simple, single-processor systems to today's complex multi-core, multi-accelerator, and multi-node architectures [1]. This advancement has brought forth a new era of computing power, capable of performing quintillions of calculations per second. However, with this increase in power comes a corresponding rise in complexity, particularly in hardware design and architecture. HPC systems now feature a diverse array of components such as CPUs and GPUs, each with memory hierarchies adding layers

P. Diehl et al. (Eds.): WAMTA 2024, LNCS 14626, pp. 22–33, 2024.
https://doi.org/10.1007/978-3-031-61763-8_3

to the computational puzzle. This complexity presents significant challenges in terms of programming and optimization, demanding innovative approaches to fully harness the potential of these sophisticated machines [2].

Parallel to the evolution of hardware, the complexity of domain-specific applications in HPC has also escalated. These applications, ranging from molecular dynamics to large-scale astrophysics, now require the processing of enormous datasets and the execution of highly complex algorithms. The computational demands of these tasks have grown exponentially, often outpacing the advancements in hardware capabilities. As a result, there is an increasing need for specialized software that can effectively leverage the available hardware resources while managing the intricacies of these domain applications. This necessity is particularly acute in areas such as climate modeling and biomedical research, where accurate and timely results are critical.

In response to these challenges, task-based runtime systems have emerged as a pivotal solution [3–8]. These systems adopt a dynamic execution model, which allows for more efficient and adaptive management of computational tasks. Unlike traditional static execution models, task-based runtimes dynamically allocate resources based on the real-time demands of each task. This flexibility is crucial for optimizing performance across a diverse range of applications and hardware architectures [9–13]. Furthermore, these systems enable better load balancing, communication-computation overlap, and reduce idle time of computational resources, thereby enhancing overall efficiency and scalability.

In this study, we delve into the multifaceted capabilities of the PaRSEC task-based runtime system [8, 14], with a special emphasis on its adept handling of diverse matrix operations, including dense, low-rank, mixed-precision, and sparse matrices. These matrix types are integral to a wide spectrum of scientific endeavors, notably in the realms of climate forecasting and 3D unstructured mesh deformation [15–21] – areas that form the cornerstone of our research. Through a series of experiments and analytical processes, we illuminate the profound impact of PaRSEC on elevating the performance and scalability of computational tasks. These tasks vary in their computational demands, yet consistently benefit from PaRSEC's robust architecture across diverse hardware platforms. This is particularly significant in an era where accuracy and efficiency are paramount.

The contributions of this paper are as follows. We go a step further to illustrate the indispensable role of task-based runtime systems like PaRSEC in the landscape of scientific computing. By adeptly balancing computational loads and optimizing resource utilization, PaRSEC not only excels in current computing environments but also paves the way for groundbreaking advancements in complex matrix computations. This study, therefore, not only showcases PaRSEC's current achievements but also sets the stage for task-based runtime's pivotal role in the evolution of scientific computing, with PaRSEC guiding the way beyond the traditional niche of dense, regular algorithms.

The remainder of this paper unfolds in the following manner. We present related work in Sect. 2 and introduce PaRSEC in Sect. 3. Section 4 details the scientific applications. Then, we present the performance analysis in Sect. 5, followed by conclusions and planned work in Sect. 6.

2   Related Work

In the realm of HPC, the emergence of task-based runtime systems has been a pivotal development, particularly in their adept handling of the intricacies and concurrent nature of contemporary computing architectures. These systems are adept at decomposing computational processes into smaller, manageable tasks. This decomposition facilitates dynamic allocation and balancing of computational load, while concurrently mitigating the overheads associated with communication and synchronization processes.

OpenMP [5], a widely recognized standard for parallel programming in shared-memory systems, includes task-based features that have transformed it into a dynamic, task-oriented environment. Parallelism is achieved through a mix of directives and library routines, enabling efficient task management by the compiler and runtime system. OmpSs [4], an extension to OpenMP, introduces support for heterogeneous systems, asynchronous tasks, and data dependencies, enhancing flexibility. Similarly, COMP Superscalar (COMPSs) [22] aims to simplify development for distributed systems with a programming interface and a runtime system that leverages application parallelism. StarPU [3] provides a framework for environments with distributed, heterogeneous multicore systems, enabling task-specific kernel annotations and efficient task scheduling and data management by the runtime system. HPX (High-Performance ParalleX) [6], based on the ParalleX model, offers a C++ runtime system optimized for high-performance computing in parallel and distributed environments. Lastly, Legion [7], a runtime system with a unique approach, is designed for distributed and heterogeneous computing architectures. Legion's programming model distinctively separates the definition of tasks and data from their actual mapping onto hardware resources. This approach not only facilitates automatic parallelism detection but also optimizes data locality, thereby enhancing both performance and scalability.

In this work, we concentrate on PaRSEC [8], which offers a set of original programming paradigms that often enable higher scalability than competing approaches; our study particular emphasis is on assessing performance efficiency and scalability of these programming concepts within the context of real-world scientific applications, instead of relying on synthetic benchmarks like in [23].

3   The PaRSEC Runtime System

The core design of PaRSEC, akin to other similar systems, leverages the concepts of tasks and dependencies. These concepts are instrumental in defining computations and their data flows, allowing for the representation of algorithms as Directed Acyclic Graphs (DAGs) where tasks are nodes and dependencies are edges. PaRSEC distinguishes itself in its ability to dynamically map these DAGs across distributed resources, ensuring that data dependencies are meticulously managed. This involves adeptly moving data across various memory spaces-be it within a node, across nodes, or between different devices-and efficiently assigning tasks to diverse computational resources. The system's interaction with users is facilitated through a range of Domain-Specific Languages (DSLs), offering users heightened flexibility and enabling scientists to express complex algorithms more intuitively. One such DSL that is used in this research, the Parameterized Task Graph (PTG) [24] provides a succinct yet expansive description of task dependencies through a format known as the Job Data Flow (JDF). This representation allows for the categorization of tasks into classes, each encompassing the necessary details for the instantiation and execution of task instances on various computational units. PaRSEC is further enhanced by integrating Template Task Graph (TTG) [25], a C++ API that expands on PTG by allowing dynamic task dependency selection with varied parameter types. Moreover, PaRSEC incorporates the Dynamic Task Discovery (DTD) [26], a DSL that focuses on sequential task insertion in DAG construction, though it shares the overhead challenges common to distributed task-insertion runtimes.

4   Applications as Testbed

Two scientific applications are utilized as testbeds, summarized in the following.

Geospatial Modeling Towards Climate and Weather Prediction [16, 20, 21]. Gaussian processes (GPs) serve as a cornerstone in machine learning and Bayesian statistics, particularly for their versatility in modeling and predicting complex behaviors. They are especially prevalent in spatial data analysis. One of the key methods in employing GPs for spatial data is through Maximum Likelihood Estimation (MLE). This involves defining a GP model with specific mean and covariance functions for a set of spatial points. The MLE method then seeks to optimize the model parameters to best fit the observed data. Consider a set of spatial observations $\mathbf{Z}$, where $\mathbf{Z} = \{Z(\mathbf{s}_1), \ldots, Z(\mathbf{s}_n)\}^\top$ corresponds to the observed values at n different locations $\mathbf{s}_1, \ldots, \mathbf{s}_n$ in a d-dimensional space $\mathbb{R}^d$. We assume these observations come from a stationary and isotropic Gaussian random field with a mean of zero. The covariance between any two points is defined by the function $C(\mathbf{h}; \boldsymbol{\theta}) = \text{cov}\{Z(\mathbf{s}), Z(\mathbf{s} + \mathbf{h})\}$, where $\mathbf{h}$ is the lag vector in $\mathbb{R}^d$, and $\boldsymbol{\theta}$ is a vector of unknown parameters. The covariance matrix for these points, denoted by $\boldsymbol{\Sigma}(\boldsymbol{\theta})$, has entries $\boldsymbol{\Sigma}_{ij} = C(\mathbf{s}_i - \mathbf{s}_j; \boldsymbol{\theta})$ for $i, j = 1, \ldots, n$, and is both symmetric and positive definite. The statistical inference of $\boldsymbol{\theta}$ is based on the Gaussian log-likelihood function: $\ell(\boldsymbol{\theta}) = -\frac{n}{2}\log(2\pi) - \frac{1}{2}\log|\boldsymbol{\Sigma}(\boldsymbol{\theta})| - \frac{1}{2}\mathbf{Z}^\top\boldsymbol{\Sigma}(\boldsymbol{\theta})^{-1}\mathbf{Z}$. The goal in GP modeling is to determine the optimal parameter vector $\widehat{\boldsymbol{\theta}}$ that maximizes this log-likelihood function. We consider the squared exponential covariance function for 2D/3D spaces, which is given by: $C(\mathbf{h}; \boldsymbol{\theta}) = \sigma^2 \exp\left(-\frac{h^2}{\beta}\right)$, where $h = \|\mathbf{h}\|$ is the Euclidean distance between spatial points, σ^2 is the variance, β represents the correlation range, and $\boldsymbol{\theta} = (\sigma^2, \beta)^\top$.

3D Unstructured Mesh Deformation [19, 27]. In simulations involving fluid-structure interactions with 3D moving bodies, handling large mesh deformations is a significant challenge. The Radial Basis Function (RBF) method offers a solution for generating high-quality adaptive meshes, which is particularly useful for determining the movement of internal nodes within a volume based on the movement of nodes on the boundary. Following the approach outlined in [28], we can express the displacement d within the entire domain as a sum of radial basis functions: $d(\mathbf{x}) = \sum_{i=1}^{n_b} \alpha_i \phi(\|\mathbf{x} - \mathbf{x}_{b_i}\|) + p(\mathbf{x})$, where $\mathbf{x}_{b_i} = [x_{b_i}, y_{b_i}, z_{b_i}]$ represents the known boundary nodes, p is a polynomial, n_b is the number of boundary nodes, and ϕ is a chosen basis function. The coefficients α_i and the polynomial p are determined by the boundary conditions $d(\mathbf{x}_{b_i}) = d_{b_i}$, with d_b containing the known displacement values at the boundary. The unknown coefficients α must satisfy the constraint $\sum_{i=1}^{n_b} \alpha_i p(\mathbf{x}_{b_i}) = 0$. We consider the Gaussian RBF, which is defined as $\phi(r) = \exp(-r^2)$, where r is the Euclidean distance. To manage the condition numbers of the RBF matrices, global support functions are scaled by a shape parameter δ, leading to the scaled RBF function $\phi_\delta(r) := \phi(r/\delta)$, with δ typically set to half the minimum distance between nodes: $\delta = \frac{1}{2} \times \min \|\mathbf{x} - \mathbf{x}_{b_i}\|$.

These two scientific applications both necessitate the solution of large-scale dense linear systems, which involve conducting a Cholesky factorization on a symmetric positive-definite covariance matrix, a process that is intensive in terms of both memory usage and computational load. HiCMA [15–21], a leading-edge solution for these applications, powered by PaRSEC, explores the data sparsity and/or sparsity in these applications and adopts tile low-rank (TLR) and mixed-precision (MP) technologies to address these challenges. In this study, we assess PaRSEC via HiCMA, focusing on several matrix computations (employing dense/MP and TLR/DP for geospatial modeling, and TLR+sparse/DP for 3D unstructured mesh deformation), as illustrated in Fig. 1.

- Figure 1(a) demonstrates the traditional approach, where the entire matrix is handled in double-precision (DP or FP64).
- Figure 1(b) presents a tile-based precision-aware approach for matrix computations. Here, the precision of each tile (DP, single-precision (SP or FP32), or half-precision (HP or FP16)) is determined by its norm relative to the overall matrix norm [20,29]. The choice of precision affects computational load, memory requirements, and communication volume.
- Figure 1(c) illustrates the use of TLR compression by condensing the off-diagonal tiles of the dense covariance matrix to a certain accuracy, specific to the application (see the heatmap in [15] for 2D/3D kernels). The varying rank of each tile, along with the rank discrepancy between on- and off-diagonal tiles, poses a new challenge in balancing computation, memory, and communication loads.
- Figure 1(d) also shows the TLR compression format, but combined with sparsity, meaning the ranks of some tiles are reduced to zero after compression. The level of sparsity is application-specific [19], further exacerbating the load imbalance challenges inherent in the TLR format.

5   Performance Results and Analysis

5.1   Experimental Settings

Experiments were carried out on four systems, each with a unique architecture.

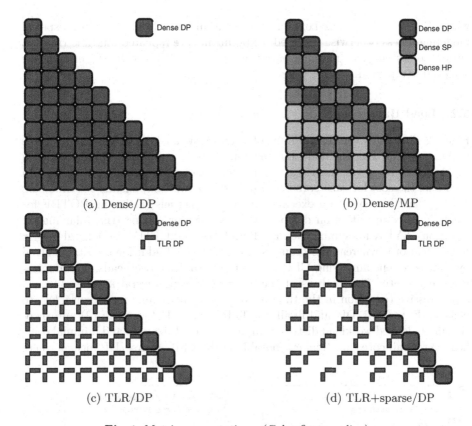

(a) Dense/DP

(b) Dense/MP

(c) TLR/DP

(d) TLR+sparse/DP

Fig. 1. Matrix computations. (Color figure online)

- Shaheen II: This is a Cray XC40 system comprising 6,174 compute nodes. Each node is equipped with two 16-core Intel Haswell CPUs operating at 2.30 GHz and has 128 GB of DDR4 main memory.
- Fugaku: This system is based on ARM architecture and includes over 150,000 compute nodes. Each node features a 48-core A64FX CPU running at a maximal 2.2 GHz (boost mode), coupled with 32 GB of HBM2 main memory.
- Haxane: An Intel-based GPU compute node, incorporating two 8-core Xeon(R) Silver 4309Y CPUs at 2.80 GHz, 63 GB of main memory, and a single NVIDIA H100 PCIe GPU.
- Frontier: This is a GPU-based AMD cluster with 9,408 compute nodes. Each node is composed of a 64-core AMD Optimized 3rd Gen EPYC CPU and four AMD MI250X GPUs, with access to 512 GB of DDR4 memory.

Accuracy thresholds are set according to the requirements of each application: 10^{-9} for geospatial modeling and 10^{-5} for 3D unstructured mesh deformation. The "band distribution" strategy [16] for TLR formats is employed, complemented by a two dimensional block cyclic data distribution (2DBCDD) strategy for tiles outside the band, using a process grid of $P \times Q$ (as square as possible), where $P \leq Q$. A 2D squared exponential covariance function is used in geospatial modeling unless otherwise specified. Experiments are repeated multiple times to ensure consistency; as minimal variation is observed, the highest performance achieved is reported.

5.2   Load Balancing

Figure 2 illustrates the distribution of computational load across the 48 cores within a single Fugaku node for the four matrix computations discussed in Fig. 1. The size of the matrices is consistent across these four evaluations. In each one, the cost for each core is represented by two components: the blue bars indicate the time spent on executing numerical kernels (including POTRF for Cholesky decomposition on diagonal tiles, TRSM for solving triangular matrix equations, SYRK for symmetric rank-k updates, and GEMM for general matrix multiplication), whereas the orange bars represent all additional costs incurred by that core, encompassing CPU idle periods, runtime overheads, communication delays, etc. The analysis of these figures reveals several key insights: (1) a progressive reduction in the time-to-solution transitioning from dense/DP, to dense/MP, to TLR/DP, and finally to TLR+sparse/DP formats; (2) an exceptionally balanced workload distribution, high CPU utilization, and minimal overhead across all cores, particularly notable in the TLR+sparse/DP format where

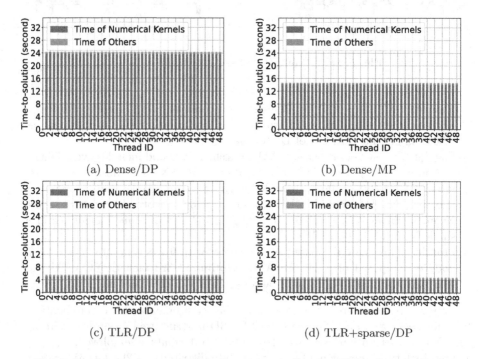

Fig. 2. Load balancing across shared memory on Fugaku. (Color figure online)

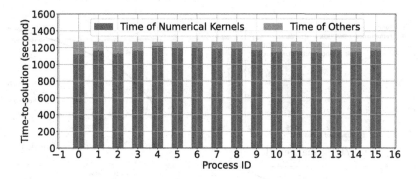

Fig. 3. Load balancing across distributed memory on Shaheen II.

variations in rank and the presence of sparsity are factors, as detailed in Sect. 4. Moreover, the sparsity level in Fig. 2(d) is approximately 2% for this smaller matrix size, explaining the modest improvement when moving from TLR/DP to TLR+sparse/DP. Similarly, Fig. 3 assesses the balance of workload distribution across nodes/processes for TLR/DP on 16 Shaheen II nodes.

5.3 GPU Efficiency

HiCMA currently lacks support for TLR computations on GPUs. Consequently, we present an analysis of GPU utilization for computations in dense formats, as illustrated in Fig. 4. Each point in these figures corresponds to the actual GPU occupancy, determined through periodic measurements using Nvidia's suite of diagnostic tools. The analysis reveals that attaining full (100%) GPU utilization is achievable during operations in both dense/DP and dense/MP formats. This observation underscores that the computational workflows are not hindered by data transfer operations (D2H and H2D), confirming that data transfers can be effectively overlapped with computational operations in PaRSEC.

5.4 Scalability

Figure 5 illustrates the performance scalability of PaRSEC on homogeneous CPU architectures. Specifically, Fig. 5(a) presents the weak scaling of dense/DP

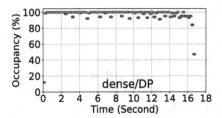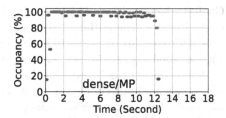

Fig. 4. GPU occupancy on H100.

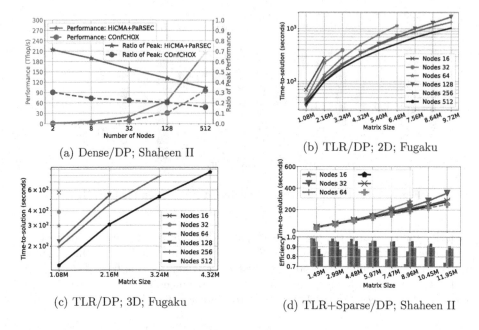

(a) Dense/DP; Shaheen II

(b) TLR/DP; 2D; Fugaku

(c) TLR/DP; 3D; Fugaku

(d) TLR+Sparse/DP; Shaheen II

Fig. 5. Performance scalability on homogenous CPU architectures.

Cholesky factorization via HiCMA on Shaheen II, benchmarked against ConfCHOX [30]. The settings follow the specifications in [30], e.g., matrix size of $8192 \times \sqrt{P}$ where P is the number of processes. In this figure, the left y-axis quantifies the achieved performance, whereas the right y-axis compares this performance to the theoretical peak. Notably, HiCMA consistently outperforms ConfCHOX, frequently securing doubled performance gains. Figure 5(b) and 5(c) detail the performance on Fugaku for TLR/DP in 2D and 3D respectively. These two figures highlight strong scalability for each matrix size, with individual graphs indicating weak scalability per node. The transition from 2D to 3D kernels represents a shift to more computationally intensive problems, thereby enhancing scalability along with smaller solvable matrices on identical resources. This effect is particularly pronounced for TLR+sparse/DP, as depicted in Fig. 5(d). Here, the upper part displays performance across varying node counts, while the lower part evaluates this performance relative to the bounded critical path in Cholesky factorization. This critical path includes the serial and incompressible steps: POTRF, the initial TRSM, and the first SYRK for each panel factorization. This analysis considers only the computational costs of these three kernels, with attainable performance reaching 90% across all matrix sizes.

Furthermore, Fig. 6 presents the performance for dense/DP and dense/MP across varying node counts on Frontier. Annotations related to the "MP effect" highlight the observed maximum performance enhancement achieved by MP over DP under different node configurations, consistently achieving a speedup exceeding 3×. Additionally, in terms of parallel efficiency, there is a notable

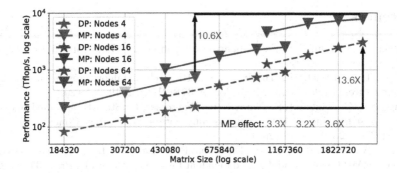

Fig. 6. Performance scalability on heterogeneous GPU system Frontier.

improvement in performance, with a 13.6× and 10.6× enhancement observed when scaling from 4 nodes to 64 nodes for dense/DP and dense/MP, respectively.

All in all, these findings highlight PaRSEC's versatility in handling complex real-world scientific applications, particularly regarding load balancing, efficiency, and scalability.

6   Conclusion and Future Work

This study focuses on PaRSEC's versatility in handling operations introduced by scientific applications, which involve dense matrices, low-rank matrices, matrices in mixed-precision formats, and sparse matrices, each presenting unique challenges. Through experiments and analysis, we demonstrate PaRSEC's remarkable capabilities in enhancing load balancing, computational efficiency, and scalability across a variety of hardware architectures. Looking forward, we aim to delve deeper into task-level behaviors and hardware counter metrics to uncover more granular insights, especially on Frontier. Furthermore, we envisage expanding our investigation to encompass additional task-based runtime systems, thereby broadening the scope of our research.

Acknowledgments. This research was supported in part by internal awards from Saint Louis University (Grant-0001651 and PROJ-000498) and the Exascale Computing Project (17-SC-20-SC). For computer time, this research used the compute node at Innovative Computing Laboratory, Shaheen II supercomputer at King Abdullah University of Science & Technology, Fugaku supercomputer at RIKEN (Group ID: ra010008), and Frontier supercomputer at Oak Ridge National Laboratory (Project ID: CSC612).

References

1. Meuer, H., Strohmaier, E., Dongarra, J., Simon, H.: The Top500 List (2020). http://www.top500.org
2. Keyes, D.E., Ltaief, H., Turkiyyah, G.: Hierarchical algorithms on hierarchical architectures. Philos. Trans. Roy. Soc. A **378**(2166), 20190055 (2020)
3. Augonnet, C., Thibault, S., Namyst, R., Wacrenier, P.: StarPU: a unified platform for task scheduling on heterogeneous multicore architectures. Concurr. Comput. Pract. Exp. **23**, 187–198 (2011)
4. Duran, A., Ferrer, R., Ayguadé, E., Badia, R.M., Labarta, J.: A proposal to extend the OpenMP tasking model with dependent tasks. Int. J. Parallel Prog. **37**(3), 292–305 (2009)
5. OpenMP. OpenMP 5.2 Complete Specifications (2021)
6. Heller, T., Kaiser, H., Iglberger, K.: Application of the ParalleX execution model to stencil-based problems. Comput. Sci. Res. Dev. **28**(2–3), 253–261 (2013)
7. Bauer, M., Treichler, S., Slaughter, E., Aiken, A.: Legion: expressing locality and independence with logical regions. In: International Conference for High Performance Computing, Networking, Storage and Analysis, SC 2012 (2012)
8. Bosilca, G., Bouteiller, A., Danalis, A., Faverge, M., Herault, T., Dongarra, J.: PaRSEC: a programming paradigm exploiting heterogeneity for enhancing scalability. Comput. Sci. Eng. **99**, 1 (2013)
9. Bosilca, G., et al.: Flexible development of dense linear algebra algorithms on massively parallel architectures with DPLASMA. In: IPDPS Workshops. IEEE (2011)
10. Akbudak, K., Ltaief, H., Mikhalev, A., Charara, A., Esposito, A., Keyes, D.: Exploiting data sparsity for large-scale matrix computations. In: Aldinucci, M., Padovani, L., Torquati, M. (eds.) Euro-Par 2018. LNCS, vol. 11014, pp. 721–734. Springer, Cham (2018). https://doi.org/10.1007/978-3-319-96983-1_51
11. Al-Harthi, N., et al.: Solving acoustic boundary integral equations using high performance tile low-rank LU factorization. In: Sadayappan, P., Chamberlain, B.L., Juckeland, G., Ltaief, H. (eds.) ISC High Performance 2020. LNCS, vol. 12151, pp. 209–229. Springer, Cham (2020). https://doi.org/10.1007/978-3-030-50743-5_11
12. Jagode, H., Danalis, A., Dongarra, J.: Accelerating NWChem coupled cluster through dataflow-based execution. Int. J. High Perform. Comput. Appl. **32**(4), 540–551 (2018)
13. Tillenius, M., Larsson, E., Lehto, E., Flyer, N.: A task parallel implementation of a scattered node stencil-based solver for the shallow water equations. In: Proceedings of the 6th Swedish Workshop on Multi-Core Computing. Halmstad University (2013)
14. Bosilca, G., Bouteiller, A., Danalis, A., Faverge, M., Herault, T., Dongarra, J.J.: PaRSEC: exploiting heterogeneity to enhance scalability. Comput. Sci. Eng. **15**(6), 36–45 (2013)
15. Cao, Q., et al.: Performance analysis of tile low-rank Cholesky factorization using parsec instrumentation tools. In: 2019 IEEE/ACM International Workshop on Programming and Performance Visualization Tools (ProTools), pp. 25–32. IEEE (2019)
16. Cao, Q., et al.: Extreme-scale task-based Cholesky factorization toward climate and weather prediction applications. In: Proceedings of the Platform for Advanced Scientific Computing Conference, pp. 1–11 (2020)

17. Cao, Q., et al.: Leveraging parsec runtime support to tackle challenging 3D data-sparse matrix problems. In: 2021 IEEE International Parallel and Distributed Processing Symposium (IPDPS). IEEE (2021)

18. Abdulah, S., et al.: Accelerating geostatistical modeling and prediction with mixed-precision computations: a high-productivity approach with parsec. IEEE Trans. Parallel Distrib. Syst. **33**(4), 964–976 (2021)

19. Cao, Q., et al.: A framework to exploit data sparsity in tile low-rank Cholesky factorization. In: 2022 IEEE International Parallel and Distributed Processing Symposium (IPDPS), pp. 414–424. IEEE (2022)

20. Cao, Q., et al.: Reshaping geostatistical modeling and prediction for extreme-scale environmental applications. In: SC 2022: International Conference for High Performance Computing, Networking, Storage and Analysis (SC). IEEE Computer Society (2022)

21. Cao, Q., Abdulah, S., Ltaief, H., Genton, M.G., Keyes, D., Bosilca, G.: Reducing data motion and energy consumption of geospatial modeling applications using automated precision conversion. In: 2023 IEEE International Conference on Cluster Computing (CLUSTER), pp. 330–342. IEEE (2023)

22. Lordan, F., et al.: Servicess: an interoperable programming framework for the cloud. J. Grid Comput. **12**(1), 67–91 (2014)

23. Slaughter, E., et al.: Task bench: a parameterized benchmark for evaluating parallel runtime performance. In: SC 2020: International Conference for High Performance Computing, Networking, Storage and Analysis. IEEE (2020)

24. Danalis, A., Bosilca, G., Bouteiller, A., Herault, T., Dongarra, J.: PTG: an abstraction for unhindered parallelism, pp. 21–30 (2014)

25. Bosilca, G., Harrison, R.J., Herault, T., Javanmard, M.M., Nookala, P., Valeev, E.F.: The Template Task Graph (TTG)-an emerging practical dataflow programming paradigm for scientific simulation at extreme scale. In: IEEE/ACM 5th International Workshop on Extreme Scale Programming Models and Middleware (ESPM2). IEEE (2020)

26. Hoque, R., Herault, T., Bosilca, G., Dongarra, J.: Dynamic task discovery in PaRSEC: a data-flow task-based runtime. In: Proceedings of the 8th Workshop on Latest Advances in Scalable Algorithms for Large-Scale Systems, ScalA 2017 (2017)

27. Alomairy, R., Bader, W., Ltaief, H., Mesri, Y., Keyes, D.: High-performance 3D unstructured mesh deformation using rank structured matrix computations. ACM Trans. Parallel Comput. **9**(1), 1–23 (2022)

28. De Boer, A., Van der Schoot, M.S., Bijl, H.: Mesh deformation based on radial basis function interpolation. Comput. Struct. **85**(11–14), 784–795 (2007)

29. Higham, N.J., Mary, T.: Mixed precision algorithms in numerical linear algebra. Acta Numer **31**, 347–414 (2022)

30. Kwasniewski, G., et al.: On the parallel I/O optimality of linear algebra kernels: near-optimal matrix factorizations. In: Proceedings of the International Conference for High Performance Computing, Networking, Storage and Analysis, pp. 1–15 (2021)

Distributed Asynchronous Contact Mechanics with DARMA/vt

Nicolas Morales[1]([✉]), Reese Jones[1], Jonathan Lifflander[1], Philippe P. Pébaÿ[2], Sean McGovern[2], Cezary Skrzyński[2], and Caleb Schilly[2]

[1] Sandia National Laboratories, Albuquerque, USA
{nmmoral,rjones,jliffla}@sandia.gov
[2] NexGen Analytics, Sheridan, USA
{philippe.pebay,sean.mcgovern,cezary.skrzynski,
caleb.schilly}@ng-analytics.com

Abstract. Contact mechanics, or the modeling of the impenetrability of solid objects, is fundamental to computational solid mechanics (CSM) applications yet is oftentimes the most challenging in terms of computational efficiency and performance.

These challenges arise from the irregularity and highly dynamic nature of contact simulation, particularly with algorithms designed for distributed memory architectures. First among these challenges is the inherent load imbalance when distributing contact load across compute nodes. This imbalance is highly problem dependent, and relates to the surface area of contact manifolds and the volume around them, rather than the distribution of the mesh over compute nodes, meaning the application load can vary drastically over different phases. The dynamic nature of contact problems motivates the use of distributed asynchronous many-tasking (AMT) frameworks to efficiently handle irregular workloads.

In this paper, we present our work on distBVH, a distributed contact solution using the DARMA/vt library for asynchronous tasking that is also capable of running on-node Kokkos-based kernels. We explore how distBVH addresses the various challenges of CSM contact problems. We evaluate the use of many of DARMA/vt's dynamic load balancers and demonstrate how our load balancing approach can provide significant performance improvements on various computational solid mechanics benchmarks. Additionally, we show how our approach can take advantage of DARMA/vt for tasking and efficient on-node kernels using Kokkos to scale over hundreds of processing elements.

Keywords: Computational Solid Mechanics · Contact Mechanics · AMT

1 Introduction

In computational solid mechanics (CSM), simulations involving contact mechanics are some of the most challenging to compute. These problems model the

P. Diehl et al. (Eds.): WAMTA 2024, LNCS 14626, pp. 34–45, 2024.
https://doi.org/10.1007/978-3-031-61763-8_4

impenetrability of solid materials and can be solved analytically only for the simplest problems [9]. Modeling contact mechanics is fundamental to accurately representing many physical phenomena, but incurs significant computational cost. For example, Puso et al. found a 30% increase in total time in some of their CSM problems when enabling contact resolution [7,18]. Even larger performance costs in real-world problems have been related to the authors of this work anecdotally.

In this paper, we will focus exclusively on explicit time-stepping 3D CSM applications. Computational contact mechanics algorithms are typically composed of two primary components. The first is the computation of the gap function between surfaces, known as *search*. The second component is the stable *enforcement* of impenetrability constraints. Depending on the enforcement technique used, the search component may be invoked multiple times per explicit time step.

The general computational flow is as follows. First, the dynamics portion of the CSM application evaluates the displacements of the finite elements. Next, overlapping elements are detected using *search*. Gaps are resolved using the *enforcement* algorithm, possibly iteratively invoking *search* multiple times. In this work, we will focus on distributed *search* with a simple penalty *enforcement* algorithm.

In a distributed setting with non-adaptive mesh techniques, elements are usually distributed evenly among processing elements (PEs) in such a way as to minimize communication cost. These elements also map to the interior of the collision bodies. From a contact point of view, the interiors can be omitted, as we are interested in the gaps between exterior surfaces. This naturally leads to a disparity between the load characteristics of mesh distributions between contact and non-contact routines in the CSM application.

This disparity is further amplified by the highly dynamic nature of contact problems. As computational load scales (nonlinearly) with the number of nodal contacts, this makes the performance characteristics of a given contact problem difficult to predict. Furthermore, given that contacts may involve elements distributed to different PEs, the problem is highly non-local. Resolving these contacts requires sparse and irregular communication with the specific PEs involved. Finally, given that contact methods typically use pruning or spatial hierarchical algorithms for winnowing potential contacts, these particular contact resolution tasks may differ greatly in their running time. This, in turn, can lead to significant load imbalance problems; if given a problem with a single point of contact (such as a ball hitting a wall), a non-dynamic load balancer might simply use one PE to resolve the contact, with other PEs remaining idle. Attaway et al. [4] summarize these problems succinctly; they describe the distributed contact problem as exhibiting *global*, *dynamic*, and *irregular* behaviors. This combination of all three behaviors, makes computational contact mechanics a challenging problem to solve.

In recent years, asynchronous many tasking (AMT) frameworks have been proposed to address the challenges around such irregular applications. Examples of these include DARMA/vt [15], Charm++ [11], HPX [10], and Legion [6]. The advantage of these approaches is that the runtime system can schedule, track, and balance tasks dynamically.

Our Contribution. We propose distBVH [1], a scalable algorithm for distributed asynchronous contact search that addresses the dynamicism challenges in contact applications. Our approach uses the DARMA/vt [15] AMT runtime for task scheduling and load balancing, while maintaining interoperability with more traditional bulk-synchronous MPI codes. We present a novel multi-phase algorithm for search that utilizes Kokkos [19] for shared-memory parallelism in conjunction with distributed AMT for minimizing communication and computation costs. Additionally, distBVH has been integrated into NimbleSM [2], a 3D MPI-based Lagrangian finite element code for solid mechanics simulations.

The rest of this paper is organized as follows. In Sect. 2, we provide an overview of previous approaches in the field. Next, we discuss our novel algorithm in Sect. 3. We present initial performance results of our code in Sect. 4, using our integration in the NimbleSM finite element code to demonstrate our results. Finally, we suggest future directions for research and conclude in Sect. 5.

2   Prior Work

Contact problems in computational solid mechanics are extensively studied due to their importance in interactions between solid matter. Johnson's often cited text [9] provides a number of analytical solutions. Barber et al. [5] provide an overview of contact problems, including a survey of various solution methods. A book by Wriggers et al. [20] goes in depth on contact problems, including different forms of contact and the finite element formulation of contact problems.

Degroot et al. [7,18] discuss the computational challenges around parallel solid mechanics applications, including the cost of contact resolution. They show up to a 30% increase in cost for their "Juicer" problem when enabling contact. Attaway et al. [4] present an early parallel, PRONTO3D, that is scalable to thousands of nodes.

An extensive body of work on contact mechanics also exists in the field of computer graphics, where soft body and cloth simulations are important for realistic visual effects. Many of these formulations focus on the scheduling of contact events, including work by Harmon et al. [8] on asynchronous contact mechanics and Ainsley et al. [3] on speculative asynchronous contact mechanics. A paper by Xiang, Kale, and Tamstorf [17] builds on the previous two works to solve scalable asynchronous contact problems for cloth simulations in Charm++. Related work on bounding volume hierarchy construction for ray tracing on the GPU was performed by Lauterbach et al. [12]. Lebrun-Grandié et al. provide an overview of ArborX [13], a performance-portable on-node and MPI-based geometric search library that supports overlap queries in addition to nearest neighbor queries.

In our work, we rely significantly on distributed dynamic load-balancing algorithms due to the varying load in our problem over time. Menon et al. [16] provide a framework for a distributed dynamic load balancer, *GrapevineLB*, that uses partial information about application loads to make informed balancing decisions in a scalable manner. Lifflander et al. [14] build on this work with a novel distributed load balancer that is included in DARMA/*vt*.

3 Algorithm

The contact search algorithm is composed of five different steps. The first step, update and tree build, handles the transition of data from the node-resident MPI portion of the time step to DARMA/*vt* virtual collections and then construction of the bounding volume hierarchy. The second, the broadphase, performs a distributed coarse pruning of potential contacts and generates tasks for the refined search steps. The refined search steps are the midphase, which performs on-node pruning of bounding volumes using shared-memory parallel constructs, and the narrowphase, which is the application-defined closest-point projection algorithm. The midphase also copies elements between nodes in order to evaluate contact on-node, in a process called *ghosting*. Finally, computational loads are migrated by the DARMA/*vt* load balancer. In this paper, we will focus on the update, tree build, and broadphase steps, as the on-node algorithms used for the midphase and narrowphase are extensively covered in other literature [12,13].

3.1 Update and Tree Build

The ideal distribution of elements for the non-contact computations over processing elements for a typical non-adaptive mesh will consider the interior (non-surface) elements of the mesh. On the other hand, contact search should only consider the surface elements. Moreover, the load distribution in contact is highly dependent on the spatial locality of contact points. For example, a problem with a singular point of contact might be isolated to the elements distributed on a single node, maximizing load imbalance.

We address this problem in our method by remapping each collision object's collections of finite elements, which we call *patches*, to different processing elements using the DARMA/*vt* load balancer. These patches will eventually be the leaves of our broadphase tree, and the "quality" of the patches is important for performance of later stages of our approach. The term "quality" requires some explanation—typical spatial culling approaches, including our own, work in a hierarchical fashion to cull large swaths of potential contacts before refining in the next step. This means partitioning a space into (typically two, for a binary tree) possibly overlapping subspaces. Ideally, the probability of a contact in each of the subspaces is roughly equivalent, meaning that the tree is balanced. Spatial culling techniques that are properly balanced can then reduce an $O\left(n^2\right)$ problem to an $O\left(n \log n\right)$ problem. Of course, there is no exact way of knowing the probability of contact without solving the contact problem itself, so instead we use a heuristic approach to maintain a balanced tree.

Our approach uses spatial clustering for building patches using a space-filling curve. This ensures that elements close to one another will be located in the same patch. We follow the same general scheme as Lauterbach et al. [12] for clustering, using a Morton encoding for the centroid of the patches. In practice, we generate just the indices of the elements that are part of the patch and the bounding volumes (BV) of the patches in this step. This saves computation cost from copying the data early on, as not all patches will be participating in the contact search.

We generate a number of clusters per compute node according to the overdecomposition factor; this gives fine-grained control over the granularity of the broadphase tree. In general, one can view this granularity as the boundary between on-node and off-node computations in the contact search. A finer granularity in the broadphase will mean less work done on-node in the narrowphase (as the height of the narrowphase trees will be smaller), but more work in the broadphase. Furthermore, the early culling before the ghosting steps of the narrowphase mean less data transfer cost. This tradeoff is explored in Sect. 4.

Patch BVs are reduced across the processor elements to produce a single list of leaves. Next, we construct a bounding volume hierarchy (BVH) from the list of leaves in a top-down fashion, splitting each successive level of the tree along the mean point of the longest axis of the scattered BV centroids. This heuristic is designed to split each level of the tree in such a way that either side is as likely to be in contact as the other. In practice, given two bodies $\mathbf{P}$ and $\mathbf{Q}$ that may potentially come into contact, only one body, without loss of generality, $\mathbf{Q}$ needs to construct the tree $\mathcal{T}_Q$. $\mathcal{T}_Q$ is then broadcast to each rank, so that every processing element has an identical representation of this broadphase tree.

3.2   Broadphase

The subsequent step, the broadphase, determines which patches are potentially in contact and initiates the ghosting and narrowphase steps for those patches. As this step compares the overlapping patches of two collision objects, the broadphase task that gets generated for a potential collision has a dependency on the update tasks for both objects, and the tree build for one of the objects.

In parallel, each broadphase patch p_i from collision object $\mathbf{P}$ will check against collision with the broadphase tree $\mathcal{T}_Q$ belonging to body $\mathbf{Q}$. In general, assuming a balanced tree, this method will take $O(|\mathbf{P}|\,|\mathbf{Q}|)$ time. For each potential collision we spawn a midphase task.

The tasks are generated by adding entries into an *insertable collection*, a DARMA/*vt* virtual collection that supports sparse indexing and insertion. This permits some state to be stored with the tasks, such as the originating ranks for the patches that are in contact, that will be used during contact enforcement. Additionally, this provides a migrateable handle for DARMA/*vt*'s load balancer to associate with a node, allowing midphase tasks to be balanced.

The results of the broadphase are then used for further initialization of element data. Per-surface-element data is required for further refined pruning of the potential contact set, but at large scales with millions of elements, copying this data over the network is expensive. We delay this copying operation until after the broadphase, and only perform it for patches that are potentially in contact. This lazy approach enables efficient interoperability with MPI codes, such as is the case with NimbleSM, as per-node data in the MPI portion is only sent over the network for later phases if the corresponding patch shows a potential collision.

3.3 Midphase and Ghosting

The midphase step further prunes the potential collisions by examining the bounding volumes of elements within a patch. Each bounding volume that is potentially in contact will then be further refined by the narrowphase, using closest-point projection algorithms that are common in contact applications.

The midphase operates on-node, so requires the per-surface-element data from each colliding patch. As mentioned in Sect. 3.2, this per-surface-element data is lazily initialized after the broadphase step. However, the elements of both patch p_i and q_j of the potential contact are not guaranteed to be collocated, and in fact might be required to be present on multiple ranks. In order to provide maximum freedom for the DARMA/vt load balancer to relocate midphase tasks, we do not even require one of the two patches to be collocated with the midphase task. This is motivated by the fact that the majority of time in our algorithm is spent in the midphase and narrowphase tasks.

The problem of collocation is addressed by copying patch element data through a ghosting step. Each midphase task generates two subtasks for patches p_i and q_i, requesting a copy of patch element data to the rank that the midphase task is mapped to. However, there is a particular issue that arises. Up to this point, our tasks have been operating in a virtual indexing space; that is, in indices $0 \leq i \leq Ro$, where R is the total number of ranks and o is the overdecomposition factor. This means that on a given rank, up to o patches may request the same patch from another rank during the ghosting step. Our algorithm performs devirtualization, where the destination rank for a given patch is recorded for each request, but duplicate requests to the same target rank are ignored. This can save theoretically a factor of o cost for each patch in particularly degenerate contact situations.

Once p_i and q_i are ghosted onto the same PE, it is possible to further cull the potential collision set by using an on-node algorithm. The choice of this algorithm is left to users of distBVH, though in Sect. 4, we utilize ArborX [13] in our experiments.

3.4 Narrowphase

Regardless of the midphase and narrowphase (closest-point projection) methods used, our distributed algorithm requires one more step: the transfer of collision results back to the originating PEs. These results typically include the gaps between elements with respect to the normals or potentially also the computed penalty force. As one of our design goals is interoperability with primarily MPI codes, this transfer of contact information back to the originating PEs is important for the MPI integrators to take into account the contact forces. Furthermore, this mapping is also important for visualization.

3.5 Load Balancing

At the end of the timestep, DARMA/*vt*'s load balancer has a chance to run. In this paper we will omit a description of DARMA/*vt*'s various load balancers, but information on this topic can be found in Lifflander et al. [14]. Dynamic load balancers are an essential part of our distributed algorithm's performance, as the midphase and narrowphase tasks can have a huge disparity in running time. At the minimum, a midphase task may simply involve checking the children of the root node of a bounding volume hierarchy before terminating. At the maximum (particularly in degenerate cases), the task may end up comparing every element in p_i and q_i, leading to roughly $O(n^2)$ asymptotic behavior.

There is some computational cost to initiating the load balancer. However, this cost can be amortized over multiple timesteps. Our algorithm relies in part on a persistence heuristic. Although in some cases contacts can be brief, lasting only a handful of timesteps, we rely on most contact states being persistent over multiple timesteps due to inertial forces. A consequence is that we load balance less often. Section 4 goes into more detail on some of our experiments with changing load balancer frequency.

4 Results

We evaluated our algorithm in the Lagrangian finite elements solid mechanics application, NimbleSM [2]. Experiments were carried out on a cluster with Dual Socket Intel E5-2683v3 2.00GHz CPUs with 28 cores each, 256 GB DDR 3 RAM, and 56 Gb/s FDR infiniband. We used two CSM problems for our benchmarks.

The first, *sphere/plate contact* with 1,530,664 total elements simulates a sphere striking a wall. This particular problem was selected in order to understand the performance characteristics of our algorithm on a severely unbalanced problem—the sphere strikes the wall at only one point. The second problem, *thin plate contact*, contains 4,374,826 total elements. This problem simulates two large, thin plates striking one another and is used to demonstrate our performance when approximately half of all elements are in contact.

In all our experiments, we configured DARMA/*vt* to record traces, which has a negligible performance penalty, and to use DARMA/*vt* supplied *HierarchicalLB*. This load balancer is based on a traditional centralized load balancing scheme. We used a recent version of Kokkos (4.2) and ArborX (1.4.1) for the on-node kernels. Kokkos was configured to use OpenMP as its backend, utilizing all 28 threads available on the node. We scaled our experiments up to 32 compute nodes, totaling 896 total cores.

Figure 1 shows the results of a strong scaling experiment we performed on *thin plate contact*. We were interested in analyzing how the overdecomposition factor

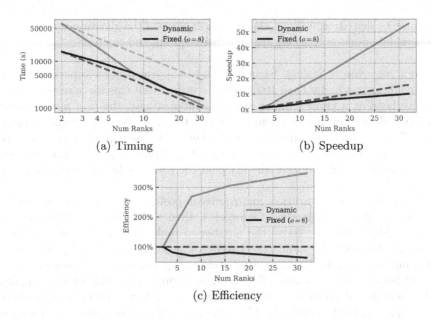

(a) Timing   (b) Speedup

(c) Efficiency

Fig. 1. Strong scaling results of the *thin plate* experiment up to 32 ranks compared between a run with a fixed overdecomposition factor $o = 8$ and one with a dynamic overdecomposition factor. Note that this problem was too large to run efficiently on a single rank. The dashed lines show ideal scaling. See Sect. 4 for a discussion of apparent superlinear scaling.

o would affect scaling. The overdecomposition factor affects the granularity of our tasks, and also affects the number of leaves in our broadphase tree. In the strong scaling study, we are maintaining the same problem size as we increase the number of ranks. The overdecomposition factor serves as a multiplier here; if the overdecomposition factor stays the same, then the patch (and task) size becomes smaller and smaller. On the other hand, if we halve the overdecomposition factor whenever we double the number of cores, we can maintain the same patch size. We call this *dynamic* overdecomposition.

Figure 2 shows a snapshot of a single time step in the *thin plate contact* problem. In this problem, roughly two-thirds of the time step is consumed by

Fig. 2. A projections plot for 8 compute nodes on the *thin plate contact* problem. This plot captures a single time step, with each row being a processing element. The red blocks are the finite element parts of the time-step, while purple is the contact ghosting and blue the midphase and narrowphase.

the contact calculation. We can also see the expense of the ghosting step—blocks in the middle portion (purple) are ghosting requests and replies.

Apparent Superlinear Scaling. Figures 1b and 1c appear to show superlinear scaling and efficiency greater than 100%. We discovered that this was a result of high task overhead at a lower number of ranks. Interestingly, the *thin plate contact* problem suffers from this overhead because of the close (but not touching) proximity of the two plates. This proximity triggers the patches of both plates to be included in the broadphase even though the midphase process exits earlier; however at this point, we have already paid the cost of scheduling the task and ghosting.

The *Dynamic* configuration for overdecomposition is as follows: we fix at 32 ranks an overdecomposition factor of 4, then multiply the overdecomposition factor by two as we halve the number of ranks. The scaling study shows advantages to inversely scaling the overdecomposition factor in this way for a higher number of ranks. Having a fixed overdecomposition factor, however, scales close to linearly before falling off at a higher number of ranks. Our conclusion is that one should be cautious with having too small of a patch size. In these cases, task overhead dominates. This is apparent from the falloff for the fixed overdecomposition factor at larger scales.

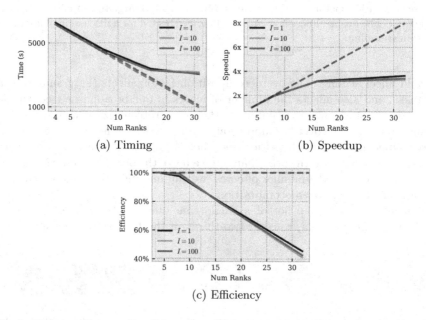

(a) Timing   (b) Speedup

(c) Efficiency

Fig. 3. Strong scaling results of the *sphere/plate contact* experiment, showing the timing, speedup, and efficiency up to 32 ranks comparing different load balancing intervals. The overdecomposition factor in this experiment uses the *Dynamic* scheme discussed above.

Figure 3 shows the result of a strong scaling experiment we performed on the *sphere/plate contact* problem. In this experiment, we modified the interval in time steps between runs of *HierarchicalLB*, in order to understand the impact of the LB on overall performance. The *sphere/plate contact* problem exhibited particular difficulties scaling, in that the problem is significantly smaller than the *thin plate contact* problem and processors are starved for data. In addition, only a small proportion of patches were involved in the contact event. Interestingly, we found that in this particular problem, load balancing frequency had little impact on performance. This is likely a result of persistence in the contact problem along with the smaller number of ranks we used in our experiments causing the load balancing step to be very cheap.

We also ran a single experiment at 16 nodes on the *sphere/plate contact* problem comparing the use of *HierarchicalLB* with no load balancer. In total, the experiment with *HierarchicalLB* took 3046.87 s over a total of 10000 time steps. Running without the load balancer totaled 4086.5 s, yielding a roughly 1.34x speedup simply from running the load balancer. Figure 4 shows a sample time step for the problem with and without LB. Note that the scales in these figures are not correlated, and were sampled from slightly different (but roughly equivalent) times. However, one can clearly see that only half the cores are utilized at all when not using the load balancer.

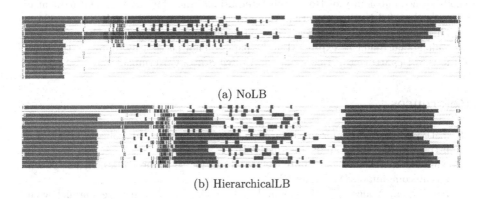

(a) NoLB

(b) HierarchicalLB

Fig. 4. Projections showing the effect of load balancing on a time step of the *sphere/plate contact* problem. Note that these were sampled at slightly different times, and their scaling does not correspond. However, one can see the severe load imbalance issues when not running the load balancer as only half of the available PEs are utilized for contact.

5   Conclusion

In this work, we have shown how distributed computational contact mechanics problems can be solved in a scalable manner using asynchronous tasking. Our approach takes advantage of dynamic load balancing and asynchronous task scheduling from DARMA/vt to solve many of the problems around irregularity that affects previous approaches. Additionally, we presented a novel lazy patch initialization and ghosting algorithm that can adapt to highly dynamic contact problems and interoperate with existing MPI code.

Some aspects of this work that we would like to explore in the future include further examining the surface decomposition of the mesh. Currently, our approach generates patches dynamically, according to our clustering heuristics. It is possible that this could be precomputed, but may generate lesser quality patches. We would like to explore this area and evaluate whether this performance trade-off is worth it.

Another aspect for exploration is understanding better the role persistence plays in load balancing. We would like to perform a more formal analysis of persistence, including measuring per-patch or per element, rather than just observing the knock-on effects on LB cost.

Finally, we would like to add GPU support to our approach. We envision GPUs being used for the midphase and narrowphase steps, but it s likely that we would have to take steps to reduce kernel scheduling overhead due to the small size of our tasks.

Acknowledgments. Sandia National Laboratories is a multimission laboratory managed and operated by National Technology & Engineering Solutions of Sandia, LLC, a wholly owned subsidiary of Honeywell International Inc., for the U.S. Department of Energy's National Nuclear Security Administration under contract DE-NA0003525.

This paper describes objective technical results and analysis. Any subjective views or opinions that might be expressed in the paper do not necessarily represent the views of the U.S. Department of Energy or the United States Government.

References

1. distBVH, a library for asynchronous parallel distributed collision detection. https://github.com/sandialabs/distBVH
2. NimbleSM, a Lagrangian finite-element code for solid mechanics. https://www.github.com/nimbleSM/NimbleSM
3. Ainsley, S., Vouga, E., Grinspun, E., Tamstorf, R.: Speculative parallel asynchronous contact mechanics. ACM Trans. Graph. (TOG) **31**(6), 1–8 (2012)
4. Attaway, S., et al.: A parallel contact detection algorithm for transient solid dynamics simulations using PRONTO3D. Comput. Mech. **22**, 143–159 (1998)
5. Barber, J.R., Ciavarella, M.: Contact mechanics. Int. J. Solids Struct. **37**(1–2), 29–43 (2000)
6. Bauer, M., Treichler, S., Slaughter, E., Aiken, A.: Legion: expressing locality and independence with logical regions. In: SC 2012: Proceedings of the International Conference on High Performance Computing, Networking, Storage and Analysis, pp. 1–11. IEEE (2012)
7. Degroot, T., et al.: Accomplishments and challenges in code development for parallel and multimechanics simulations. In: Palma, J.M.L.M., Amestoy, P.R., Daydé, M., Mattoso, M., Lopes, J.C. (eds.) VECPAR 2008. LNCS, vol. 5336, pp. 214–227. Springer, Heidelberg (2008). https://doi.org/10.1007/978-3-540-92859-1_20

8. Harmon, D., Vouga, E., Smith, B., Tamstorf, R., Grinspun, E.: Asynchronous contact mechanics. In: ACM SIGGRAPH 2009 Papers, pp. 1–12 (2009)

9. Johnson, K.L., Johnson, K.L.: Contact Mechanics. Cambridge University Press, Cambridge (1987)

10. Kaiser, H., Heller, T., Adelstein-Lelbach, B., Serio, A., Fey, D.: HPX: a task based programming model in a global address space. In: Proceedings of the 8th International Conference on Partitioned Global Address Space Programming Models, pp. 1–11 (2014)

11. Kale, L.V., Krishnan, S.: CHARM++ a portable concurrent object oriented system based on C++. In: Proceedings of the Eighth Annual Conference on Object-Oriented Programming Systems, Languages, and Applications, pp. 91–108 (1993)

12. Lauterbach, C., Garland, M., Sengupta, S., Luebke, D., Manocha, D.: Fast BVH construction on GPUs. In: Computer Graphics Forum, vol. 28, pp. 375–384. Wiley Online Library (2009)

13. Lebrun-Grandié, D., Prokopenko, A., Turcksin, B., Slattery, S.R.: ArborX: a performance portable geometric search library. ACM Trans. Math. Softw. (TOMS) **47**(1), 1–15 (2020)

14. Lifflander, J., Slattengren, N.L., Pébaÿ, P., Miller, P., Rizzi, F., Bettencourt, M.: Optimizing distributed load balancing for workloads with time-varying imbalance. In: Proceedings of the 2021 IEEE International Conference on Cluster Computing. Virtual Conference (2021). https://doi.org/10.1109/Cluster48925.2021.00039

15. Lifflander, J., Miller, P., Slattengren, N.L., Morales, N., Stickney, P., Pébaÿ, P.P.: Design and implementation techniques for an MPI-oriented AMT runtime. In: 2020 Workshop on Exascale MPI (ExaMPI), pp. 31–40. IEEE (2020). https://doi.org/10.1109/ExaMPI52011.2020.00009

16. Menon, H., Kalé, L.: A distributed dynamic load balancer for iterative applications. In: Proceedings of the International Conference on High Performance Computing, Networking, Storage and Analysis, SC 2013, pp. 1–11. ACM, New York (2013). https://doi.org/10.1145/2503210.2503284

17. Ni, X., Kale, L.V., Tamstorf, R.: Scalable asynchronous contact mechanics using CHARM++. In: 2015 IEEE International Parallel and Distributed Processing Symposium, pp. 677–686. IEEE (2015)

18. Puso, M., et al.: Accomplishments and challenges in code development for parallel and multimechanics simulations. Technical report, Lawrence Livermore National Lab. (LLNL), Livermore, CA (United States) (2008)

19. Trott, C.R., et al.: Kokkos 3: programming model extensions for the exascale era. IEEE Trans. Parallel Distrib. Syst. **33**(4), 805–817 (2022). https://doi.org/10.1109/TPDS.2021.3097283

20. Wriggers, P.: Computational Contact Mechanics. Springer, Cham (2006)

IRIS Reimagined: Advancements in Intelligent Runtime System for Task-Based Programming

Narasinga Rao Miniskar$^{(\boxtimes)}$, Seyong Lee, Johnston Beau,
Aaron Young, Mohammad Alaul Haque Monil, Pedro Valero-Lara,
and Jeffrey S. Vetter

Oak Ridge National Laboratory, Oak Ridge, TN 37831, USA
{miniskarnr,lees2,youngar,monilm,valerolarap,vetter}@ornl.gov

Abstract. Task-based programming models are gaining traction in scientific computing. IRIS is a portable runtime system that exploits multiple heterogeneous programming systems and can discover available resources and manage multiple diverse programming systems (e.g., CUDA, Hexagon, HIP, Level Zero, OpenCL, and OpenMP) simultaneously. It accounts for the constraints of task dependencies and provides customizable scheduling policies to map those tasks to heterogeneous devices. In this paper, we present new capabilities added to IRIS to improve its portability for heterogeneous programming, build-friendliness, and performance efficiency. The new additions include vendor-specific kernel support, a runtime system with a foreign function interface to eliminate writing wrapper or boilerplate code for heterogeneous kernels, an easy-to-use and configurable CMake-based build environment, automatic and efficient data transfers and orchestration, and the Hunter and DAGGER toolchains to evaluate IRIS's task scheduling algorithms.

Keywords: Heterogeneous Computing · Runtime System · IRIS · DMEM · CUDA · HIP · Task based programming

This manuscript has been authored by UT-Battelle, LLC under contract DE-AC05-00OR22725 with the US Department of Energy (DOE). The US government retains and the publisher, by accepting the article for publication, acknowledges that the US government retains a nonexclusive, paid-up, irrevocable, worldwide license to publish or reproduce the published form of this manuscript, or allow others to do so, for US government purposes. DOE will provide public access to these results of federally sponsored research in accordance with the DOE Public Access Plan (http://energy.gov/downloads/doe-public-access-plan).

P. Diehl et al. (Eds.): WAMTA 2024, LNCS 14626, pp. 46–58, 2024.
https://doi.org/10.1007/978-3-031-61763-8_5

1   Introduction

The current trend in computer architectures is a transition toward extreme heterogeneity, with a focus on domain-specific computing. Initially observed in mobile and embedded markets, this trend is expanding into high-performance computing (HPC), machine learning, enterprise, and cloud computing [8]. Contemporary architectures such as NVIDIA Xavier and Qualcomm Snapdragon are notable examples that indicate the movement toward systems-on-chip (SOCs) containing multiple heterogeneous processors for diverse applications. In HPC, most of the top systems are heterogeneous [17], and this trend is expected to persist. However, the challenge lies in the lack of programming systems that span these architectures while ensuring performance portability. Various programming models exist—from directive-based high-level programming (OpenMP [16], OpenACC [15], etc.) and C++ template metaprogramming (Kokkos [5], RAJA [4], SYCL [7], etc.) to low-level device-specific programming (CUDA [14], HIP [1], etc.). However, these models' implementation and portability are inconsistent. One common feature among these heterogeneous programming models is the reliance on runtime systems (RTS), which necessitates efficient management of resources and data dependencies, as well as dynamic balancing of goals during execution.

To address the challenges posed by increasingly diverse heterogeneous systems, IRIS [8] was developed to provide enhanced capabilities in heterogeneous RTSs. IRIS includes features such as online adaptive scheduling, dynamic resource discovery, proactive data movement, support for simultaneous execution of multiple heterogeneous devices, and an interface for online code generation. These advancements aim to achieve performance portability by dynamically adapting to system constraints and dependencies that are often unknown until execution time, offering a solution to the complex scheduling challenges inherent in heterogeneous architectures. This paper presents work that builds on the original IRIS framework by adding new, more advanced capabilities to IRIS to make it more portable, easier to program and build, and more performant. The summary of enhancements and contributions to IRIS is given below.

- Vendor-specific kernels: IRIS was extended to allow vendor-specific kernel calls. These are written with host wrapper kernel functions to enable vendor-specific libraries (e.g., cuBLAS) to be callable from IRIS instead of having to write the kernels in their native device languages (e.g., CUDA).
- Foreign function interface: this contribution extends IRIS to use the foreign function interface (FFI) library [6] to call the device-specific kernels with parameters. This means that users can avoid writing the explicit boilerplate code or wrapper code (written in C++) for each IRIS kernel and each of its parameters.
- Distributed data memory management: IRIS was extended with a new heterogeneous and distributed memory handling mechanism (DMEM) to automate data movement across devices based on the requirements—but without the need for the programmer to explicitly specify the host-to-device (H2D) and

device-to-host (D2H) data transfer APIs. DMEM reduces the overall data transfers by 4× and achieves performance gains of 5× when compared to the performance of manually handled memory management through H2D and D2H APIs.

- A heterogeneous build environment was added for IRIS-based applications to ease the development for heterogeneous systems.
- Support for Hunter: a new framework developed for exploration of scheduling algorithms. It also offers a runtime simulator for heterogeneous platforms.
- Support for DAGGER: another framework developed to create the artificial task graphs for evaluating the task scheduling policies of IRIS. A brief example of its usage is included in this paper to highlight the device-scaling performance portability of IRIS.

The rest of the paper is organized as follows: Sect. 2 provides a description of the IRIS runtime framework. Section 3 discusses the state-of-the-art runtime systems and a comparison with IRIS. The extensions of IRIS and new capabilities are described in Sect. 4. Section 5 provides the results for each of IRIS's new capabilities. Finally, we conclude the paper and describe future work in Sect. 6.

2 Background: IRIS

IRIS is a task-based programming model for extremely heterogeneous devices in a system [8,10,11]. It enables application developers to write applications for diverse heterogeneous programming platforms with native device-specific programming models, including CUDA, HIP, Level Zero, OpenCL, and OpenMP. IRIS orchestrates multiple programming platforms and consolidates them into a single execution/programming environment by providing portable tasks and shared virtual device memory. IRIS provides shared virtual device memory across multiple disparate physical device memories to achieve application portability and flexible task scheduling with effective data orchestration [12]. It does so by automatically transferring data across multiple devices to maintain memory consistency across tasks. This memory-model abstraction allows developers to prioritize the application's primary feature set and overall function rather than worrying about coding for device-specific memory spread across multiple heterogeneous devices (unscalable and less portable).

A *Task* is a scheduling unit in IRIS and is mapped to a device by the customizable scheduling policy available in IRIS to run on a single device of heterogeneous system. A task comprises zero or more commands; these can be either data transfer commands or kernel execution commands on an accelerator. The data transfer commands can be H2D, D2H, or device to device (D2D). The DMEM methodology added to IRIS automatically derives these data transfer commands for each task based on the data required for the task, data availability on other devices, and data dependency on other tasks. IRIS provides APIs to indicate the dependency of a task on other tasks.

3   Related Work

Task-based dynamic runtimes are positioned as part of the solution to some of the most important challenges in HPC today [2,11], such as programming productivity, performance portability, and extreme heterogeneity. However, novel developments are needed in software abstractions to increase application portability using fully dynamic runtime systems to schedule and control highly varied resources. Existing standard approaches rely mostly on static mapping and scheduling, such that the programmer must decide which device to use for each task, such as OpenMP tasking [18] or others [9]. We can find two dynamic runtime systems with good support for the aforementioned challenges: StarPU [3] and IRIS [8]. Although StarPU provides a relatively easy-to-use interface and has support for heterogeneous architectures, IRIS goes further by supporting a simpler interface for a greater variety of devices and programming models. Moreover, IRIS eliminates the need for a wrapper for the codes to be computed in the tasks and provides highly optimized memory management that can scale up performance on a high number of disparate accelerators [13].

4   IRIS Re-imagined

This paper presents work done to extend the IRIS framework with new capabilities to further increase its performance, portability, and programming efficiency.

4.1   Vendor-Specific Kernels

HPC vendor libraries (such as math libraries) face important challenges caused by the explosion of in-node heterogeneity. Due to this increasing heterogeneity, manual computation orchestration across runtimes and devices is becoming intractable. Historically, vendors and open-source BLAS libraries have mostly focused on a single architecture. However, recently, some math libraries from the open-source community have been focusing on supporting heterogeneity in their software stack (e.g., Chameleon). However, the need to support heterogeneity across a diversity of architectures is still a challenge. The IRIS runtime system was developed to provide the orchestration: it provides functionalities such as task offloading, whereby, the computation uses vendor-optimized kernels according to the device to which the task is issued. Using this feature, IRIS facilitates newer abstractions to solve larger math problems by ensuring that most appropriate processors for a given task to harness scalability and performance. Several vendor library abstractions are built on top of IRIS using these capabilities, such as MatRIS [13], which encapsulates previous efforts such as IRIS-BLAS [11], and LARIS [12]. Because of this feature support in IRIS, MatRIS is fully heterogeneous and portable across heterogeneous systems.

4.2 Foreign Function Interface (FFI)

IRIS requires boilerplate (wrapper) code for each kernel implementation for an OpenMP device. Adding support for vendor-specific kernel calls [11] highlighted that for each call, IRIS also needs boilerplate code—often multiple versions for each type of supported device (such as CUDA, HIP, and OpenMP). Figure 1(a, b) shows the boilerplate code requirement for IRIS-native kernels and vendor-specific kernels. The boilerplate code contains an implementation of method APIs to set the positional kernel arguments as well as a method to call the actual kernel with positional parameters. The positional parameters are stored in a temporary run-time memory chunk. It is tedious to write boilerplate code for each kernel. A simple SAXPY kernel for OpenMP device requires ~100 lines of boilerplate code to be written, and this effort is required for all vendor-specific kernels and for all devices. IRIS was extended to use *libFFI* so that programmers need not write boilerplate code for IRIS kernels, as shown in Fig. 1(c).

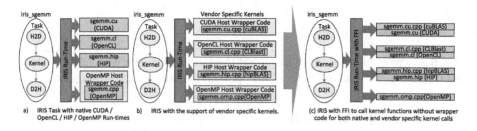

Fig. 1. IRIS with FFI

4.3 Distributed Data Memory Management (DMEM)

Orchestrating memory objects and their copies across heterogeneous devices during execution plays a vital role in heterogeneous systems. Data movement between heterogeneous devices often becomes a bottleneck in achieving strong performance because the data transfer overhead nullifies the impact of greater parallelism. Moreover, accelerators such as GPUs in contemporary HPC nodes have faster connections with higher bandwidth to transfer data. Such a connection requires one D2D transfer as opposed to two transfers (i.e., D2H and H2D). To orchestrate memory object copies in different devices and efficiently utilize the data transfer among them, IRIS introduces DMEM, which provides transparent and efficient data communication (such as invoking faster D2D data transfer when possible) and managing the set of copies of memory in a heterogeneous system.

As a logical memory handler, DMEM stores the addresses of an application's data objects in host and device memory. By keeping a *dirty flag*, DMEM keeps

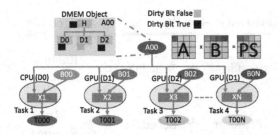

Fig. 2. IRIS DMEM data object example for tiled matrix multiplication. A and B are input tiled matrices, and PS denotes the partial sum tiled matrix

track of which copy of a particular memory object is the most recent. As the execution progresses, the DMEM logic controller continues updating the flags when a change occurs in a memory object. Because IRIS dependencies in a directed acyclic graph (DAG) prevent race conditions, only one device can write to a particular memory object. As seen in Fig. 2, the *A00* tile is a shared IRIS–DMEM memory object for all tasks (*X1, X2, ..., XN tiled matrix multiplication kernels*). Programmers do not need to use H2D and D2H command APIs for DMEM memory objects because the DMEM controller handles data transfers at runtime, based on the data requirements of the task kernels.

The DMEM memory handler acts like a write-back cache to prevent unnecessary data movement to host memory. The data transfer to output host memory object is required in two scenarios: (1) when the application accesses it after the execution of tasks or task graphs and (2) when the device lacks valid data that is available in another device but a direct D2D data transfer is not possible. DMEM cannot avoid the second scenario, but it can postpone the first scenario's D2H data transfer until the application is really needed. The application programmer musr call an IRIS API with an explicit DMEM flush-out command and submit it as a part of the last task or as a standalone task. For more technical details about the DMEM methodology and data transfer priorities, refer to the HPEC conference paper [10].

4.4 Heterogeneous Build Environment for IRIS Applications

The CMake build utility was added to IRIS to build applications, along with heterogeneous kernels. This utility enables the developers to configure the CMake variables with appropriate sources, and it builds the necessary libraries for each heterogeneous device. It also supports application sources that developers can use to build application libraries and executables with the included IRIS library links for IRIS APIs.

4.5 Hunter

The Hunter Framework is designed to enable the exploration of scheduling algorithms for large-scale heterogeneous architectures. Hunter was developed and

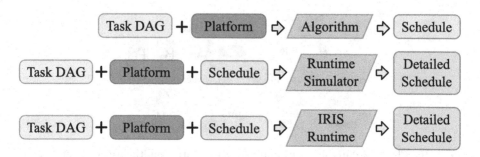

Fig. 3. Block diagram highlighting the use flows for the Hunter Framework.

leveraged for this work to model heterogeneous platforms and evaluate the performance of various scheduling algorithms on these platforms. Hunter is tightly coupled with the IRIS runtime API, which allows task graphs within IRIS to be exported to Hunter. Likewise, schedules within Hunter can be run using the IRIS runtime.

Hunter is a Python library with multiple components designed to work together. Hunter uses an object-oriented programming style; a parent class defines the API and multiple derived classes, which can each have their own implementation of the API. The main input components of Hunter are a task DAG to define the application task graph and a platform to define the model of the computer system. Scheduling algorithms implemented in Hunter takes a task DAG and platform as inputs to provide scheduling decisions (i.e., schedule). The task DAG and platform, along with a schedule, can then be passed to the Hunter runtime simulator or the IRIS runtime for evaluation. The output of the evaluation includes scheduling with additional execution details, more accurate simulated execution times, and the actual execution times from running on the hardware using IRIS. These evaluation flows are highlighted in Fig. 3.

4.6 DAGGER

The Directed Acyclic Graph Generator to Evaluate Runtimes (DAGGER) is a tool developed to synthesize payloads, generating task DAGs of arbitrary complexity. It was initially built to test interesting corner cases easily missed when building a runtime system, and so was used to verify the scheduling decisions when developing IRIS. This functionality was extended for evaluations of different desired DAG characteristics—allowing us to examine and evaluate scheduling policies, and the general performance of IRIS, without having to write an exhaustive corner cases (on the order of hundreds of diverse applications).

DAGGER is composed of a generator and a runner program. The generator accepts a range of parameters used to statistically determine the structure and shape of the DAG. Additionally, the user provides the kernel names (with appropriate kernel arguments) with the probabilities to which each generated task will be assigned. The resultant DAG is recorded as an IRIS-readable JSON file. The DAGGER runner accepts the same arguments and loads the JSON file by handing it directly to IRIS, but it serves, importantly, as a proxy application by allocating the correct number of memory objects and other kernel arguments. It also uses IRIS's internal profiling information but controls where it is logged—for recording results.

Users adjust variables that allow varying the width and depth, and the number of tasks, whereas the shape of the DAG and distribution of tasks are determined by adjusting the cumulative distribution functions' mean and standard deviation variables. Finally, complexity in the generated DAG can be set by increasing the number of skips, which can lead to interesting interactions among tasks by increasing the potential interactions of tasks between levels. Additionally, it allows each task to be assigned kernel names that are statistically selected by providing the associated probability, the dimensionality of the kernels, and the memory buffers associated with each kernel task. DAGGER allows the synthetic generation of DAGs with interesting shapes and interactions.

New features recently added to DAGGER include the ability to specify the number of concurrent memory buffers allowed for each kernel name and the sharing of memory objects used between tasks; both allow the user to indicate the potential concurrency by mitigating data dependencies between tasks. Finally, both the runner and generator can generate explicit D2H and H2D memory transfers (to get the memory into IRIS when submitting the task graph) or using IRIS's DMEM, which replaces the final tasks in the graph from D2H with the required *DMEM_ FLUSH_ OUT_ CMD*.

5   Results

The effectiveness of IRIS's new capabilities was evaluated using a tiled matrix multiplication benchmark running on a truly heterogeneous system—comprising four NVIDIA A100 and four AMD MI100 GPUs. The tiled matrix multiplication algorithm is implemented using vendor-specific kernels support in IRIS and is part of the MatRIS framework [11–13]. We then explored the scaling of IRIS's scheduling policies by running an identical DAG on multiple systems, each with different combinations of GPUs from multiple vendors.

5.1   FFI

The effectiveness of FFI was measured using a tiled matrix multiplication benchmark. We varied the matrix and tile size to scale over the number of tasks and measured the performance of the FFI version versus the traditional IRIS-based boilerplate code. It has been observed that FFI-based kernel calls have no additional overhead compared to that of boilerplate code. Moreover, in some cases, the performance is slightly better than explicit boilerplate code (Table 1).

Table 1. Matrix multiplication performance with and without FFI. Each experiment is run for 10 times and present the median values.

Matrix Size	Tile Count	Tasks	FFI (GFLOPS)	Boilerplate code (GFLOPS)
4096	2×2	8	5.1	4.2
8192	2×2	8	11.3	9.8
16384	2×2	8	20.8	20.8
16384	4×4	64	19.9	19.2
16384	8×8	512	18.6	17.9
16384	16×16	4096	0.76	0.78

5.2 DMEM

The capabilities of distributed memory objects (DMEM) in IRIS are demonstrated in Table 2. For this experiment, we ran MatRIS [13] LU factorization on a CADES cloud node with four NVIDIA A100 and four AMD MI100 GPUs. We considered a $\approx 32K \times 32K$ matrix with 16×16 tiling, which created around 1500 tasks scheduled to eight GPUs (both NVIDIA and AMD). The first data row of Table 2 shows H2D and D2H data transfer considering each task-initiated data transfer from the host, and, after computing, returned the updated data to the host: it shows around 5000 data transfers in total. However, the use of DMEM (second row of the table) significantly reduced both H2D and D2H transfers because DMEM can find the last location of the data and initiate the appropriate transfer when required. Also, DMEM uses D2D transfers when possible, which provides an additional performance boost. When data needs to be transferred from an AMD GPU to an NVIDIA GPU, DMEM orchestrates the corresponding D2H and H2D transfer. Because of these strategies employed by DMEM, IRIS yields an order of magnitude lower number of total data transfers, which enables superior performance. We also observed nearly $5\times$ gains on matrix multiplication using our intelligent DMEM memory handling technology, as shown in Fig. 4. The gains are due to a reduced number of data transfers and using optimal data transfer APIs.

Table 2. Count of data transfers and their type for DMEM and without DMEM on the $8\times$ GPUs (NVIDIA and AMD). Benchmark: LU factorization on $32,678 \times 32,768$ dense matrix

System	CADES			
Transfer	H2D	D2H	D2D	total
Without DMEM	4,219	1,497	0	5,716
With DMEM	567	395	426	1,388

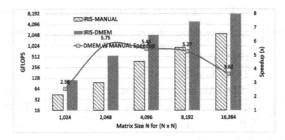

Fig. 4. Performance improvement by DMEM for a tiled matrix multiplication benchmark. Platform: four NVIDIA A100 CUDA GPUs and four AMD MI100 GPUs. The y-axis is on a log scale. Each experiment was run 10 times, and median values are presented.

5.3   DAGGER

In this experiment, an identical DAGGER-generated DAG was run on several systems to highlight the scaling of IRIS's dynamic scheduling policies. Each system is different, featuring unique combinations of the number of GPUs, from both NVIDIA and AMD, in different generations, as shown in Table 3. For brevity, we excluded OpenMP and OpenCL runtimes from the evaluation. IRIS provides the abstract task view given by the DAG; it can automatically link and resolve the appropriate kernel to the underlying backend/runtime on the system—so no code changes are needed. Additionally, IRIS honors data locality, internally tracking ownership/modification of memory buffers of devices; thus, we can change the scheduling policy to affect performance, and it will add the required memory movement to ensure correctness.

The generated task DAG used for this experiment contains 240 `bigk` kernel tasks with 6 concurrent duplicates of memory objects at each level; the instance of each memory object used by each task is stochastic, resulting in a large workload of complex dependencies. This synthetic workload is largely compute-bound, featuring a double-nested `for loop` to compute a sum. The width of the DAG is 6 at each level and is thus 40 levels deep. Each kernel invocation was run at a size of 1024 (i.e., the largest possible number of work items on AMD GPU-based systems).

The results are shown in Fig. 5. Typically, we see systems with fewer GPUs benefit less from scheduling policy selection, whereas systems with more devices benefit from dynamic policy selection. A good example of this effect can be seen by focusing on the 2× speedup achieved by the *Explorer* system when using **ftf**, **random, roundrobin,** or **sdq** over the **depend** or **profile** policies. By experimental design, we assigned all memory to one device at the start of the graph submission, and both *depend* and *profile* policies aim to avoid unnecessary memory movement, yielding a sequential baseline for our comparison. In contrast, the speedups gained by the First-to-Finish **ftf** (only assigns the next task to an idle device, effectively work-stealing), Shortest-Device-Queue **sdq** (assigns each task to the device with the fewest tasks in its queue), **roundrobin**, and **random**

Table 3. The GPU configuration of systems used in the evaluation.

System	Vendor	Generation	Card Name	# of GPUs	Runtimes
Oswald	NVIDIA	Pascal	P100	1	CUDA
Radeon	AMD	Vega II	Vega 20	1	HIP
Zenith	NVIDIA	Ampere	GA102	1	CUDA
	AMD	Navi II	Navi 21	1	HIP
Explorer	AMD	Vega II	MI60	2	HIP
Equinox	NVIDIA	Volta	V100	4	CUDA
Leconte	NVIDIA	Volta	V100	6	CUDA

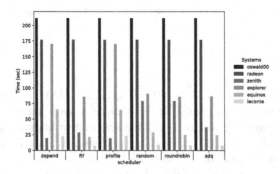

Fig. 5. Execution times of DAG on systems with varying dynamic scheduling policies.

ignore the cost of memory transfers and thus can fully saturate the devices—provided the DAG has enough parallelism, which our experiment ensures. Systems with more devices further highlight this trend, achieving a 3× speedup on *Equinox* and *Leconte*: there are memory movement costs that prevent this workload from reaching the theoretical limit of 4 and 6×, respectively.

The only system that was observed to go against this trend is *Zenith*, which, unfortunately, is the only truly heterogeneous machine in this study. The penalty here is in moving memory between two different runtimes: (D2D) memory movement in this case defaults to moving memory through the host (as separate H2D and subsequent D2H calls), which both have their own synchronization points. Performance is worsened here when we consider the hardware. Each stage of this communication must occur over the PCI-E interconnect, whereas this cost is notapplicable for single runtime systems that have vendor-specific interconnects (NVLink and Infinity Fabric) for fast D2D memory transfers. This results in more reckless policies (in terms of ignoring memory locality) such as **roundrobin** and **random** suffering by taking 3–4× longer than the memory-aware scheduling decisions (**depend** or **profile**), whereas **ftf** and **sdq** performance falls in between because these policies do not consider memory locality but do rely on feedback from the device queues.

The older generation and single-card systems (*Oswald* and *Radeon*) were not affected by the choice of scheduling policy since they do not have enough hardware to exploit the concurrency in DAG. Here, the discrepancy in absolute performance is attributed to hardware differences in the P100 and Vega II GPUs.

6 Conclusion

This paper presents the new capabilities added to IRIS to achieve better performance efficiency, higher portability, improved programmability, and a more convenient build environment. The IRIS DMEM memory handler has achieved $2.5\times$ to $5.7\times$ improvement in performance when compared to manually introduced data transfer calls. Features such as FFI in IRIS allow programmers to avoid writing boilerplate code for each kernel, which is usually 70 to 100 extra lines of code per kernel. Moreover, the addition of the DAGGER and Hunter frameworks enhanced IRIS capabilities for verification and scalability by providing an unbounded range of task and device experiments. This paper shows the scaling performance of IRIS using dynamic scheduling policies on a fixed DAGGER workload. In the future, we will present the performance of static scheduling policies—leaning heavily on the Hunter framework.

References

1. AMD: HIP: C++ heterogeneous-compute interface for portability (2020)
2. Ang, J., et al.: Reimagining codesign for advanced scientific computing: report for the ASCR workshop on reimaging codesign (2022). https://www.osti.gov/biblio/1822199. Accessed 6 July 2022
3. Augonnet, C., Thibault, S., Namyst, R., Wacrenier, P.: STARPU: a unified platform for task scheduling on heterogeneous multicore architectures. In: Sips, H.J., Epema, D.H.J., Lin, H. (eds.) Euro-Par 2009. LNCS, vol. 5704, pp. 863–874. Springer, Heidelberg (2009). https://doi.org/10.1007/978-3-642-03869-3_80
4. Beckingsale, D.A., et al.: RAJA: portable performance for large-scale scientific applications. In: 2019 IEEE/ACM International Workshop on Performance, Portability and Productivity in HPC (P3HPC), pp. 71–81 (2019)
5. Edwards, H.C., Sunderland, D.: Kokkos array performance-portable manycore programming model. In: Guo, M., Huang, Z. (eds.) Proceedings of the 2012 PPOPP International Workshop on Programming Models and Applications for Multicores and Manycores, PMAM 2012, New Orleans, LA, USA, 26 February 2012, pp. 1–10. ACM (2012). https://doi.org/10.1145/2141702.2141703
6. Group, F.W.: libffi: A Portable Foreign Function Interface Library. GNU Project (Year of the latest version). https://sourceware.org/libffi/
7. Khronos Group: SYCL: C++ single-source heterogeneous programming for openCL (2019)
8. Kim, J., Lee, S., Johnston, B., Vetter, J.S.: IRIS: a portable runtime system exploiting multiple heterogeneous programming systems. In: 2021 IEEE High Performance Extreme Computing Conference, HPEC 2021, Waltham, MA, USA, 20–24 September 2021, pp. 1–8. IEEE (2021)
9. Korakitis, O., Gonzalo, S.G.D., Guidotti, N., Barreto, J.P., Monteiro, J.C., Peña, A.J.: Towards OmpSs-2 and OpenACC interoperation. In: Lee, J., Agrawal, K., Spear, M.F. (eds.) PPoPP 2022: 27th ACM SIGPLAN Symposium on Principles and Practice of Parallel Programming, Seoul, Republic of Korea, 2–6 April 2022 (2022)

10. Miniskar, N.R., Haque Monil, M.A., Valero-Lara, P., Liu, F.Y., Vetter, J.S.: IRIS-DMEM: efficient memory management for heterogeneous computing. In: 2023 IEEE High Performance Extreme Computing Conference (HPEC), pp. 1–7 (2023)
11. Miniskar, N.R., Mohammad, A.H.M., Pedro, V.L., Liu, F., Vetter, J.S.: IRIS-BLAS: towards a performance portable and heterogeneous blas library. In: 29th IEEE International Conference on High Performance Computing, Data, and Analytics, HiPC 2022, Bengaluru, India, 18–21 December 2022, pp. 1–10. IEEE (2022)
12. Monil, M.A.H., Miniskar, N.R., Liu, F., Vetter, J.S., Valero-Lara, P.: LaRIS: targeting portability and productivity for LaPACK codes on extreme heterogeneous systems using IRIS. In: IEEE/ACM Redefining Scalability for Diversely Heterogeneous Architectures Workshop, Dallas, TX, USA, 13–18 November 2022. IEEE (2022)
13. Monil, M.A.H., Miniskar, N.R., Teranishi, K., Vetter, J.S., Valero-Lara, P.: MatRIS: multi-level math library abstraction for heterogeneity and performance portability using IRIS runtime. In: Proceedings of the SC 2023 Workshops of the International Conference on High Performance Computing, Network, Storage, and Analysis, pp. 1081–1092 (2023)
14. Nickolls, J., Buck, I.: NVIDIA CUDA software and GPU parallel computing architecture. In: Microprocessor Forum (2007)
15. OpenACC: OpenACC Application Programming Interface (2024). https://www.openacc.org. Accessed 24 Jan 2024
16. OpenMP: OpenMP Application Programming Interface (2024). https://www.openmp.org/specifications/. Accessed 24 Jan 2024
17. TOP500.org: November 2023 TOP500 (2023). https://www.top500.org/lists/top500/2023/11/. Accessed 24 Jan 2024
18. Valero-Lara, P., Kim, J., Hernandez, O., Vetter, J.S.: OpenMP target task: tasking and target offloading on heterogeneous systems. In: Chaves, R., et al. (eds.) Euro-Par 2021. LNCS, vol. 13098, pp. 445–455. Springer, Cham (2021). https://doi.org/10.1007/978-3-031-06156-1_35

MatRIS: Addressing the Challenges for Portability and Heterogeneity Using Tasking for Matrix Decomposition (Cholesky)

Mohammad Alaul Haque Monil[✉], Narasinga Rao Miniskar,
Pedro Valero-Lara, Keita Teranishi, and Jeffrey S. Vetter

Oak Ridge National Laboratory, Oak Ridge, TN 37831, USA
{monilm,miniskarnr,valerolarap,teranishik,vetter}@ornl.gov

Abstract. The ubiquitous in-node heterogeneity of HPC and cloud computing platforms makes software portability and performance optimization extremely challenging. Described here, the MatRIS multilevel math library abstraction framework employs tasking to alleviate these difficulties. MatRIS includes the IRIS task-based runtime on the bottom level and exposes different layers of abstraction to render algorithms architecturally agnostic. MatRIS ensures the decomposition and creation of tasks that represent the necessary encapsulation of the optimized kernels from both vendor and open-source math libraries. Once built, MatRIS can select different combinations of accelerators at runtime, making it portable even on diverse heterogeneous architectures. By leveraging the IRIS runtime's features for managing heterogeneity, MatRIS deploys algorithms that remove the need to specify orchestration and data transfer. This study describes how the serial task abstraction of a tiled Cholesky factorization is made portable and scalable in the case of multi-device and multi-vendor heterogeneity on a node with NVIDIA and AMD GPUs by using MatRIS. First, we demonstrate that Cholesky in MatRIS provides multi-GPU scalability that offers competitive performance versus cuSolverMG. Then, we present the challenges and opportunities for heterogeneous execution.

Keywords: Math Library · Runtime System · POTRF · Cholesky Decomposition · Portability · Heterogeneity · Task based programming

1 Introduction

Diverse in-node heterogeneity introduces significant scalability, scheduling/management, portability, and programming productivity challenges. The challenges for heterogeneity can be broken down into three sub-problems: (1) **portability** to different heterogeneous systems, (2) **scalability** across homogeneous architectures (e.g., multi-GPU execution) in a node, and (3) **utilization** of different

© The Author(s), under exclusive license to Springer Nature Switzerland AG 2024
P. Diehl et al. (Eds.): WAMTA 2024, LNCS 14626, pp. 59–70, 2024.
https://doi.org/10.1007/978-3-031-61763-8_6

heterogeneous devices to solve a single problem. Providing solutions for each of these problems requires significant programming effort. Memory management across heterogeneous devices and computation orchestration adds another layer of challenges. Some efforts provide portable abstractions [12], and some support heterogeneity [5]; however, a solution that targets all the aforementioned challenges has proven elusive.

To overcome these challenges, we have developed MatRIS [10,11]. MatRIS provides layers of abstractions that hide the detail of the *IRIS* task-based runtime [3,6] and different Math libraries. The *IRIS runtime layer* is the lowest layer of MatRIS and orchestrates different runtimes. The *kernel layer* of MatRIS operates above the *IRIS runtime layer* and provides unified APIs by abstracting kernels from various math libraries. The *algorithm layer* provides the highest level of abstraction for BLAS/LAPACK APIs and enables the creation of architecture-agnostic algorithms.

Through these abstractions, MatRIS expresses a linear algebra problem using architecture-agnostic task APIs that create a set of tasks to form directed acyclic graphs (DAG). The computation associated with the tasks in a DAG is dynamically invoked based on different architectures. Hence, MatRIS algorithms are portable to different hardware architectures and can utilize all devices in a node. MatRIS leverages the heterogeneous memory and runtime orchestration of IRIS and therefore does not require specifying any memory transfer details. Once written, MatRIS algorithms are portable across different processor hardware (**portability**), can be executed across different numbers of GPUs (**scalability**), and can be run on a combination of devices in a heterogeneous system (**utilization**). *By doing so, MatRIS essentially reduces the problem set of heterogeneity into a DAG scheduling problem.*

The following work demonstrates that, by using Cholesky decomposition, MatRIS can tackle portability, scalability, and utilization issues of heterogeneous systems. We describe the potential of MatRIS by providing a deep dive on how MatRIS makes Cholesky decomposition portable and heterogeneous; a demonstration of no-source-change portability to different heterogeneous devices; an example of the scalability of Cholesky in a multi-GPU environment for both AMD and NVIDIA GPUs; a comparison with vendor libraries, cuSolverMG, cuSolver, and hipSolver; and a demonstration of how MatRIS lowers the programming productivity challenge of diverse heterogeneity to a flexible scheduling problem.

2   Background: Cholesky Decomposition, IRIS, and MatRIS

2.1   Cholesky Decomposition

In linear algebra, a matrix decomposition transforms a matrix through factorization. This is a well-known technique to parallelize the operation to solve a linear system of equations $Ax = b$, which is a key component of many applications.

Depending on the characteristics of the matrix to be decomposed, there are many different matrix decompositions. This study focuses on the Cholesky decomposition, a popular factorization that can be made on Hermitian and positive-definite matrices. The decomposition of matrix A can be represented as $A = LL^T$, where L and L^T are the lower triangular of the matrix and its conjugate transpose, respectively.

2.2 IRIS

Figure 1a shows the IRIS task-based runtime [3,6]. Focused on supporting heterogeneity, IRIS supports CPUs and GPUs from different vendors (AMD and Intel CPUs and AMD and NVIDIA GPUs). Moreover, it also supports Qualcomm Hexagon DSPs and FPGAs from different vendors. Kernels written in different programming languages can be invoked from IRIS, including OpenMP, OpenACC, HIP, CUDA, XilinxCL, OpenCL, Hexagon C++, and IntelCL. However, mapping between the programming language and the architecture is constrained because each programming model typically supports only a subset of architectures. One important feature of the IRIS runtime is its scheduler, which can dynamically or statically map different tasks onto different architectures, on which the IRIS runtime invokes APIs for the native runtime of that architecture. IRIS can also orchestrate different platforms in a system simultaneously to bind them into a unified environment. Currently, it can perform scheduling and memory management by providing a unified abstraction for different runtimes.

2.3 MatRIS

MatRIS [10,11] provides multilevel abstraction for *Mat*h libraries that use the *IRIS* task based runtime [3,6]. The MatRIS software stack shown in Fig. 1b provides different abstractions in a layered fashion. The *IRIS runtime layer* at the bottom provides necessary abstractions for runtimes and architectures. The *kernel layer* in the middle provides unified APIs for different kernels that abstract different math libraries and their kernels. Architecture-agnostic algorithms are expressed through the support of the lower level in the *algorithm layer*. Empowered by these abstractions, seamless inclusion of new algorithms can be achieved in MatRIS by considering new libraries, architectures, and devices at different layers without impacting others. MatRIS provides portable and heterogeneous implementations for GETRF, POTRF, TRSM, GEMM, POSV and GESV. All the algorithms in MatRIS APIs and algorithms follow standard BLAS/LAPACK interfaces and can be ported to nodes with diverse heterogeneity. This paper focuses on the Cholesky decomposition of MatRIS.

3 Related Work

The literature is fairly sparse in terms of math libraries that use tasking. Two examples are PLASMA [4] and LASs (Linear Algebra routines on OmpSs) [14].

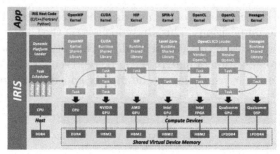

(a) IRIS Runtime.

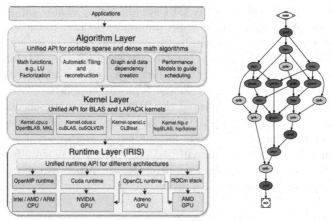

(b) Performance comparison between (c) Cholesky DAG for
MatRIS and cuSolverMG for POTRF.   a 4 × 4 decomposition.

Fig. 1. IRIS, MatRIS, and POTRF DAG from MatRIS.

PLASMA supports dense linear algebra operations by using OpenMP, whereas
LASs supports both dense and sparse operations by using OmpSs. However,
both libraries target CPU platforms. Other libraries such as Chameleon [7] use
task-based abstraction from the StarPU runtime. Powered by the StarPU runtime, Chameleon supports heterogeneity but does not support extreme cases
of heterogeneity, such as GPUs from different vendors in a single node. Also,
DPLASMA [2] uses a task-based approach by using PaRSEC [1] runtime; however, it focuses on distributed execution. GPU offloading capability has been
added in OpenMP as of version 4.0. Valero-Lara et al. [15] explored a case of
heterogeneous TRSM (a BLAS kernel) by leveraging the offloading feature of
OpenMP 4.5. In that study, the authors used static mapping of different parts
of the algorithm (tiles) on a one-CPU and one-GPU configuration and showed
promising results when using a task-based approach on a single node of Summit
supercomputer located at Oak Ridge National Laboratory.

4   Cholesky Decomposition in MatRIS

This section provides a deep dive into how different abstraction levels of MatRIS make Cholesky decomposition portable and heterogeneous by using tasking. This section also describes how Cholesky in MatRIS can mitigate the challenges of **portability, scalability**, and **utilization** inherent in today's heterogeneous HPC architectures.

4.1   Abstractions for Memory and Computation

The IRIS runtime provides the necessary abstraction for memory and computation at the bottom layer of MatRIS (Fig. 1b). Memory objects in MatRIS are heterogeneous thanks to the DMEM [9] feature of the IRIS runtime. These DMEM objects are tied to system malloced memory, which is translated into device memory accompanied by necessary memory transfers at run time. For this reason, Cholesky decomposition in MatRIS does not need to specify any memory transfer. Moreover, MatRIS provides tiling features [8] that can decompose and reconstruct a large memory object to/from smaller chunks of heterogeneous memory, thereby alleviating the need for traditional tile-to-flat and flat-to-tile operations. Unlike the conventional tile-to-flat operation, MatRIS reconstructs the resultant matrix during execution, which is asynchronous to the flow of DAG execution.

MatRIS uses IRIS tasks that encapsulate the kernel signature, necessary memory objects, and parameters for the abstraction of computation in the Cholesky decomposition. The tasks are then inserted into a graph (DAG) that dictates the execution flow. During execution, IRIS invokes the necessary kernels from the vendor library for the device on which the task is scheduled. The kernel APIs are described in Subsect. 4.2.

```
IRIS_TASK_APIS(
        IRIS_FUNC(matris_core_, POTRF_TYPE),
        IRIS_FUNC(matris_task_, POTRF_TYPE),
        "matris_" IRIS_C_STR(POTRF_TYPE) "_kernel", 1,
        NULL_OFFSET, GWS(M), NULL_LWS,
        PARAM(major, MatrisBlasType),
        PARAM(uplo, MatrisBlasType),
        PARAM(M, int32_t),
        PARAM(N, int32_t),
        IN_OUT_TASK(A, DTYPE*, DTYPE, A, sizeof(DTYPE)*M*N),
        PARAM(lda, int32_t));
```

Listing 1.1. Task generation API.

4.2   Kernel APIs for Cholesky

Kernel APIs are defined in the kernel layer of MatRIS (Fig. 1b). The kernel layer provides two functionalities: (1) task generation API and (2) a connection between the task and the optimized kernel. Listing 1.1 shows the task generation

API. This API generates the necessary sources to create an IRIS task and place it in a DAG. Inputs and output memory objects are also defined here. Our implementation of tiled Cholesky needs four types of kernels: POTRF, TRSM, SYRK, and GEMM. Hence, four kernel APIs are defined and can be used in any other algorithm in MatRIS, thereby demonstrating the flexibility through the inclusion of new kernel APIs. The third parameter of Listing 1.1 is the name of the kernel, which makes it possible to invoke different architecture-specific kernels. The kernel layer has back-end support for the kernels from open-source and vendor math libraries (e.g., cuBLAS, hipBLAS, MKL, OpenBLAS). The unified kernel function for MatRIS (e.g., `matris_dpotrf_kernel`) is then instantiated for different back ends by pointing to the actual function call in that library and providing the necessary translation (e.g., `MATRIS_BLAS_LEFT` to `CUBLAS_SIDE_LEFT`). This invocation to the specific architecture-optimized kernel only happens at run time, which makes kernel APIs **portable**.

```
Tiling2D <DTYPE> A_til(A, M, N, tile_size_r, tile_size_c,..);
if (uplo == MATRIS_BLAS_LOWER) {
    for (int k = 0; k < A_til.row_tiles_count(); k++) {
        IRIS_FUNC(laris_graph_common_, POTRF_TYPE)
            ( graph... A_til.GetAt(k,k).IRISMem()...);
        for (int m = k+1; m < A_til.row_tiles_count(); m++) {
            IRIS_FUNC(laris_graph_common_, TRSM_TYPE)
                ( graph...A_til.GetAt(k,m).IRISMem()...);
        }
        for (int m = k+1; m < A_til.row_tiles_count(); m++) {
            IRIS_FUNC(laris_graph_common_, SYRK_TYPE)
                ( graph...A_til.GetAt(m,m).IRISMem());
            for (int n = k+1; n < m; n++) {
                IRIS_FUNC(laris_graph_common_, GEMM_TYPE)
                    ( graph...A_til.GetAt(n,m).IRISMem());
            }
        }
    }
}
```

Listing 1.2. Sequential pseudo code of Cholesky in MatRIS using kernel APIs.

4.3 Tiled Cholesky in MatRIS

In the algorithm layer of MatRIS (Fig. 1b), architecture-agnostic tiled algorithms are specified and utilize unified kernel APIs and memory abstractions of the kernel and runtime layers. Listing 1.2 provides a sequential pseudo code of the Cholesky decomposition. This algorithm is inspired by PLASMA [16] and LASs [13]. However, in contrast to PLASMA and LASs, MatRIS provides a fully portable and heterogeneous solution for Cholesky decomposition. At first, MatRIS uses system malloced memory (memory A in the first line of Listing 1.2) to decompose it into tiles and to tie corresponding memory addresses to the IRIS memory objects. Then, the Cholesky loop calls the kernel APIs to serially generate the tasks needed for computation. Listing 1.2 contains several notable features: (1) there is no architecture-specific information, (2) all device memory and transfers are hidden, (3) there is no dependency specification to construct the DAG, and (4) task creation and addition to the graph is also hidden. The benefit of such implementations is twofold: (1) the addition of a new hardware back end does not change the algorithm, and (2) a serial tiled algorithm from any state-of-the-art library can be adopted without worrying about task and dependency creation.

While the tasks are created, MatRIS utilizes the data flow features in the IRIS runtime to create dependencies required for the DAG, which exposes the concurrency to be exploited by different heterogeneous devices. Figure 1c depicts the DAG created from the Cholesky decomposition in Listing 1.2 and shows the available concurrency at different levels. Each of the tasks shown in Fig. 1c is portable across all the heterogeneous devices in a node. Hence, MatRIS algorithms such as the Cholesky decomposition can run on any combination of homogeneous and heterogeneous devices in a node by providing necessary data transfer between devices. Therefore, MatRIS provides a solution to **scalability** and **utilization**.

Although MatRIS provides functional portability, scalability, and utilization, we must scrutinize the factors that impact performance. Section 5 describes the performance and shows how MatRIS reduces the problem set of heterogeneity into a DAG scheduling problem.

5   Experiments

In this section, we describe our evaluation of the MatRIS Cholesky decomposition in terms of portability, scalability, and utilization. We used a Compute and Data Environment for Science (CADES) cloud node from Oak Ridge National Laboratory to evaluate MatRIS. This node has four A100 GPUs from NVIDIA, four MI100 GPUs from AMD, and an AMD EPYC 7763 CPU with 128 cores, thereby representing a node with diverse heterogeneity. We used the GNU-8.5.0 compiler along with ROCm-5.1.2 and CUDA-11.7. We relied on cuBLAS, hipBLAS, cuSolver, hipSolver, and OpenBLAS for architecture-specific kernels. We used block-cyclic and dynamic scheduling of the IRIS runtime. We performed several experiments. First, we investigated how Cholesky achieves functional portability, scalability, and utilization. Second, we scrutinized Cholesky's multi-GPU scalability performance. Third, we compared the performance of tiled Cholesky in MatRIS with cuSolverMG and single-task (or tile) POTRF from cuSolver and hipSolver. Finally, we demonstrated how MatRIS translates the portability and heterogeneity problem into a scheduling problem.

5.1   Portability, Scalability, and Utilization of Cholesky

Once built, Cholesky in MatRIS can run on any combination of heterogeneous devices by setting an environment variable. For example, setting `IRIS_ARCHS=cuda` makes Cholesky run on the available CUDA GPUs, and setting `IRIS_ARCHS=cuda:openmp:hip` utilizes all available devices in the CADES

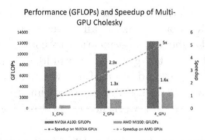
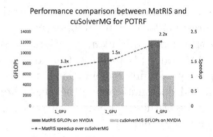

(a) Performance and speedup of multi-GPU Cholesky.

(b) Performance comparison between MatRIS and NVIDIA cuSolverMG for POTRF.

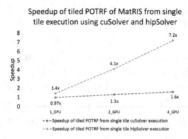

(c) Speedup of tiled POTRF of MatRIS from single tile execution using cuSolver and hipSolver.

Fig. 2. Performance and speedup comparison of POTRF in MatRIS.

node by respecting the specified scheduler. Therefore, it provides functional portability and the capability to utilize all available devices. Moreover, one can set the number and types of GPUs to utilize, which provides better scalability control.

5.2 Multi-GPU Scalability of Cholesky

The performance of Cholesky decomposition when using a different number of the same GPU type is demonstrated in Fig. 2. We considered a $32,768 \times 32,768$ matrix, where the tile sizes are $2,048 \times 2,048$, which generates ~ 800 tasks. The impact of increasing the number of GPUs is shown in Fig. 2a. As anticipated, the NVIDIA A100 provided better performance than the AMD MI100. However, the MI100 provided better scalability when the number of GPUs kept increasing (up to a 5× speedup is observed for AMD GPUs compared to a 1.6× speedup on NVIDIA GPUs, where speedup = multi-GPU execution/single GPU execution). This behavior can be correlated with the trade-off between kernel execution versus inter-GPU data transfer. With more parallelism offered with multiple GPUs, the need for more inter-GPU data transfers increases. NVIDIA's cuBLAS and cuSolver provide faster kernel execution, making data transfer a bottleneck.

The more expensive data transfer (compared to kernel execution) offsets some of the benefits of parallelism. However, the slower execution of each kernel for the AMD MI100 GPUs successfully hides the data transfer penalty. For this reason, the execution of Cholesky enjoys more benefit from the device-level parallelism on AMD GPUs.

5.3 Comparison of Cholesky with Vendor Libraries

A comparison with NVIDIA's multi-GPU implementation of Choleksy in cuSolverMG[1] is shown in Fig. 2b. MatRIS provided better performance than

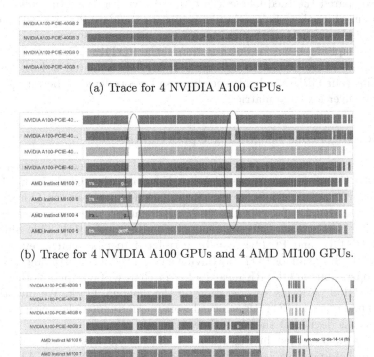

(a) Trace for 4 NVIDIA A100 GPUs.

(b) Trace for 4 NVIDIA A100 GPUs and 4 AMD MI100 GPUs.

(c) Trace for 1 CPU, 4 NVIDIA A100 GPUs, and 4 AMD MI100 GPUs.

Fig. 3. Trace of Cholesky decomposition on an A100 and an M100 GPU with 16×16 decomposition of a $16,384 \times 16,384$ matrix. This trace shows MatRIS's ability to simultaneously utilize multiple devices from multiple vendors. The gap demonstrates the need for better scheduling. Diagonal POTRF on the slower MI100 GPU is creating the gap.

---

[1] https://github.com/NVIDIA/CUDALibrarySamples/tree/master/cuSOLVER/MgPotrf.

the cuSolverMG for different GPU configurations. MatRIS provided up to 2.2×
performance for four GPUs versus cuSolverMG. The cuSolverMG library did
not provide scalability for more than two GPUs. These performance gaps could
be coming from the differences in the implementation of the tiled algorithm.
MatRIS decomposes row and column-wise like other state-of-the-art libraries
(e.g., PLASMA), whereas cuSolverMG decomposes in one dimension. Another
difference could be that MatRIS uses pinned memory; however, when we ran
MatRIS without memory pinning, it still provided better performance than
cuSolverMG. We did not find a comparable multi-GPU implementation from
AMD.

We compared the tiled Cholesky of MatRIS with a single-tile cuSolver and
hipSolver in which the cuSolver/hipSolver use the standard POTRF call. Surpris-
ingly, Cholesky with MatRIS provides a 7.2× speedup compared to a single-tile
hipSolver, implying room for optimization of the POTRF in hipSolver for large
matrix sizes. When compared to cuSolver, MatRIS achieved a 1.6× speedup
when using four GPUs, and this speedup can be correlated to better optimization in cuSolver for large matrices.

5.4 Heterogeneous Scheduling Opportunities

The previous experiments showed performance of homogeneous devices (same
kinds of GPUs) to demonstrate scalability. However, when Cholesky in MatRIS
uses different types of devices, we see a degradation in performance. Our previous
effort showed that LU factorization in MatRIS can provide better performance
when using GPUs from different vendors simultaneously [11]. This difference
between GETRF and POTRF can be correlated to more concurrency in the
DAG for GETRF than for POTRF. Having a larger set of embarrassingly parallel
GEMM operations in GETRF means a better chance of occupying other GPUs
when one GPU performs an operation on the diagonal block. We investigated
traces to find out why POTRF achieved worse performance when using multiple
heterogeneous devices at the same time.

The traces presented in Fig. 3 show that slow devices create gaps in the
trace when heterogeneity is introduced. The trace for four NVIDIA A100 GPUs
(Fig. 3a) does not show many gaps. However, in the case of four A100 GPUs and
four MI100 GPUs, some gaps are observed because the POTRF kernels in the
critical path were scheduled in a slower MI100 GPU, which makes other devices
wait. The same is observed when all devices, including the CPU, are used. In
this case, the CPU turned out to be the slowest device and produced larger
gaps that further degraded the performance. So, careful scheduling based on
performance models is necessary to harness meaningful performance in the heterogeneity described here. In summary, the results shown in Fig. 3 demonstrate
that the flexible task-level portability of MatRIS essentially lowered the problem set of heterogeneity to a scheduling problem. Future work includes exploring
performance model–guided scheduling.

6 Conclusion

MatRIS provides multilevel abstractions to express tiled linear algebra algorithms to a DAG of tasks using the IRIS runtime. By using architecture-agnostic unified Kernel APIs that can instantiate tasks to invoke optimized kernels from vendor and open-source libraries at runtime, MatRIS makes algorithms portable, capable of scaling to multiple devices, and able to use any combination of processors in a node. Using Cholesky decomposition, MatRIS demonstrates speedup while using multiple GPUs and provides comparable performance to vendor libraries. Moreover, by having the flexibility to choose any heterogeneous device at runtime, MatRIS reduces the problem set of heterogeneity to a DAG scheduling problem. Exploring performance model–guided DAG scheduling is future work.

Acknowledgements. This work is funded, in part, by Bluestone, a X-Stack project in the DOE Advanced Scientific Computing Office with program manager Hal Finkel. This manuscript has been authored by UT-Battelle LLC under contract no. DE-AC05-00OR22725 with the US Department of Energy. The publisher, by accepting the article for publication, acknowledges that the US government retains a non-exclusive, paid up, irrevocable, world-wide license to publish or reproduce the published form of the manuscript, or allow others to do so, for US government purposes. The DOE will provide public access to these results in accordance with the DOE Public Access Plan (http://energy.gov/downloads/doe-public-access-plan).

References

1. Bosilca, G., Bouteiller, A., Danalis, A., Faverge, M., Hérault, T., Dongarra, J.J.: PaRSEC: exploiting heterogeneity to enhance scalability. Comput. Sci. Eng. **15**(6), 36–45 (2013)
2. Bosilca, G., et al.: Distibuted dense numerical linear algebra algorithms on massively parallel architectures: DPLASMA (2010)
3. Cabrera, A.M., Hitefield, S., Kim, J., Lee, S., Miniskar, N.R., Vetter, J.S.: Toward performance portable programming for heterogeneous systems on a chip: a case study with qualcomm snapdragon SoC. In: 2021 IEEE High Performance Extreme Computing Conference, HPEC 2021, Waltham, MA, USA, 20–24 September 2021, pp. 1–7. IEEE (2021). https://doi.org/10.1109/HPEC49654.2021.9622794
4. Dongarra, J.J., et al.: PLASMA: parallel linear algebra software for multicore using OpenMP. ACM Trans. Math. Softw. **45**(2), 16:1–16:35 (2019). https://doi.org/10.1145/3264491
5. Farhan, M.A.A., et al.: MAGMA templates for scalable linear algebra on emerging architectures. Int. J. High Perform. Comput. Appl. **34**(6), 645–658 (2020). https://doi.org/10.1177/1094342020938421
6. Kim, J., Lee, S., Johnston, B., Vetter, J.S.: IRIS: a portable runtime system exploiting multiple heterogeneous programming systems. In: 2021 IEEE High Performance Extreme Computing Conference, HPEC 2021, Waltham, MA, USA, 20–24 September 2021, pp. 1–8. IEEE (2021). https://doi.org/10.1109/HPEC49654.2021.9622873

7. Klinkenberg, J., Samfass, P., Bader, M., Terboven, C., Müller, M.S.: CHAMELEON: reactive load balancing for hybrid MPI+ OpenMP task-parallel applications. J. Parallel Distrib. Comput. **138**, 55–64 (2020)
8. Miniskar, N.R., Monil, M.A.H., Valero-Lara, P., Liu, F., Vetter, J.S.: Tiling framework for heterogeneous computing of matrix-based tiled algorithms (2023)
9. Miniskar, N.R., Monil, M.A.H., Valero-Lara, P., Liu, F.Y., Vetter, J.S.: IRIS-DMEM: efficient memory management for heterogeneous computing. In: 2023 IEEE High Performance Extreme Computing Conference (HPEC), pp. 1–7. IEEE (2023)
10. Monil, M.A.H., Miniskar, N.R., Liu, F., Vetter, J.S., Valero-Lara, P.: LaRIS: targeting portability and productivity for LaPACK codes on extreme heterogeneous systems using IRIS. In: IEEE/ACM Redefining Scalability for Diversely Heterogeneous Architectures Workshop, RSDHA@SC 2022, Dallas, TX, USA, 13–18 November 2022. IEEE (2022)
11. Monil, M.A.H., Miniskar, N.R., Teranishi, K., Vetter, J.S., Valero-Lara, P.: MatRIS: multi-level math library abstraction for heterogeneity and performance portability using IRIS runtime. In: Proceedings of the SC 2023 Workshops of the International Conference on High Performance Computing, Network, Storage, and Analysis, pp. 1081–1092 (2023)
12. Trott, C.R., et al.: Kokkos 3: programming model extensions for the exascale era. IEEE Trans. Parallel Distrib. Syst. **33**(4), 805–817 (2022). https://doi.org/10.1109/TPDS.2021.3097283
13. Valero-Lara, P., Catalán, S., Martorell, X., Labarta, J.: BLAS-3 optimized by OmpSs regions (lass library). In: 2019 27th Euromicro International Conference on Parallel, Distributed and Network-Based Processing (PDP), pp. 25–32. IEEE (2019)
14. Valero-Lara, P., Catalán, S., Martorell, X., Usui, T., Labarta, J.: sLASs: a fully automatic auto-tuned linear algebra library based on OpenMP extensions implemented in OmpSs (LASs library). J. Parallel Distrib. Comput. **138**, 153–171 (2020). https://doi.org/10.1016/j.jpdc.2019.12.002
15. Valero-Lara, P., Kim, J., Hernandez, O., Vetter, J.S.: OpenMP target task: tasking and target offloading on heterogeneous systems. In: Chaves, R., et al. (eds.) Euro-Par 2021. LNCS, vol. 13098, pp. 445–455. Springer, Cham (2021). https://doi.org/10.1007/978-3-031-06156-1_35
16. YarKhan, A., Kurzak, J., Luszczek, P., Dongarra, J.: Porting the PLASMA numerical library to the OpenMP standard. Int. J. Parallel Program. **45**, 612–633 (2017)

ParSweet: A Suite of Codes for Benchmarking and Testing Mutex-Based Parallel Systems

Max Morris$^{(\boxtimes)}$ and Steven R. Brandt

Center of Computation and Technology, Louisiana State University,
Baton Rouge, USA
{mmorris,sbrandt}@cct.lsu.edu

Abstract. We present ParSweet, a collection of parallel codes in various programming languages covering common uses and implementations of mutual exclusion. This provides us with a basis for evaluating existing parallel systems for speed and efficiency, and a robust test suite for evaluating the correctness of new parallel systems. We also present benchmark results comparing the performance of various lock implementations, including our own and those from the std:: and hpx:: libraries. We have made the suite publicly available, with a process in place for accepting and incorporating additional codes submitted by the community.

1 Introduction

Parallel programming is challenging both in terms of performance and correctness. Data-parallel applications, where operations can be performed repetitively on a large array of data are the most common parallel codes. However, some applications use a more complex task-based form of parallelism. Mutexes, atomic memory operations, or both are needed for these.

This domain of problems is particularly challenging because programming with locks is not composable, i.e., it is not always possible to look at isolated subroutines within a larger body of code and reason about the behavior of the program. In addition, due to the complexity of many applications which require mutual exclusion, the race conditions which may arise tend to be more subtle than those found in data parallel codes. While some frameworks and languages, e.g., Rust, can protect against low-level memory races, higher-level memory races can still exist. We will discuss an example of a higher-level race later on.

We had set out to create programming tools and paradigms to mitigate the problems inherent to parallel programming with mutexes. As a part of this work, we sought out a database of codes using mutual exclusion for the purposes of verifying the correctness and applicability of our tools. We needed code samples which covered a wide range of use cases while also being neither too trivial nor too complex.

The repositories we found, such as the "Software-artifact Infrastructure Repository (SIR)" [3,6] database, did not meet these requirements. SIR is self-described as containing real-world codes along with build scripts and fault data.

P. Diehl et al. (Eds.): WAMTA 2024, LNCS 14626, pp. 71–83, 2024.
https://doi.org/10.1007/978-3-031-61763-8_7

Although SIR does not have an explicit focus on parallel programming, the repository includes parallel codes. However, most were either too large to fit our needs (e.g., an entire relational database management system) or too trivial (e.g., a simple deadlock).

It is our belief that the needs of complex real-world parallel applications can be accurately modeled and evaluated on a smaller scale. For this reason, we created ParSweet, a database of small-to-medium-sized codes exemplifying a range of common use cases of mutexes. When constructing the database, we avoided establishing dependencies on any specific lock implementation. Many exist, and each has different semantics, overheads, affinities for certain configurations, and performance under load.

We do not imagine that ParSweet is complete in its current form. We plan to expand the database ourselves in addition to accepting pull requests from other researchers. The fully-realized intention of ParSweet is to provide a dynamic and growing set of examples which allow researchers to test new tools and ideas that address the problems inherent to this class of parallel programs.

2 Mutex Implementations

For our initial set of lock implementations, we rely on samples from literature. We made use of "The Art of Multiprocessor Programming" [7] (hereafter the AoMP) as a general reference. We also contributed three of our own designs: the IdLock, TIdLock, and TwoCounterLock. Included in our benchmarks are also `std::mutex` & `std::recursive_mutex` from the C++ standard library, and `hpx::mutex` & `hpx::spinlock` from HPX [8]. Of the list below, only the Anderson, Optimized Anderson, CLH, MCS, and TwoCounter locks provide fairness guarantees.

TAS Lock. The "Test and Set" or TAS Lock is a very simple design. It attempts to use a get-and-set atomic instruction to flip a memory location from zero to one. If it succeeds, it has the lock. To unlock, it sets the value back to zero.

TTAS Lock. The "Test and Test and Set" or TTAS Lock tests the atomic memory location to see whether it is zero before attempting to get-and-set its value. This is intended to reduce cache invalidations caused by the get-and-set operation while attempting to get the lock. The benefit realized from this optimization seems to be hardware-dependent; sometimes the speed of the lock is doubled, but other times it is actually a pessimization of the TAS Lock.

Anderson Lock. The Anderson Lock [4], or array lock, uses an array of values. Threads waiting for the lock spin on different memory locations to avoid cache invalidations. This locking strategy is potentially vulnerable to false sharing.

Optimized Anderson Lock. The Optimized Anderson Lock attempts to mitigate false sharing by ensuring the elements in the array are located far enough away from each other in memory so as to be on different cache lines. As with the TTAS Lock, this optimization is not consistently helpful.

Backoff Lock. The Backoff Lock lock is a variation on the TTAS lock designed to reduce contention. Each time a thread attempts and fails to acquire the lock, it goes to sleep for a short, random interval. The maximum interval that can be chosen increases each time contention is encountered. It is difficult to tune these parameters properly see a performance benefit. Our repository includes a tuner which attempts to find the best duration parameters.

CLH Lock. The CLH Lock [5,9] is a complex lock with an implicit queue of nodes, providing each thread with a distinct memory location to spin on. This lock ensures that a maxmimum of two nodes ever access the same node at the same time. Nodes are cycled between threads and reused, which is a potential source of slowdown on NUMA machines.

MCS Lock. The MCS Lock [10] is similar to the CLH Lock, but it uses an explicit queue. It avoids the cycling of nodes required by the CLH Lock, which potentially results in better performance on NUMA machines.

ID Lock. The ID Lock uses a compare-and-set operation to update an atomic variable from a null thread id to the id of the thread attempting to get the lock. To unlock, it puts the null value back.

Two Counter Lock. The Two Counter Lock is loosely inspired by the classic Bakery Lock. When attempting to acquire the lock, each thread increments an atomic counter to obtain a unique 'ticket'. The thread will then spin on a second atomic counter which indicates which ticket number may proceed. The latter counter is incremented upon unlock.

hpx::mutex and hpx::spinlock. While the mutexes presented above can be switched out by the scheduler, any mutex used in a work-queue system will stop the thread it is executing on from progressing. This is not the case with HPX locks and work queues, which can swap out any blocked thread and keep working. For some applications, this capability may be the most important.

3   Parallel Codes

As an example of a higher-order race condition, consider a naïve implementation of a parallel set using a singly-linked list. Internally, the items of the set are kept in sorted order. Threads may add items, remove items, and check if an item is contained in the set. Each node has a "next" pointer to its successor. Each node also has its own mutex that threads must own before they are able to read or write to the node, thus preventing a low-level race condition.

However, consider the remove operation: To delete some node N_p from the linked list, its predecessor N_{p-1} must be updated to point to N_{p+1}. Since the only node being written to is N_{p-1}, it is the only node the thread locks. A high-level race condition arises when another thread simultaneously attempts to delete N_{p-1}. Because N_{p-2} is not locked by the first thread, the second thread is free to acquire the lock and update N_{p-2}, setting its successor to be N_p, before the first thread has finished its operation. This effectively causes the first delete to be "forgotten."

Even when the programmer is careful to ensure that any variable being written to is protected by a mutex, higher-level race conditions can still arise and cause programs to behave incorrectly. Careful understanding of the structure of an algorithm is required to mitigate these types of data races; locks have no intrinsic mechanism to help with this.

3.1   Sets

ParSweet includes several correct implementations of the parallel set described above. We draw these implementations from AoMP, except that we exclude the coarse-grained locking set and the lock-free set. In this paper, we will discuss and analyze one of these implementations: the Fine-Grained Set.

Fine-Grained Set. The Fine-Grained Set protects each node with its own lock. Each thread owns at most 2 locks at any given time. Before a thread is allowed to operate on a node, it must own the node's lock in addition to its predecessor's lock. Compared to the other set implementations, this set is guaranteed to traverse the list of nodes only once per operation, potentially halting before reaching the end. However, since nodes must be locked as they are visited, more time may be spent waiting to acquire locks.

3.2   Maps

ParSweet also includes implementations of a parallel hash map. In this paper, we will discuss and analyze one of these: the Partitioned Hash Map.

Partitioned Hash Map. The Partitioned Hash Map maintains an array of B buckets, for some integer $B > 0$. Each bucket contains a linked list, guarded by a lock. Each linked list has no internal locking; a thread accessing any part of it must own the bucket's lock.

4   Benchmarks and Tests

Each benchmark is parameterized by the number of threads T, and the amount of work W_T done per thread. Each benchmark also performs tests to verify correctness. W_T was tuned for each machine to avoid excessive run times on the less powerful configurations. Values of W_T are shown below each table. In all cases, T was set to be the number of processors in the machine. Benchmarks for HPX locks use the HPX runtime and HPX versions of standard interfaces, e.g., hpx::thread and hpx::async. All other locks run in the standard C++ runtime.

4.1   Machines

The following machines were used to run the benchmarks.

- **mike**: Intel(R) Xeon(R) Platinum 8358 CPU @ 2.60 GHz, 64 threads [1].
- **qbc**: Intel(R) Xeon(R) Platinum 8260 CPU @ 2.40 GHz, 48 threads [2].
- **medusa**: Intel(R) Xeon(R) Gold 6148 CPU @ 2.40G Hz, 40 threads.
- **melete05**: Intel(R) Xeon(R) CPU E5-2698 v4 @ 2.20 GHz, 80 threads.
- **skeleton**: Intel(R) Core(TM) i5-10600K CPU @ 4.80 GHz, 12 threads.
- **twilight**: Intel(R) Core(TM) i7-10850H CPU @ 2.70 GHz, 12 threads.
- **buran**: AMD EPYC 7352 CPU @ 2.30 GHz, 48 threads.

4.2   Lock Benchmark

The lock benchmark purposefully enacts extremely high contention. Each thread must increment a shared counter W_T times, locking and unlocking a shared mutex each time. This test measures the locks' performance in high contention scenarios.

4.3   Set Benchmark (SetByLock)

Each thread performs the add, remove, and contains operations over a thread-unique collection of values to a shared set. In this paper, we selected the Fine-Grained Set as the baseline set implementation and ran the benchmark with each of the lock implementations.

4.4   Map Benchmark (MapByLock)

Each thread performs the put, get, and delete operations over a thread-unique collection of values to a shared map. In this paper, we selected the Partitioned Hash Map as the baseline map implementation and ran the benchmark with each of the lock implementations.

5   Results

The highest and lowest ten percent of measurements for each benchmark were discarded to reduce the effect of system noise. In addition, we implemented a cooling-off period between runs to avoid processor throttling. Table 1 lists the abbreviated lock names which are used in Figs. 1, 2, 3, 4, 5, 6 and 7. In addition, Fig. 8 shows an overview of the results across all locks, benchmarks, and machines.

Table 1. Abbreviations of lock names.

Abbreviated Name	Lock Name
T	TASLock
TT	TTASLock
C	TwoCounterLock
I	IdLock
IT	TIdLock
L	CLHLock
M	MCSLock
B	BackoffLock< 1, 17 >
A	ALock
AO	OptimizedALock
SM	std::mutex
SR	std::recursive_mutex
HM	hpx::mutex
HS	hpx::spinlock

Lock	Time(ms)	σ(ms)
HS‡	58.72	0.45
T	92.21	5.67
C†	92.28	5.43
I	110.00	0.00
TT	118.15	5.84
SM	118.48	0.50
B	119.26	5.32
M†	120.97	0.17
SR	123.00	0.00
IT	124.20	0.96
L†	162.06	0.23
A†	164.75	0.71
AO†	182.41	0.84
HM‡	243.04	0.21

(a) medusa

Lock	Time(ms)	σ(ms)
B	63.61	5.09
SM	152.63	13.18
SR	174.89	11.99
M†	633.63	47.31
HS‡	642.38	24.95
AO†	650.32	42.84
L†	664.50	24.49
IT	1005.26	78.03
TT	1014.19	84.68
HM‡	1496.00	30.78
C†	1035.67	85.39
A†	1576.00	161.03
I	1903.89	215.10
T	2111.67	369.95

(b) qbc

Lock	Time(ms)	σ(ms)
T	31.00	0.00
C†	34.00	0.00
I	34.42	0.49
IT	37.88	0.33
B	38.00	0.00
TT	38.45	0.50
M†	39.00	0.00
SM	39.27	0.45
SR	42.00	0.00
HS‡	277.20	32.89
L†	277.90	842.36
A†	530.20	957.91
AO†	761.80	1306.89
HM‡	2330.35	41.61

(c) melete05

Fig. 1. Figure (a) Lock benchmark for medusa, $W_T = 200000$; Figure (b) Lock benchmark for qbc, $W_T = 20000$; Figure (c) Lock benchmark for melete05, $W_T = 20000$. † denotes a lock with a fairness guarantee. ‡ denotes a lock which requires HPX to use.

Lock	Time(ms)	σ(ms)
HS‡	2.29	0.45
T	3.46	2.02
SR	3.54	0.50
I	3.67	1.65
IT	4.04	1.93
TT	4.29	1.90
SM	5.38	1.65
B	5.54	1.96
C†	14.42	3.97
M†	19.00	5.77
A†	21.62	4.71
AO†	21.96	3.43
L†	23.54	3.87
HM‡	27.83	3.88

(a) twilight

Lock	Time(ms)	σ(ms)
B	63.50	18.83
HS‡	89.75	9.44
TT	144.75	11.63
IT	149.08	10.42
SM	149.21	18.23
SR	161.19	14.39
T	238.56	28.99
I	252.90	28.45
C†	512.69	52.79
M†	616.25	50.34
A†	635.52	53.72
L†	636.73	56.40
AO†	671.94	62.62
HM‡	954.60	124.48

(b) skeleton

Lock	Time(ms)	σ(ms)
HS‡	10.00	0.00
C†	17.54	0.91
L†	18.00	0.00
T	18.59	0.89
I	19.50	0.94
M†	22.35	0.48
SM	22.88	0.33
B	24.36	1.19
TT	24.42	1.15
SR	25.21	1.26
IT	25.32	1.26
A†	30.00	0.00
AO†	31.23	0.42
HM‡	35.00	0.00

(c) mike

Fig. 2. Figure (a) Locks benchmark for twilight, $W_T = 4800$; Figure (b) Locks benchmark for skeleton, $W_T = 200000$; Figure (c) Locks benchmark for mike, $W_T = 20000$. † denotes a lock with a fairness guarantee. ‡ denotes a lock which requires HPX to use.

5.1 Locks

We did not expect there to be a single best lock implementation. The best lock will always be dependent on the needs of the application and the architecture of the machine. Still, we were surprised at the variation in the results and at the discrepancy between the observed and expected lock performance.

The MCS lock can be thought of as an optimization of the CLH lock, designed for better performance on NUMA architectures. However, the two locks exhibited similar performance on qbc, which is a NUMA machine. The backoff lock exhibited fairly good performance on all machines, but on qbc it was by far the fastest; the second-fastest lock on that machine, `std::mutex`, was over twice as slow. These effects highlight the non-uniformity and unpredictability of lock behavior, and points to the necessity of performing benchmarking to determine the best lock for each machine and application.

The TAS and TTAS locks were another surprise. Generally, the TAS lock either outperformed or remained on par with the TTAS lock. We had expected that the latter would always be the best. This would suggest that, on some machines, the atomic get operation is implemented in terms of something like compare-and-set, rather than being natively supported.

Similarly, OptimizedALock significantly outperformed ALock on some machines, but not others. OptimizedALock simply stores its elements further away from each other in memory to mitigate false sharing. On machines like qbc, where OptimizedALock is over twice the speed of ALock, this appears to have the intended effect. It would seem that, on machines where OptimizedALock has poorer performance, the false sharing problem either does not occur at all, or does occur and is not mitigated by OptimizedALock. It has been suggested that, due to prefetching, the OptimizedALock would need to increase its padding size to be a greator factor of the cache line size in order to see a performance benefit. We feel that further benchmarking of this lock type with varying padding sizes is needed.

Among the fair locks, the TwoCounter lock performs well on most platforms. On melete05 and medusa, TwoCounterLock is the fastest fair lock and the second fastest lock overall, only narrowly slower than TASLock. On twilight, TwoCounterLock is still the fastest fair lock, but is slower than the non-fair locks. On qbc, TwoCounterLock is one of the slowest locks, regardless of fairness. In general, the TwoCounterLock seems to be a good choice in high-contention applications where fairness is important, especially due to its simplicity in implementation compared to the other fair locks we tested.

In this benchmark, the HPX locks demonstrate two extremes: hpx::spinlock was consistently one of the fastest locks, and hpx::mutex was consistently one of the slowest.

Lock	Time(ms)	σ(ms)	Lock	Time(ms)	σ(ms)	Lock	Time(ms)	σ(ms)
HS‡	58.00	0.00	SM	1931.11	14.97	HS‡	116.00	0.00
M†	101.09	0.29	SR	2047.62	22.92	C†	122.90	0.43
L†	104.18	0.47	HM‡	2327.80	15.72	I	122.91	0.45
IT	108.15	0.35	B	2523.49	211.54	IT	123.21	0.46
I	108.93	0.26	TT	2588.61	148.41	TT	123.26	0.44
C†	112.00	0.00	IT	2612.70	128.06	T	123.45	0.57
B	116.02	4.42	C†	2679.10	192.57	SR	126.29	0.53
TT	116.25	4.46	A†	2840.25	83.11	B	126.33	0.47
T	116.27	4.35	T	2886.41	137.30	M†	130.34	0.55
SR	116.29	0.53	I	2940.79	166.14	L†	141.34	0.57
SM	124.04	0.38	AO†	2990.43	101.39	HM‡	151.39	0.49
AO†	187.25	0.43	L†	3280.26	134.06	A†	154.26	0.46
A†	188.45	0.50	HS‡	3340.79	400.52	AO†	193.72	0.52
HM‡	418.94	2.28	M†	3466.61	187.56	SM	296.08	724.02
	(a) buran			(b) melete05			(c) medusa	

Fig. 3. Figure (a) Locks benchmark for buran, $W_T = 200000$. Figure (b) SetByLocks benchmark for melete05, $W_T = 200$; Figure (c) SetByLocks benchmark for medusa, $W_T = 200$. † denotes a lock with a fairness guarantee. ‡ denotes a lock which requires HPX to use.

5.2   SetByLocks

The SetByLocks benchmark has lower contention than the Lock benchmark and more instructions performed while holding the lock. As before, no lock

Lock	Time(ms)	σ(ms)
HS‡	312.49	13.43
IT	401.19	24.40
TT	406.72	21.90
HM‡	416.70	4.78
M†	418.57	43.07
SR	435.47	12.39
SM	451.67	16.96
C†	453.79	43.78
B	467.28	36.67
T	488.34	24.59
L†	527.34	59.33
I	544.21	23.75
A†	571.91	81.53
AO†	664.57	51.06

(a) qbc

Lock	Time(ms)	σ(ms)
TT	9.00	1.32
IT	9.04	1.37
T	9.33	1.49
HS‡	11.09	1.78
I	11.50	1.00
HM‡	11.73	1.45
C†	12.62	2.50
M†	14.00	2.92
B	15.25	4.99
A†	18.96	5.49
L†	20.54	5.66
AO†	26.00	9.33
SM	75.42	10.28
SR	81.83	10.34

(b) twilight

Lock	Time(ms)	σ(ms)
IT	26.95	1.78
TT	27.90	2.32
T	28.71	2.16
C†	33.10	5.72
B	34.85	3.14
HM‡	35.95	2.47
M†	36.17	5.17
I	36.24	3.98
HS‡	40.39	5.68
L†	45.63	7.61
A†	46.68	9.71
AO†	59.22	14.61
SM	93.93	13.27
SR	130.90	23.60

(c) skeleton

Fig. 4. Figure (a) SetByLocks benchmark for qbc, $W_T = 100$; Figure (b) SetByLocks benchmark for twilight, $W_T = 50$; Figure (c) SetByLocks benchmark for skeleton, $W_T = 100$. † denotes a lock with a fairness guarantee. ‡ denotes a lock which requires HPX to use.

Lock	Time(ms)	σ(ms)
HS‡	185.32	0.55
T	200.60	0.66
B	200.92	0.76
C†	201.50	0.67
TT	201.60	0.66
M†	215.00	0.95
SM	229.98	114.36
SR	234.92	180.09
HM‡	239.60	0.49
A†	251.67	0.85
AO†	287.10	1.30
IT	4111.88	14675.65
I	4978.12	14828.38
L†	9068.06	18182.25

(a) mike

Lock	Time(ms)	σ(ms)
HS‡	141.00	0.00
SR	151.98	0.15
SM	153.00	0.00
C†	153.78	0.41
T	154.83	0.38
B	155.49	0.50
TT	155.51	0.50
I	155.54	0.50
L†	156.32	0.47
M†	158.05	6.65
IT	163.78	37.17
HM‡	174.51	0.50
A†	180.26	0.44
AO†	193.54	0.50

(b) buran

Lock	Time(ms)	σ(ms)
B	190.89	6.00
L†	195.05	2.64
AO†	197.81	7.08
A†	210.01	3.51
IT	211.31	4.79
C†	211.38	4.31
TT	212.53	3.70
HS‡	212.82	4.09
HM‡	223.89	2.10
M†	250.41	9.49
SM	256.55	4.25
SR	280.74	5.74
I	290.70	11.96
T	290.77	12.31

(c) melete05

Fig. 5. Figure (a) SetByLocks benchmark for mike, $W_T = 200$; Figure (b) SetByLocks benchmark for buran, $W_T = 200$; Figure (c) MapByLocks benchmark for melete05, $W_T = 600$. † denotes a lock with a fairness guarantee. ‡ denotes a lock which requires HPX to use.

Lock	Time(ms)	σ(ms)
HS‡	6.00	0.00
B	8.00	0.00
T	8.00	0.00
TT	8.00	0.00
C†	8.00	0.00
I	8.17	0.37
IT	8.44	0.50
SM	9.00	0.00
SR	9.00	0.00
M†	9.00	0.00
HM‡	9.58	0.49
A†	10.00	0.00
L†	10.03	0.16
AO†	10.22	0.42

(a) medusa

Lock	Time(ms)	σ(ms)
SM	43.48	0.74
AO†	45.05	4.57
TT	46.15	1.94
IT	46.80	1.40
HS‡	49.08	0.98
SR	49.40	0.49
A†	49.88	3.77
C†	51.62	3.28
M†	52.20	5.33
L†	52.38	5.76
I	54.42	4.40
B	57.42	1.22
T	57.88	3.98
HM‡	58.02	1.71

(b) qbc

Lock	Time(ms)	σ(ms)
SR	9794.05	2393.95
A†	10023.64	4038.06
C†	10097.24	3729.44
SM	10170.50	2111.68
L†	10538.68	3635.48
B	10840.14	2456.43
M†	10896.59	4243.30
AO†	11215.59	4486.94
TT	13393.43	4876.77
T	13509.38	2735.81
I	13509.45	3885.76
IT	14076.05	5578.14
HM‡	15030.81	812.88
HS‡	16964.81	1358.74

(c) twilight

Fig. 6. Figure (a) MapByLocks benchmark for medusa, $W_T = 500$; Figure (b) MapBy-Locks benchmark for qbc, $W_T = 300$; Figure (c) MapByLocks benchmark for twilight, $W_T = 30000$. † denotes a lock with a fairness guarantee. ‡ denotes a lock which requires HPX to use.

Lock	Time(ms)	σ(ms)
A†	757.12	76.86
L†	776.85	62.72
M†	818.08	97.26
C†	819.98	61.33
AO†	857.98	92.03
SR	957.00	86.80
SM	964.23	63.78
IT	978.33	247.79
TT	994.90	235.05
T	1035.33	231.51
B	1050.65	86.67
I	1112.97	223.80
HM‡	1119.45	20.99
HS‡	1646.62	148.02

(a) skeleton

Lock	Time(ms)	σ(ms)
HS‡	5.23	0.42
T	8.00	0.00
C†	8.00	0.00
TT	8.80	0.40
B	9.00	0.00
I	9.00	0.00
SR	9.10	0.30
IT	9.20	0.40
SM	9.90	0.30
M†	10.00	0.00
A†	12.00	0.00
L†	12.00	0.00
HM‡	12.00	0.00
AO†	12.30	0.46

(b) mike

Lock	Time(ms)	σ(ms)
HS‡	58.00	0.00
M†	101.09	0.29
L†	104.18	0.47
IT	108.15	0.35
I	108.93	0.26
C†	112.00	0.00
B	116.02	4.42
TT	116.25	4.46
T	116.27	4.35
SR	116.29	0.53
SM	124.04	0.38
AO†	187.25	0.43
A†	188.45	0.50
HM‡	418.94	2.28

(c) buran

Fig. 7. Figure (a) MapByLocks benchmark for skeleton, $W_T = 10000$; Figure (b) Map-ByLocks benchmark for mike, $W_T = 600$; Figure (c) MapByLocks benchmark for buran, $W_T = 500$. † denotes a lock with a fairness guarantee. ‡ denotes a lock which requires HPX to use.

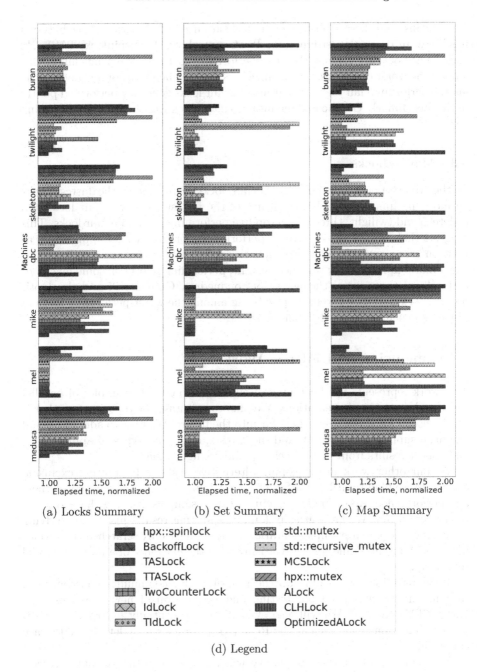

(a) Locks Summary   (b) Set Summary   (c) Map Summary

hpx::spinlock	std::mutex
BackoffLock	std::recursive_mutex
TASLock	MCSLock
TTASLock	hpx::mutex
TwoCounterLock	ALock
IdLock	CLHLock
TIdLock	OptimizedALock

(d) Legend

Fig. 8. Summary of lock performance across machines and benchmarks.

clearly wins, and there is a large amount of variance in lock performance between machines. In particular, std::mutex, TwoCounterLock, hpx::spinlock, TASLock, and TTASLock are among the best-performing locks on some machines, but among the worst on others. On all machines except qbc, TwoCounterLock is the fastest-performing fair lock. As a group, the fair locks generally performed poorly in this benchmark. On qbc and medusa, hpx::spinlock was the fastest-performing lock.

5.3   MapByLocks

In the MapByLocks benchmark, the fair locks were among the fastest locks on most machines. On skeleton, all five of the fastest locks were fair locks. On melete05 and twilight, three of the top five performing locks were fair locks. This suggests that lock fairness improves performance for this type of application, at least on some configurations. hpx::mutex consistently performed poorly in this benchmark. hpx::spinlock was inconsistent, performing poorly on some machines and well on others; it was the fastest lock on medusa. On melete05 and qbc, OptimizedALock performed well, despite being among the worst-performing locks in previous benchmarks on the same machines.

6   Conclusion and Future Work

This work represents the beginning of our effort to collect examples of parallel codes and mutex implementations. We plan to maintain the repository so that it can be useful for other researchers far into the future. We plan to add additional language support (e.g., Rust), add more tests, add more types of applications, and collect results from more machines and configurations.

As our other work in developing alternative systems for mutual exclusion continues, we plan to utilize ParSweet for verifying the new systems' correctness and performance. Accordingly, we will add code samples utilizing those systems to the repository. We have already found interesting results just from studying the current set of mutex implementations, and we have only scratched the surface in terms of potential lines of study arising from the existence of a unified parallel repository.

In preparation for opening up the repository for community contributions, we will implement automated testing and verification of new additions with Github(TM) Actions. We will also evaluate and potentially incorporate third-party verification tools, such as the Relacy [11] library which detects subtle race conditions.

It is our hope that the community will contribute to this ongoing project. The repository can be found at: https://github.com/mmor115/ParSweet.

The results are striking both in the difficult-to-explain variances in performance, and in how often our expectations were defied. Programmers tend not to think carefully about mutex implementations, and may not even be aware that alternatives exist. The results from our benchmarks show that performance in parallel applications is affected in significant and unpredictable ways by the choice of mutex implementation. Blindly choosing one, such as the default implementation in a given language or framework (e.g., std::mutex or hpx::mutex) will likely result in suboptimal performance. Accordingly, when choosing a mutex implementation, benchmarking of multiple lock implementations on a per-machine *and* per-application basis is needed to find the most efficient lock for a given circumstance.

We will attempt to improve the locks we currently have. Because the TwoCounterLock knows how many threads are ahead of it, it may be able to benefit from a backoff component that sleeps only when it anticipates a long wait.

Acknowledgements. We thank LSU HPC and CCT IT Services for making available the mike, qbc, medusa, and buran compute resources, and we thank Vicenç Beltran Querol for his helpful insight.

References

1. Mike-III. https://www.hpc.lsu.edu/resources/hpc/system.php?system=SuperMike-III
2. Qb3. http://www.hpc.lsu.edu/resources/hpc/system.php?system=QB3
3. Software-artifact infrastructure repository. https://sir.csc.ncsu.edu/portal/index.php
4. Anderson, T.E.: The performance of spin lock alternatives for shared-memory multiprocessors. IEEE Trans. Parallel Distrib. Syst. **1**(1), 6–16 (1990)
5. Craig, T.: Building fifo and priorityqueuing spin locks from atomic swap. Technical report TR 93-02-02, Department of Computer Science, University of Washington (1993)
6. Do, H., Elbaum, S., Rothermel, G.: Supporting controlled experimentation with testing techniques: an infrastructure and its potential impact. Empir. Softw. Eng. **10**, 405–435 (2005)
7. Herlihy, M., Shavit, N., Luchangco, V., Spear, M.: The art of multiprocessor programming. Newnes (2020)
8. Kaiser, H., et al.: HPX-the C++ standard library for parallelism and concurrency. J. Open Source Softw. **5**(53), 2352 (2020)
9. Magnusson, P., Landin, A., Hagersten, E.: Queue locks on cache coherent multiprocessors. In: Proceedings of 8th International Parallel Processing Symposium, pp. 165–171. IEEE (1994)
10. Mellor-Crummey, J.M., Scott, M.L.: Algorithms for scalable synchronization on shared-memory multiprocessors. ACM Trans. Comput. Syst. (TOCS) **9**(1), 21–65 (1991)
11. Vyukov, D.: Relacy race detector. https://github.com/dvyukov/relacy

Rethinking Programming Paradigms in the QC-HPC Context

Silvina Caino-Lores[3], Daniel Claudino[1], Eugene Dumitrescu[1], Travis S. Humble[1], Sonia Lopez Alarcon[2], and Elaine Wong[1(✉)]

[1] Oak Ridge National Laboratory, Oak Ridge, TN, USA
{claudinodc,dumitrescuef,humblets,wongey}@ornl.gov
[2] Rochester Institute of Technology, Rochester, NY, USA
slaeec@rit.edu
[3] University of Rennes, Inria, CNRS, IRISA, Rennes, France
silvina.caino-lores@inria.fr

Abstract. Programming for today's quantum computers is making significant strides toward modern workflows compatible with high performance computing (HPC), but fundamental challenges still remain in the integration of these vastly different technologies. Quantum computing (QC) programming languages share some common ground, as well as their emerging runtimes and algorithmic modalities. In this short paper, we explore avenues of refinement for the quantum processing unit (QPU) in the context of many-tasks management, asynchronous or otherwise, in order to understand the value it can play in linking QC with HPC. Through examples, we illustrate how its potential for scientific discovery might be realized.

Keywords: quantum computing · high performance computing

1 Introduction

A quantum computer is a physical system in which an initial quantum state evolves in time quantum mechanically to reach a new state that will contain the solution to a certain problem. Like other accelerators such as GPUs, ASICs and FPGAs, quantum computers have their own niche applications at which they excel, and are not meant to universally outperform classical computing. The set of problems that will benefit from quantum computing (QC) is still being defined,

This manuscript has been authored by UT-Battelle, LLC, under contract DE-AC05-00OR22725 with the US Department of Energy (DOE). The US government retains and the publisher, by accepting the article for publication, acknowledges that the US government retains a nonexclusive, paid-up, irrevocable, worldwide license to publish or reproduce the published form of this manuscript, or allow others to do so, for US government purposes. DOE will provide public access to these results of federally sponsored research in accordance with the DOE Public Access Plan (https://www.energy.gov/doe-public-access-plan).

P. Diehl et al. (Eds.): WAMTA 2024, LNCS 14626, pp. 84–91, 2024.
https://doi.org/10.1007/978-3-031-61763-8_8

but some research points to Hamiltonian simulation as a good first candidate, which has practical applications that will enhance drug development [3]. QC has also shown advantages over classical implementations in very specific, but arguably not useful problems [1, 6]. More optimistically, however, research on all aspects of QC from the technology to the software stack and high performance computing (HPC) integration is advancing the field to reach quantum advantage on real life problems.

QC is intricate in its workings, but as the software stack advances, and applications are defined, non-quantum experts should be able to take advantage of these accelerators without deep knowledge of quantum entanglement, quantum superposition, or quantum noise mitigation [4, 5, 9]. One aspect that users will need to be aware of is the *probabilistic nature of quantum mechanics*. The quantum state of a quantum system cannot be observed by classical means. The quantum state can be in a superstition of waves similar to the way sound can contain waves on different frequencies. But in quantum mechanics, a classical observation can only see one of these frequencies, and the others will collapse and be un-observable. For that reason, the measurement is done by repeated observation, through which each specific frequency or wave is observed with a certain probability. The building of this probability distribution contains information that can be used to solve computational problems. Therefore, quantum measurement requires repeated stochastic runs (shots) and measurements to extract the quantum state's probability distribution on a certain quantum basis.

Accelerated computing has become a leading architectural approach for HPC systems. This paper explores the possibility of quantum computers claiming their role as hardware accelerators, with the understanding that their architectures rely on the presence of specialized devices to process specialized workloads or tasks. The ways that this can be combined effectively remains to be seen and for the moment, a concrete realization of how to integrate a quantum computer with a HPC system would not necessarily demonstrate a performance advantage with current systems, but would be able to show that testing such an integration is *feasible with current programming tools*. In this paper, we outline how computation tasks might interact with each other in this context on known quantum programs.

2   Quantum Programming Tools

Despite the nascent technology underlying QC, there has been substantial progress in the development of programming tools that integrate QPUs with conventional systems. Issuing instructions to a quantum control unit plays a pivotal role in the execution of a quantum program, while the recovering of data from the QPU depends on subsequent post-processing of measurement results. This interplay between the QPU and the calling system–depicted in Fig. 2–can be developed to be either synchronous or asynchronous depending on the algorithm, but the latter is more generally used at the moment (Fig. 1).

One way of classifying programming paradigms involves its distance from the program to the hardware. Thus, how tasks are to be viewed might be relative to

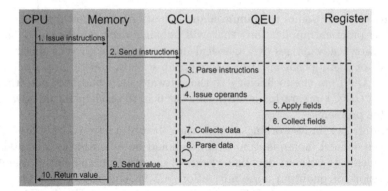

Fig. 1. A sequence diagram detailing the interactions between a CPU, memory, and a QPU [2]. Operands are the sequence of quantum gates that implement an input instruction logic, the quantum control unit (QCU) parses these instructions while the quantum execution unit (QEU) initiates the corresponding gates through applied fields that modify the quantum physical state of the quantum register. The return process generates data that corresponds with measured results from hardware.

how easy it is to access hardware and manage its latency, resources, and general effectiveness. At the analog level, pulse sequences drive the transformation of a quantum state, circumventing the need to involve the full stack in computation. At the digital level, the instructions to manage computations can range from low-level (close to hardware) assembly languages, which can be transformed to signals for physical implementation, to a higher level that can support algorithmic descriptions closer to the user's natural language, and then brought down closer to hardware via a compiler. Recent integration attempts [7,8] were motivated by the desire to balance ease-of-use for the general user and flexibility for the domain scientists, but those frameworks and paradigms still sit quite close to the hardware without a consensus on how to approach quantum high performance computing (QHPC) task management at a system level.

We begin to consider a higher-level perspective revolving around the idea of runtimes, task-oriented and workflow-oriented approaches in QC and HPC integration for the purpose of *interoperability*. An example of this is shown in Fig. 2. This might be most akin to hybrid runtime environments with multi-processing, multi-threading and accelerator offloading capabilities (e.g., MPI, OpenMP and CUDA, respectively), where similar challenges inherent in the handling of heterogeneous systems arise: there are trade-offs with respect to the overhead of offloading a computation to an accelerator vs. the obtained performance improvement. A vast amount of literature exists on this topic, with years of experience and incremental optimizations. But, while popular solutions in HPC exist, there is a shift to try to find more flexible, productive, and higher-level mechanisms to define tasks, dependencies, resource requirements and other constraints, especially with systems that operate different physical systems from traditional computing platforms.

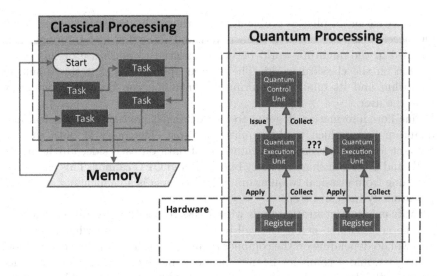

Fig. 2. An example of a high-level view of the task-based interactions in a hybrid quantum-classical system.

For example, let's consider a machine learning model implemented in Tensor-Flow running on CUDA/OpenACC vs. an AI-powered workflow doing ensemble molecular dynamics at scale through a true workflow management system (e.g., PyCOMPSs). In this scenario, the level of integration moves away from the inter-action between the accelerator and the CPU to involve multiple nodes potentially dedicated to different types of tasks. HPC systems are remotely accessible with resources assigned for a particular task via a scheduler and resource manager. In QC, existing approaches for this kind of system-level integration usually go through similar remote access by necessity, as there are strict environmental con-straints for operating a quantum system. However, such system integration is not tightly-coupled and would not be managed as in HPC, but is nevertheless a tangible scenario for actual workflow composition, and we already see solutions that allow writing hybrid quantum-classical workflows running on cloud-based QC-HPC systems (e.g., Covalent, which supports AWS Braket and IBM Quantum on the QC side).

We can begin to understand the interoperability challenges of a hybrid appli-cation use case by analyzing it holistically in a top-down manner (i.e., starting from the high-level workflow and finishing at the low-level programming of the hardware instructions). For example, one might consider the following progres-sion of analysis:

1. Identify the high level steps.
2. Identify, out of those steps, which ones will be suitable for the classical side and which ones will be suitable for the quantum side. For the parts that can be accelerated by quantum computers, one needs to understand the existing quantum algorithm and how to encode the information. Such translations

might be easier for physics problems. Since the applications that benefit from QC acceleration are not well-defined yet, understanding how information is handled in the quantum world becomes essential to make use of this information on the classical world. The desired approach is that this quantum algorithm and its quantum information encoding can be abstracted away from the user.

3. Define how information is going to be exchanged between the classical and quantum sides, which would require some sort of memory at both ends to account for the different representations of data on each side. Furthermore, CPU and GPU can share memory but CPU and QPU cannot. This encoding-decoding from classical to quantum and vice-versa is a challenging and computationally intensive step.

4. Identify existing integration tools with access to possibly several backends. It will be necessary to define the call to quantum kernels and what those kernels will do depending on the compiler requirements. The runtime or workflow manager would account for latency, memory management, and task interactions, while the compiler takes care of generating a synthesizable quantum instruction stream from a high level quantum program description.

3   Task Modeling in Quantum Computation

This section frames quantum programs in terms of their related tasks and where asynchronous multi-tasking requirements might appear in the context of a hybrid workflow management. However, we note that existing QC hardware is suitable for both synchronous and asynchronous operations, and we provide **two examples** to illustrate this. The distinction here represents a choice for how the QPU behaves in response to instructions accepted from the parent node within the accelerator architecture. This choice depends on the desired behavior of the QPU and, for purposes of performance, on the ability for the QPU to process an assigned workload in a well-characterized time. For example, synchronous operations of a QPU place a timing constraint on the compute response that depends intimately on the size of the quantum program, i.e., the depth of the circuit, and the number of measurements samples generated through repeated execution of the program. While these parameters are well-defined prior to execution, the subsequent impact on the execution time varies with the technology and communication methods.

For our **first example**, we take quantum phase estimation, a ubiquitous quantum procedure that is used in many other fundamental quantum algorithms. This presents a first opportunity to look at task modeling from a QC perspective. The phase estimation problem is formulated as follows: *Given a unitary operator U and eigenstate $|\Psi\rangle$ with an unknown eigenvalue $e^{i2\pi\varphi}$, estimate the value φ.*

Some of the assumptions on this problem come from the underlying physics and hardware, that U (as well as any of its corresponding control operations) can be efficiently implemented by a quantum circuit, and that we have the ability to efficiently prepare the state $|\Psi\rangle$. Furthermore, we impose the mathematical assumption that (for simplicity) φ can be written in an exact binary representation,

$$\varphi = 0.\varphi_1\varphi_2\cdots\varphi_m.$$

One way to construct φ is by iteratively determining φ_i from the least significant to the most significant bit. To illustrate a synchronous model, for each φ_i we require two quantum bits for computation and a classical bit to store measured results. To determine the least significant bit φ_m, we (1) initialize the two qubits (one auxiliary, one in the eigenstate); (2) apply a certain operation (in this case, controlled $U^{2^{m-1}}$); (3) measure the auxiliary qubit in a certain basis (in this case, Pauli X); and (4) store the result in the classical register.

After this process is complete, the auxiliary qubit is reinitialized and then a *phase correction* is performed in order to remove the contribution from φ_m in order to identify the next significant bit, φ_{m-1} in pretty much the same manner as described above (but now with the new phase), and so on and forth until φ_1. This is the notion of *classical feedback*: the next stage of computation depends on the value of the classical register holding the previous result. This example relies on a synchronous execution paradigm, in which results from programs submitted to the QPU depend on successful execution of an ordered sequence of computations with the final result collected when available.

To contrast this, the φ construction process can be executed in a *parallel* fashion, where each precision bit is realized in its own sequence of initialization and control-U operations with the results stored in its own classical register. This would require more qubits, larger circuit depth, and more classical registers to store the precision data. However, it is an illustration of asynchronous quantum tasks, introducing the potential to manage them at a higher level. The caveat here is that the synchronicity requirement is still imposed before the final measurement in the form of the inverse quantum Fourier transform that is applied to the results of the previous asynchronous steps. The inverse QFT is necessary for producing the correct transformation for estimating the phase. In this sense, the example would not be illustrative of a 'fully asynchronous' process.

For our **second example**, we consider an algorithm that uses a quantum computer to create and measure the properties of a parameterized trial wave function, and a classical computer to optimize the wave-function parameters. In this case, error detection during the quantum computation could present a different kind of opportunity for synchronous task modeling within a hybrid quantum-classical computation [10]. (a) In the first stage of the quantum computation, the circuit would use an ancilla qubit, a_1, to detect an error in the preparation of the initial logical state. The detection of an error from the measurement of this ancilla qubit would reset the stage. (b) In the second stage of the quantum computation, a second ancilla qubit, a_2, is entangled with the logical qubit and is utilized to perform an arbitrary angle rotation; the result for its measurement indicates which angle θ was used in the computation. (c) From there, the expectation values (depending on θ) are computed. The classical computation would then identify the angle that minimizes the algorithm's cost function.

In principle, the actions on the two ancillas are independent of each other and can be performed asynchronously. However, the synchronous model applies when both the detection of an error in state preparation and the determination of the angle θ are combined into a single ancilla. In such a scenario, upon the right measurement outcome on a_1, this qubit is reset and the circuitry on a_2 follows on the same qubit.

Ultimately, noisy intermediate-scale quantum (NISQ) and fault-tolerant operation of QHPC systems will introduce separate requirements for asynchronous multi-tasking. In the NISQ context, we need to periodically characterize the quantum processors to estimate noise parameters and perform error mitigation to finalize QPU results. There is also the concern of making calls to multiple QPUs as they lack the reliability and reproducibility of traditional technology; this introduces additional programming concerns.

In the context of fault-tolerant quantum error correction (FTQEC), we need to process conditional statements that may affect the runtime of the QPU themselves. This will lead to uncertainty in device operation times and, hence, will be better treated as an asynchronous request. Moreover, the devices are inherently probabilistic and post-processing will require gathering statistical confidence that affects runtime. This leads to an intersection between requirements for QC and other probabilistic computing paradigms.

4   Perspective on the Role of Quantum Technology

Coupling HPC and QC systems will affect the way we interact with the latter. For instance, a QC system might only be accessible through a cloud environment, potentially leading to queue waiting and larger communication latency. Conversely, a tighter coupling with the HPC system will result in more efficient execution due to the availability of specialized encoding and a tailored instruction set, but this will also require the runtime to be more responsive, thus increasing the computational load of the classical side.

A leading performance concern is the choice of a system-level/compiled programming model versus an interpreted (Python) programming model that is very common for QC today. We advocate for more integration at the system level, notably via libraries and their direct management of system resources. In addition, the examples described in Sect. 3 are relatively simple but illustrate that quantum data types and a standardizing format of data structures can lead to performance advantages, especially when leveraged to take advantage of classical resources.

In task-based models for irregular, dynamic and heterogeneous applications, critical paths are probabilistic and we cannot estimate them a priori. Schedulers, resource managers, and runtimes will have to face a challenging transformation in order to minimize idle times and leverage asynchronous operations. Furthermore, the ability to manifest the probabilistic behavior expected from quantum computers is hindered by noise from the environment, and how this kind of additional complexity affects quantum-classical task management might reveal its importance in the future.

Acknowledgements. EW, DC, TSH, and ED acknowledge that this work was performed at Oak Ridge National Laboratory, operated by UT-Battelle, LLC under contract DE-AC05-00OR22725 for the US Department of Energy (DOE). EW, DC, and TSH acknowledge that support for the work came from the DOE Advanced Scientific Computing Research (ASCR) Accelerated Research in Quantum Computing (ARQC) Program under field work proposal ERKJ332. ED is supported by the DOE Office of Science Advanced Scientific Research Program Early Career Award under contract number 3ERKJ420. SLA acknowledges that this material is partially based upon work supported by the National Science Foundation under Award No. 2300476.

References

1. Arute, F., Arya, K., Babbush, R., Bacon, D., et al.: Quantum supremacy using a programmable superconducting processor. Nature **574**, 505–510 (2019). https://doi.org/10.1038/s41586-019-1666-5

2. Britt, K.A., Mohiyaddin, F.A., Humble, T.S.: Quantum accelerators for high-performance computing systems. In: 2017 IEEE International Conference on Rebooting Computing (ICRC), pp. 1–7 (2017). https://doi.org/10.1109/ICRC.2017.8123664

3. Chen, C., et al.: Accelerating Computational Materials Discovery with Artificial Intelligence and Cloud High-Performance Computing: From Large-Scale Screening to Experimental Validation (2024). https://doi.org/10.48550/arXiv.2401.04070

4. Lopez Alarcon, S., Elster, A.C.: Quantum computing and high-performance computing: compilation stack similarities. Comput. Sci. Eng. **24**(06), 66–71 (2022). https://doi.org/10.1109/MCSE.2023.3269645

5. Lopez Alarcon, S., Wong, E., Humble, T., Dumitrescu, E.: Quantum programming paradigms and description languages. Comput. Sci. Eng. (2024). To appear

6. Madsen, L.S., et al.: Quantum computational advantage with a programmable photonic processor. Nature **606**, 75–81 (2022). https://doi.org/10.1038/s41586-022-04725-x

7. McCaskey, A., Lyakh, D., Dumitrescu, E.F., Powers, S., Humble, T.: XACC: a system-level software infrastructure for heterogeneous quantum-classical computing. Quantum Sci. Technol. **5**(2), 1–23 (2020). https://doi.org/10.1088/2058-9565/ab6bf6

8. Mintz, T.M., McCaskey, A.J., Dumitrescu, E.F., Moore, S.V., Powers, S., Lougovski, P.: QCOR: a language extension specification for the heterogeneous quantum-classical model of computation. J. Emerg. Technol. Comput. Syst. **16**(2) (2020). https://doi.org/10.1145/3380964

9. Schulz, M., Ruefenacht, M., Kranzlmuller, D., Schulz, L.: Accelerating HPC with quantum computing: it is a software challenge too. Comput. Sci. Eng. **24**(04), 60–64 (2022)

10. Urbanek, M., Nachman, B., de Jong, W.A.: Error detection on quantum computers improving the accuracy of chemical calculations. Phys. Rev. A **102**, 022427 (2020). https://doi.org/10.1103/PhysRevA.102.022427

Dynamic Tuning of Core Counts
to Maximize Performance
in Object-Based Runtime Systems

Kavitha Chandrasekar[✉] and Laxmikant V. Kale

University of Illinois at Urbana-Champaign, Urbana, IL 61801, USA
{kchndrs2,kale}@illinois.edu

Abstract. Relatively recent developments in supercomputer nodes, such as higher physical and virtual core counts per node, aim to speed up HPC application execution time. However, not all applications benefit from increased thread level parallelism and may exhibit performance degradation with increased concurrency. Additionally, the best performing thread count may not be known apriori as it can vary with application or with input size for a given application.

This motivates the need for dynamically tuning the number of threads or cores used by an application, at run-time. However, such tuning of core counts in popular object-based or task-based runtime system is non-trivial since objects or tasks are anchored to processing elements (PEs) for locality. In this work, we identify the steps for adaptive tuning of core count to the most performant configuration, at run-time, for an object-based runtime system, Charm++. We show performance benefit of dynamic profiling and adaptively selecting core (physical or virtual) count for a variety of applications including compute, memory and cache-intensive applications. Specifically, we show that our mechanism can improve performance by almost 40% in presence of cache and memory contention, by over 20% with SMT in Skylake nodes and by about 35% in KNL nodes. We also show energy savings, and in some cases power savings alongside performance improvement.

1 Introduction

There has been a steady increase in machines with higher core counts in supercomputers, in the recent years. In Top500 supercomputers, we have seen a steady increase in node size, with core counts per socket in last 10 years alone having gone up from 16 upto 260 cores. Additionally, support for upto 4 virtual cores (Simultaneous Multithreading or SMT) per phyiscal core has also become prevalent in machines. Each node also can have multiple sockets further increasing the number of cores in a shared memory processor. The reason for increasing cores per node has been to a) to increase available parallelism on a node without increasing power usage significantly and b) also due to limitations in scaling of CPU frequency in modern machines. Additionally, SMT aims to improve core usage efficiency by hiding cache and memory access costs by executing multiple hardware threads on a single physical core.

P. Diehl et al. (Eds.): WAMTA 2024, LNCS 14626, pp. 92–104, 2024.
https://doi.org/10.1007/978-3-031-61763-8_9

With the increase in number of physical and virtual cores in a socket, there is a need to examine if HPC applications always see a speedup or improvement in performance with increase in cores. For instance, applications that are memory-bound or communication-bound might see an increase in memory contention or network contention with increased concurrency from higher number of cores or increased contention in shared data structures, such as, using locks. This might lead to poorer performance and/or efficiency with use of higher core counts. Additionally, cache-bound applications might see better performance with 1-way SMT compared with 2 or 4-way SMT which may encounter L1-level cache trashing. There are other factors that can affect performance like turbo boost and uncore power usage that favor the use of fewer cores per node or socket.

Given the possibility of potential application performance degradation with increased thread counts and similar issues observed in other works [1,2] we recognize the need for dynamic tuning of threads at run-time, with a focus on maximizing performance. This is especially needed since different applications have different compute, cache, memory and communication metrics and such characteristics are not know apriori. Additionally, the same application can exhibit different characteristics for different input data. With runtimes like OpenMP and OMPSs, it is fairly easy to tune the number of cores at run-time [3] since tuning of threads in a parallel region can be done in user program and underlying implementation can make threads sleep or add threads without affecting remaining functionality of the runtime system.

However, runtime systems like OpenMP focus on within-node parallelism and rely on a hybrid model MPI+X for capabilities like multi-node execution. Other shared-memory-only systems like Kokkos [4] and StarPU [5] also integrate with MPI, providing a hybrid model for multi-node or distributed execution. Whereas, our focus is on runtime systems like Charm++ [6] and HPX [7] which are object-based or task-based provide support for Shared Memory Parallelism or SMP on single and multi-node execution. Object-based runtimes like Charm++ divide work into units or chares and provide features like load balancing and migratability. This also makes the task of tuning the number of threads or processes at run-time a more complex task. Our focus is on tuning adaptively at run-time, within-node resources, mainly threads or PEs per node. For our work, we use the capability in Charm++ to migrate objects at run time, to move objects away from PEs before suspending the pthread for the PE. The ability to migrate objects in Charm++ provides a unique opportunity for saving state in memory. We describe our implementation in later sections. Additionally, our example applications are iterative in nature, i.e. subsequent iterations follow the same pattern in terms of load, allowing us to perform adaptive tuning for future iterations.

Our work applies to the Shared Memory Parallelism (SMP) model or multicore model in Charm++. This is opposed to the "MPI-everywhere" model, where a process runs on each core of a node. In the SMP model, typically a process runs on a node or socket and within the process, parallelism is realized using thread level parallelism, by launching one thread (PE) on each core. A few notable benefits of this model are: a) sharing data structures across threads in a shared address space b) sharing objects and their tasks between threads and c) less overall memory usage compared to one process per core.

While there can be many objectives for adaptive tuning of PE counts within a node, such as performance, energy, energy-delay product (EDP), our goal in this work is to *maximize performance*. Our contributions in this paper are as follows:

1. Identify the steps and mechanism for changing the cores being used at run-time for task or object-based runtime systems
2. Describe implementation of online profiling and adaptive tuning of core counts (ppn or wpn) in Charm++. 'ppn' stands of PEs per process, used interchangeably with 'wpn' for workers per process
3. With the above techniques, we show performance improvement for production SKX and KNL machines on Stampede2 and additionally, we show energy and power benefits as well
4. Demonstrate ease of addressing application load imbalance while performing tuning of core count. Several other works that perform tuning of core count using OpenMP cannot perform load balancing simultaneously

2   Backgroud and Implementation

In this section, we describe the steps to tune core counts adaptively in an object-based runtime system and our implementation of this dynamic tuning mechanism in Charm++. We add support for adaptive tuning of cores in Charm++ SMP or multicore build which uses pthreads as PEs to achieve within-node parallelism. The SMP build is used to run Charm++ on multiple nodes typically with one process per node and one pthread on each PE.

We first introduce the Charm++ runtime system and programming model. Charm++ work units named chares are objects that are scheduled to run on PEs. Work is overdecomposed into chares such that there are multiple chares on each PE. This enables overlapping of computation and communication. Additionally, Charm++ supports migra-

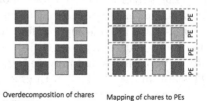

Overdecomposition of chares in Charm++   Mapping of chares to PEs

Fig. 1. Charm++ programming model

tion of chares across PEs (nodes or cores), which is used to perform functions like load balancing, fault tolerance and others, by the runtime system. Figure 1 shows the overdecomposition in Charm++, where multiple chares are mapped to each PE (enclosing boxes). If different chare arrays (different colors) are present, objects from each array will be mapped to each PE.

2.1   Implementation of Tuning Core Counts in Charm++

For tuning the number of cores at run-time in Charm++, we utilize the *object migration and load balancing* capability in Charm++ and profiling is performed at *application iteration boundaries*, described in the steps below:

1. User program starts with maximum number of cores per node
2. User code supplies all possible core counts configuration at start of the program. This is useful since some core counts that do not divide work equally may create load imbalance
3. User code also supplies instrumentation boundaries, for Charm++, this is achieved by using *AtSync()* calls from load balancing framework
4. Runtime system uses these AtSync boundaries to record iteration time per configuration, sets a new configuration from available ones (at every 5 iterations) and consequently picks the best performing configuration
5. When performing a decrease or increase of core counts per node, load-balancer TuneCoreLB moves objects away from idle cores or to active cores
6. TuneCoreLB, implemented as a load balancer in Charm++ uses a greedy strategy (mapping objects with higher load to PEs with lower load), redistributing objects only among active cores on the node
7. Typically, idle PEs call conditional wait (cv.wait()) on their pthreads and this suspends the thread. To resume pthreads becoming active PEs, corresponding notify call (cv.notify_all()) is used

2.2 AdditionalChanges to Charm++ features

Supporting adaptive tuning of core counts in Charm++ requires various changes to the Charm++ runtime.

Reduction Trees: In Charm++, every PE participates in the reduction tree whether it has objects or not. The reduction tree at the lowest level has PEs as leaf nodes and PE-0 on each node (process) is the immediate parent. When we turn cores off and idle PEs are no longer available to participate in the reduction tree. We have updated the reduction implementation to ignore idle PEs and use an updated total children count for PE-0 on each node. Additionally, the reduction step uses total object count, computed as the sum of objects created on each PE, supplied by each PE. With our dynamic tuning feature, PE-0 on each process stores and supplies the initial object count on behalf of idle PEs.

Message Delivery: Message delivery in Charm++ is managed by location manager chares, with one chare per PE. When an object migrates, query for the object location are sent to the homePE which provides new destination PE mapping after migration of the object. This is used to deliver messages to the new PE for the migrated object. With our tuning mechanism, when idle PEs are suspended, the homePEs associated with the idle PEs are no longer available to object location queries. To address this issue, we broadcast the location of migrating objects to all PEs, thereby bypassing the need to query idle homePEs.

Load Balancing: Load-balancing framework in Charm++ allows for different load balancers to be implemented. Each PE contributes local objects' load and PE load information for aggregating load statistics before load balancing is performed. When suspending PEs for our implementation, the idle PEs can no longer contribute to load collection. As a solution, we currently resume all threads for load balancing, before suspending them again. We plan on improving this implementation to not require load information from idle PEs.

Other features requiring changes, used by a wider range of Charm++ applications, are **group chares**, **multicast** and **quiescence detection**. Production use will require relatively simple modifications to these features.

2.3 Turning Cores Off Without Suspending

Our approach to turning cores off, firstly, moves objects away from cores changing to idle. Then, idle threads on unused cores are suspended by calling conditional wait (using pthreads conditional variable) to save power and possibly memory/cache bandwidth from busywaiting. However, another approach to turning idle cores off without suspending them is to pin unused PEs or pthreads to a small number of dedicated unused cores. This is useful for more complex applications like LeanMD which uses multicast, that is not yet supported with tuning core counts. With this approach of CPU pinning of idle PEs, the tradeoff is the use of some cores on a node for idle PEs when turning cores off.

2.4 Programming API

To invoke configuration exploration, the user adds familiar AtSync calls (from Charm++ load balancing framework) marking (re-)configuration steps. A reportTime() call logs iteration time. Configuration exploration steps through user provided configurations. If increasing core counts results in improved iteration time, the next configuration picked by the runtime is a higher core count, proportional to the improved time, else a lower core count configuration is picked. This is repeated for maximum trials allowed. For our experiments, the auto-tuning mechanism picks the correct configuration without having to explore all provided configurations, hence pruning the steps needed. At the end of configuration exploration, the remaining iterations are set to the best configuration by the runtime system. A simplified example for Stencil3d is listed below.

```
1  void Stencil: next_iteration() {
2    iteration++;
3    ... // Perform Computation
4    if(converged) { // If profiling complete, set best config
5      set_active_pes(pick_best());
6      AtSync();
7    } else if(iteration % profile_freq == 0 && !converged) {
8  // If profiling step, pick next config and call LB
9      reportTiming(CkWallTimer());
10     set_active_pes(pick_next());
11     AtSync();
12   } else
13     contribute(cb_next_iter); //application logic
14 }
```

Listing 1.1. Stencil3D with turning cores off capability

3   Evaluation

3.1   System and Benchmarks

We demonstrate performance improvements from our adaptive tuning mechanism on production Stampede2 nodes. We use Stampede2 Skylake node, Intel Xeon Platinum 8160 model, with two sockets (24 cores/socket). We used only one socket for our runs to avoid NUMA effects. For running Charm++ on two sockets, we would launch two logical nodes (i.e. processes) per physical node, and our results apply to this scenario as well. The Skylake node has support for 2-way SMT (48 virtual cores per socket) and 2.1 GHz CPU frequency (varies from 1.4–3.7 GHz), turbo-boost enabled. For measuring package energy and DRAM energy, we use perf tool system calls available on Stampede2. We also show results on the older KNL nodes from Stampede2, where we use 64 cores and upto 4-way SMT on each. For all experiments, we perform single node runs of Charm++, multicore build. On Skylake nodes, recent Charm++ version 7.0 was used, for older KNL runs Charm++ version 6.8.2 was used. Our results would apply to multiple node runs, where one core is left aside for communication thread in SMP build.

The Charm++ applications used are LeanMD, a moelcular dynamics code which is compute-intensive. Stencil3d where each cell exchanges data with neighboring cells in 3D grid. We add iterations around the stencil computation kernel to mimic Gauss-Seidel iterations. Changing the block size that makes stencil3D cache-intensive and memory intensive, hence we use stencil3d with different working set size for two examples, Stencil3d-cache and mem. Another benchmark used is matrix multiply, of which we perform several iterations to allow profiling and run-time adaptive configuration. We pick an input size for matrix multiply makes it cache intensive for our use-case. Choosing a different blocksize can make it more compute-bound. We use the default gcc compiler, version 6.3.0, for the Stencil and LeanMD benchmarks. We compile matrix-multiply with AVX-512 flag and icc compiler, version 18.0.2, to note the effects of increased FLOPs on cache performance. We describe the inputs for each application in the following Table 1.

3.2   Tuning Physical/virtual Core Count for Performance (and Energy and Power Savings)

For performance on Skylake node, in Fig. 2a, we observe performance for different core counts in static configuration and with auto-tuning. The normalized metric used is application iteration time compared to the best performing static configuration's iteration time. Overheads resulting from online profiling of configurations are discussed separately. In Fig. 2a, we observe that Stencil3d-cache and mem both have improved performance of about 40% and 25% when fewer cores (12 cores and 8 cores, respectively) are used instead of all the cores with SMT on a node. Our auto-tuning mechanism is able to pick the best configuration in each case. Similarly, for LeanMD (with load imbalance), our auto-tuning

Varying core count on Skylake-Stampede2

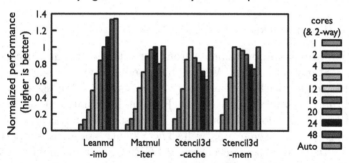

(a) Normalized Performance comparison for different core counts and auto-tuning

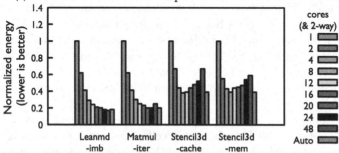

(b) Normalized Energy usage comparison for different core counts and auto-tuning

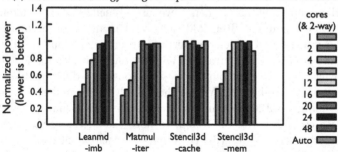

(c) Normalized Power Usage comparison for different core counts and auto-tuning

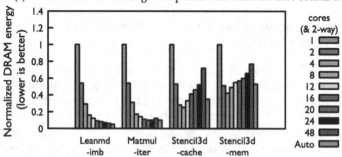

(d) Normalized DRAM energy usage comparison for different core counts and auto-tuning

Fig. 2. Application performance, energy and power with autotuning - for Charm++ benchmarks, 24 = all cores, 48 = 2-way SMT

Table 1. Input sizes for applications

Application	Input Size
Stencil3D-cache	Grid Size = 384 × 256 × 256, Block Size = 64 × 64 × 64
	Gauss-Seidel iter = 300, Chares # = 96
Stencil3D-mem	Grid Size = 384 × 256 × 256, Block Size = 64 × 64 × 128
	Gauss-Seidel iter = 600, Chares # = 48
LeanMD	Cells: 4 × 4 × 6, size: 15 15 30
	Computes (migratable) chares: 3648
Matrix multiply	# of Blocks: 24 × 24, Block size: 64 × 64
	Chares #=576

mechanism is able to determine the best performing configuration as using 2-way SMT. Since our implementation of TuneCoreLB uses a greedy strategy, it simultaneously performs within-node load balancing. For multi-node runs, TuneCoreLB in coordination with across-node load balancing can address load imbalance. LeanMD performance results showcase benefits of load balancing as the results are normalized against best configuration with load imbalance. For matrix multiply, auto-tuning performs 20% better by utilizing all cores and no-SMT, compared to 2-way SMT. We further analyzed the performance of matrix multiply to understand the benefits of turning SMT cores off. Stall cycles and cache-related hardware counters indicate significant L1 cache-trashing with two SMT threads for the working set size of about 100KiB, resulting in significant performance degradation with use of 2-way SMT. In Fig. 2b, we note that in all examples, with auto-tuning, picking the best performing configuration also results in lowest energy usage. Package and DRAM energy, in Joules, are normalized against the static configuration with highest energy usage (hence lower is better). The energy savings are primarily from reduced execution time resulting from our goal to maximize for performance. Reducing core counts on Skylake node may not always result in power savings since any surplus power may automatically be used to increase frequency to turbo range for the active cores. However, as core count is considerably lowered, we observe power savings. In Fig. 2c, power, in Watts, is normalized against configuration with highest power usage, hence lower is better. In Stencil3d-mem case, we note 12% power savings from leaving cores idle. This results in more energy savings as well for Stencil3d-mem compared to other configurations. We can generalize that when the performance benefit is smaller, picking the smaller core count is likely to save more package power. In Fig. 2d, we observe that, in all cases where fewer than all cores are used, DRAM energy usage is lower than when all cores used. There is significant savings in DRAM energy used for Stencil3d-cache and mem example, since using fewer cores results in reduced memory contention. We note that DRAM energy, in our experiments, contributes to 15% or less of the total energy usage for an application run.

We further analyze why Stencil3d-cache performance improves with reducing core counts. For this we instrument a single compute_kernel in each chare for different core counts. We see that after 4 cores, there is a significant degradation in performance of compute_kernel with an increase in number of cores active with Stencil3d-cache chares. We instrument the compute_kernel with PAPI counters PAPI_RES_STL and PAPI_TOT_CYC to measure cycles stalled on any resource and total cycles (to compute frequency), using the papi module available on Stampede2. We find that total stalled cycles (higher resource contention, eg. cache and memory, for higher cores) and frequency achieved (from turbo on fewer active cores) affect the computation time per chare. We show this in Fig. 3.

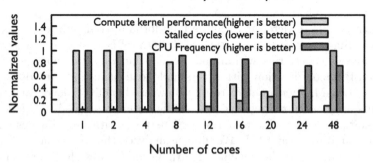

Fig. 3. Deep-dive into stencil3d-cache performance on stampede2: Performance for a single chare's computation code

On Stampede2, Skylake (any other skylake or similar config as well), we generalize that performance differences arise due to a few reasons for turning off cores that result in improved performance. 1. Cache and memory contention 2. Cache contention in presence of SMT and 3. Turbo boost: Cores are at nominal frequency when all cores are active and shutting off a few cores boosts frequency for remaining cores. In fact, we observe that the effective frequency on Stampede2 Skylake nodes is about 3.65 GHz with 1 active core, 3.3 GHz at 8 active cores and drops to 2.78 GHz at 24 active cores.

For previous generation of Intel machines, Knights Landing, we showcase the usefulness of our auto-tuning mechanism, in Fig. 4, especially to pick the right number of SMT cores. We show comparison with SMT configurations only since examples/input sizes used scale till before SMT. 4-way SMT cores tuning on older KNL machines would likely apply to similar systems like Summit super-computer, with IBM Power9 nodes where 4-way SMT is the default. For input sizes, given larger PE counts, we use LeanMD with 29184 chares and Stencil and KNeighbor with 512 for the runs on KNL.

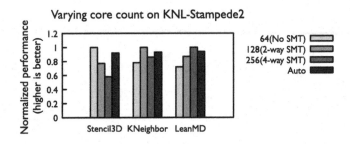

Fig. 4. Auto-tuning core counts on KNL - Benefits over 4-way SMT

3.3 Overheads

Overheads associated with our mechanism to adaptively tune core counts, *at run-time* can be categorized as follows:

1. Load balancing cost for TuneCoreLB (strategy and object migration)
2. Cost of profiling multiple configurations
3. Time taken for slower configurations

The number of configuration steps is relatively smaller than total iterations. Additionally, it is not possible to predict any prolonged iteration time when profiling slower configurations. It is important to note that our mechanism performs a search based on iteration time per configuration. This helps prune the slower configurations. We summarize the LB cost of Stencil, LeanMD and matrix multiply using average of a few LB (for turning core off) steps. For Skylake node runs, for Stencil-cache, the average LB cost is 0.09 s, for Stencil-mem it is 0.36 s, LeanMD it is 0.26 s and matrix multiply the cost for LB is 0.075 s. We observe that for larger working set size and higher object count, the LB cost is higher, from object copies during migration. We will be able to significantly reduce this cost by passing pointers as a means of migrating objects within a process (logical node).

We show a sample run for Stencil3d-cache example with 300 iterations, where auto-tuning explores different configuration, based on iteration time, in Fig. 5.

4   Related Work

There has been previous research related to tuning number of threads dynamically. Under a power-constraint, Conductor [3], uses OpenMP to change number of threads for OpenMP sections and DVFS settings, by profiling different configurations for iterative applications, using MPI+X model. Our mechanism is applicable for object or task-based runtime systems similar Charm++ like Legion and HPX. Additionally, our primary goal is to tune core count *without* a power-constraint. Other works [8], on overprovisioning hardware for a power budget explore using fewer physical cores (or nodes) than those available for

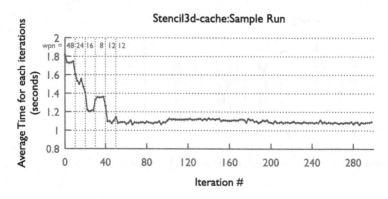

Fig. 5. Adaptive tuning timeline on Skylake

improved performance, with and without a power-constraint. However, our work addresses mechanisms for dynamically changing the number of cores.

PuPil [9], another work that looks at automatically tuning threads for disabling physical or virtual cores at run-time uses CPU affinity for reducing thread count. We find that task or object-based runtime systems that poll for new messages or tasks use a spin loop and using oversubscription of threads to turn cores off can result in interference between threads and is less efficient than suspending idle PEs. Recent work on using a combination of DCT, DVFS and uncore frequency knobs [1] optimizes for energy. We, on the other hand, use only concurrency throttling to show benefits on a production system where DVFS knobs may not be available. Our goal also differs as we maximize for performance. Prediction-based methods [10] use machine learning models to predict thread level parallelism and CPU and uncore frequency. While providing good accuracy, they differ from our approach of using online feedback to tune core count adaptively.

CRUST [2] performs tuning of SMT cores at run-time using OpenMP parallel regions. It uses system-level metrics like IPC for profiling steps. Our focus is on task/object-based runtime system tuning and additionally, we use application iteration time as performance metric during profiling.

Kokkos performs similar auto-tuning of resources dynamically, specifically for tuning the number of GPUs at run-time [11]. Other works on auto-tuning are geared towards automatically mapping of tasks to hardware, for example, for efficient computation and data movement [12].

5   Conclusion and Future Work

With increasing number of cores and architecture changes like turbo frequency, aimed to improve performance in HPC applications, there is a need for runtime systems to provide adaptive mechanisms that can tune available knobs based on application behavior. In our study, we showcase the methodology for adaptive tuning of the number of active cores in object-based runtime systems, where such tuning requires significant runtime system changes. We demonstrate the capability and evaluate our mechanism in Charm++ on production supercomputers for tuning physical and virtual (SMT) cores. Our mechanism for tuning cores count by migrating objects between cores on each node, while implemented in Charm++ runtime system, can be applied to other object and task-based runtimes with support for migration of objects or tasks.

As future work, having studied the tuning core counts to maximize performance, we plan to explore other opportunities from tuning core counts dynamically for object-based runtime systems. This includes, for instance, running another application, such as in-situ analytics, concurrently on a node to improve resource utilization. We will also extend our implementation for scenarios where different nodes may decide on a different configuration setting or core count due on load differences or variations in processor speeds. We also plan on handling application phase changes in the future.

References

1. Navarro Muñoz, A.F., Lorenzon, A., Ayguadé Parra, E., Beltran Querol, V.: Combining dynamic concurrency throttling with voltage and frequency scaling on task-based programming models. In: Proceedings of the 50th International Conference on Parallel Processing, ser. ICPP '21. Association for Computing Machinery, New York, NY, USA (2021). https://doi.org/10.1145/3472456.3472471
2. Heirman, W., Carlson, T.E., Van Craeynest, K., Hur, I., Jaleel, A., Eeckhout, L.: Automatic SMT threading for OpenMP applications on the intel Xeon phi co-processor. In: Proceedings of the 4th International Workshop on Runtime and Operating Systems for Supercomputers, ser. ROSS '14, pp. 7:1–7:7. ACM, New York, NY, USA (2014). http://doi.acm.org/10.1145/2612262.2612268
3. Marathe, A., Bailey, P.E., Lowenthal, D.K., Rountree, B., Schulz, M., de Supinski, B.R.: A run-time system for power-constrained HPC applications. In: Kunkel, J.M., Ludwig, T. (eds.) ISC High Performance 2015. LNCS, vol. 9137, pp. 394–408. Springer, Cham (2015). https://doi.org/10.1007/978-3-319-20119-1_28
4. Trott, C.R., et al.: Kokkos 3: programming model extensions for the exascale era. IEEE Trans. Parallel Distrib. Syst. **33**(4), 805–817 (2022)
5. Augonnet, C., Thibault, S., Namyst, R., Wacrenier, P.-A.: StarPU: a unified platform for task scheduling on heterogeneous multicore architectures. Concurr. Comput. Pract. Exp. **23**(2), 187–198 (2011). https://inria.hal.science/inria-00550877
6. Acun, B., et al: Parallel Programming with Migratable Objects: Charm++ in Practice, ser. SC, 2014
7. Kaiser, H., Heller, T., Adelstein-Lelbach, B., Serio, A., Fey, D.: HPX: a task based programming model in a global address space. In: Proceedings of the 8th International Conference on Partitioned Global Address Space Programming Models, ser. PGAS '14. Association for Computing Machinery, New York, NY, USA (2014). https://doi.org/10.1145/2676870.2676883
8. Patki, T., Lowenthal, D.K., Rountree, B., Schulz, M., de Supinski, B.R.: Exploring hardware overprovisioning in power-constrained, high performance computing. In: Proceedings of the 27th International ACM Conference on International Conference on Supercomputing, ser. ICS '13, pp. 173–182. ACM, New York, NY, USA (2013). http://doi.acm.org/10.1145/2464996.2465009

9. Zhang, H., Hoffmann, H.: Maximizing performance under a power cap: a comparison of hardware, software, and hybrid techniques. In: Proceedings of the Twenty-First International Conference on Architectural Support for Programming Languages and Operating Systems, ser. ASPLOS '16, pp. 545–559. ACM, New York, NY, USA (2016). http://doi.acm.org/10.1145/2872362.2872375

10. Kunas, C.A., Rossi, F.D., Luizelli, M.C., Calheiros, R.N., Navaux, P.O.A., Lorenzon, A.F.: Neuropar, a neural network-driven EDP optimization strategy for parallel workloads. In: 2023 IEEE 35th International Symposium on Computer Architecture and High Performance Computing (SBAC-PAD), pp. 170–180 (2023)

11. Valero-Lara, P., Vetter, J.S.: A MultiGPU performance-portable solution for array programming based on Kokkos. In: Proceedings of the 9th ACM SIGPLAN International Workshop on Libraries, Languages and Compilers for Array Programming, ser. ARRAY 2023, pp. 1–12. Association for Computing Machinery, New York, NY, USA (2023). https://doi.org/10.1145/3589246.3595369

12. SFX Teixeira, T., Henzinger, A., Yadav, R., Aiken, A.: Automated mapping of task-based programs onto distributed and heterogeneous machines. In: Proceedings of the International Conference for High Performance Computing, Networking, Storage and Analysis, ser. SC '23. Association for Computing Machinery, New York, NY, USA (2023). https://doi.org/10.1145/3581784.3607079

Enhancing Sparse Direct Solver Scalability Through Runtime System Automatic Data Partition

Alycia Lisito[1(✉)], Mathieu Faverge[1], Grégoire Pichon[2], and Pierre Ramet[1]

[1] Univ. Bordeaux, CNRS, Bordeaux INP, Inria, LaBRI, UMR 5800, 33400 Talence,
France
`{alycia.lisito,mathieu.faverge,pierre.ramet}@inria.fr`
[2] Univ Lyon, EnsL, UCBL, CNRS, Inria, LIP, 69342 Lyon Cedex 07, France
`gregoire.pichon@inria.fr`

Abstract. With the ever-growing number of cores per node, it is critical for runtime systems and applications to adapt the task granularity to scale on recent architectures. Among applications, sparse direct solvers are a time-consuming step and the task granularity is rarely adapted to large many-core systems. In this paper, we investigate the use of runtime systems to automatically partition tasks in order to achieve more parallelism and refine the task granularity. Experiments are conducted on the new version of the PASTIX solver, which has been completely rewritten to better integrate modern task-based runtime systems. The results demonstrate the increase in scalability achieved by the solver thanks to the adaptive task granularity provided by the STARPU runtime system.

Keywords: Sparse Direct Solver · Task scheduling · Data partitioning · Runtime systems

1 Introduction

In this paper, we are interested in solving linear systems of the form $Ax = b$ where the matrix A is usually large and sparse. This kind of problem appears in many scientific applications, such as electromagnetism or computational fluid dynamics, and is in general one of the most expensive operations in numerical models. In order to solve this problem, a wide range of methods is available: direct, iterative and hybrid methods. In this work, we will focus on direct methods, which are more time and memory consuming, but provide more robust solutions. The objective of direct methods is to factorize A into LL^h, LDL^h or LU with L, D and U respectively unit lower triangular, diagonal and upper triangular matrices, depending on the numerical properties of the problem.

The common approach to solve a sparse system is divided into four main steps: 1) ordering of the unknowns, 2) block-symbolic factorization, 3) numerical factorization, and 4) triangular system solves. The two initial steps focus

P. Diehl et al. (Eds.): WAMTA 2024, LNCS 14626, pp. 105–110, 2024.
https://doi.org/10.1007/978-3-031-61763-8_10

on computing a blocked representation of the factorized matrix to take advantage of efficient Level-3 BLAS operations [6] while minimizing the computational complexity of the last two steps. Therefore, these first two steps determine the granularity of the computation without taking into account the target architectures, which may have an impact on performance and/or scalability. There are two ways to address this issue: using parallel implementation of the computational kernels to delegate the optimization to a third-party library, or splitting the workload internally to feed the computational resources. In this paper, we focus on the latter to work with one task per core and use a runtime system to schedule the tasks. We show how the use of an external task-based runtime system such as STARPU [2] helps to easily divide the workload without adding complexity to the original algorithm.

Section 2 describes the global approach of sparse direct solvers and discusses the different levels of task granularity that can be expressed in terms of code complexity in such an algorithm. Section 4 shows some preliminary results of the new implementation of the PASTIX solver with the internal scheduler, and with the help of an external runtime system. Section 5 presents related work in other sparse direct solvers. Finally, Sect. 6 concludes and presents future work.

2   Task-Based Sparse Factorization

Sparse direct solvers are by nature very similar to dense solvers to perform LL^h (Cholesky), LDL^h, or LU factorization. They can simply be summed-up by the classic three nested loop presented in Fig. 1, and the difference lies in the non continuous range of the inner loops due to the sparsity. When one wants to apply task-based parallelism to these algorithms, three choices, from large to fine, naturally appear.

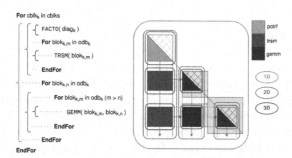

Fig. 1. Pseudo code of the factorization algorithm and visual representation of a factorization iteration with the *1D*, *2D* and *3D task level* represented in orange, pink and purple respectively. (Color figure online)

First, one can define a task as being a complete iteration of the first loop level, *1D task level*, as shown by the orange brace in Fig. 1. This kind of task distribution works well when the top left diagonal block to factorize is small because it groups together many small updates (*gemm*) and it allows using multi-threaded BLAS for large tasks. This is close to what is commonly used in sparse solvers using multi-frontal algorithms. Sparse solvers based on the multifrontal approach commonly use this task level as frontal matrices compact contributions into a temporary contiguous buffer, allowing better parallelization for additional memory consumption. One of the problems here is also that due to the large scattering of the contributions, it requires a fine protection mechanism to allow multiple tasks to be computed in parallel. It also presents a large number of data dependencies that are not suitable for all sequential task flow runtime systems (StarPU [2], OpenMP [3], PaRSEC-DTD [8]...).

Then, to create more parallelism, some implementations consider the task granularity to be defined by the second loop level, *2D task level*, shown in pink in Fig. 1. This creates two types of tasks, those that factorize a panel (set of columns) of the matrix, and those that perform panel updates (one per off-diagonal block). This solution has nice advantages: the number of data dependencies is fixed for all tasks (1 or 2 panels), so it is suitable for a task-based runtime system, and the computation of the number of contributions made to each panel is straightforward. However, at the end of the factorization, the problem becomes dense, and as it has been shown in many dense linear algebra libraries, this can be insufficient to achieve a good level of performance. It is also a problem when used on the small panels at the beginning of the factorization due to the overhead it generates with respect to the computational tasks.

Finally, the task-based approach of dense linear algebra can be applied and tasks can be defined at the inner loop level, *3D task level*, shown in purple in Fig. 1. This model is well suited when the solver needs to manage its own parallelism and use sequential tasks to reduce iteration synchronization as much as possible. As before, the number of data dependencies per task is limited, making it well suited for task-based runtime systems, and the task granularity can be properly adapted to many-core architectures on the final large blocks. However, in the case of sparse systems, the extremely large number of tasks can flood the runtime system or make it difficult and expensive to manage with a dedicated scheduler.

3   Implementation Within the PASTIX Solver

The PASTIX solver implements the LL^h *(Cholesky)*, LDL^h, and LU factorizations, and has been completely rewritten in its version 6 to improve modularity and support for external runtime systems. The numerical factorization is currently implemented using the first two levels of task parallelism, and in this paper we propose to study the use of the STARPU runtime systems to enable the third level of parallelism when needed.

PASTIX already offers a choice between two solutions: a *Dynamic* internal scheduler and a version built on top of the STARPU runtime system. The *Dynamic* scheduler uses a mixture of the first two levels *1D* and *2D* to achieve the best computational efficiency with enough parallelism to serve a large number of cores. For each factorization task, the scheduler checks the size of the update operation. If it is larger than a given threshold, the update is split and submitted with the *3D task level* scheme to be performed in parallel by other threads, otherwise the operation is performed immediately by the current working thread. This limits oversized tasks without creating too many microtasks. However, the task size can still be too large, especially for the GEMM operation. The STARPU version uses the *2D task level* algorithm by default due to the complexity of managing the large set of data dependencies in *1D*. In this paper, we have extended this version to use STARPU's automatic data partitioning to divide panels into blocks to switch for a *3D task level* algorithm. Note that we could have done this without this feature, but by using it we can dynamically select the best strategy in the same way as the *Dynamic* scheduler. In fact, based on a user threshold, the panel is split or not in order to use the best task granularity, STARPU then automatically handles the data dependencies to scatter/gather the data as needed for the different operations.

| Scheduler | Task level | Number of | | tasks | Mflop/t | Factorization | | 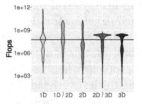 |
		cblks	bloks			s.	GFlop/s	
Dynamic	1D			17 307	5 976.6	66.07	1424.86	
	1D / 2D	17 307	193 887	73 125	1 414.7	**51.27**	**1851.64**	
	2D			157 835	655.5	52.63	1801.16	
STARPU	2D			157 835	655.5	45.89	2050.21	
	2D / 3D	17 307	193 887	908 256	105.5	**23.64**	**3980.67**	
	3D			1 114 228	81.4	24.99	3767.27	

(a) Statistics and performances of the variants.   (b) Task distribution.

Fig. 2. Statistics of all the variants for the *Cube_Coup_dt0* matrix factorization on 4 bora nodes.

Figure 2 illustrates the effect of the different strategies. As expected, adding extra levels of tasks reduces the average number of flops per task and also the maximum number of flops per task. Figure 2a illustrates the fact that mixed 2D/3D and 2D strategies drastically reduce the number of tasks above the defined threshold. Here we target tasks of similar size to those used in dense linear algebra on CPU cores, which corresponds to dense matrix multiply of 384×384 or 56, 6MFlops. On the other hand, it can be observed that increasing the task level drastically increases the number of tasks in the systems, which leads to an overload of both the *Dynamic* scheduler and the STARPU runtime system, and too many fine-grained tasks that degrade performance.

4   Experiments

Experiments were conducted on the bora cluster of the *Plafrim*[1] platform. Each bora node is equipped with two INTEL CascadeLake 18-cores running at 2.60

---
[1] https://www.plafrim.fr.

GHz and 192 GB of memory. The environment was handled with GUIX and used: INTEL MKL 2020 for BLAS kernels, OPENMPI 4.1.5, STARPU 1.4.3, and SCOTCH 7.0.1 to perform the ordering of the unknowns.

The experiments are based on PASTIX 6.3.2 available on the public git repository[2] and used a set of 19 matrices issued from The SuiteSparse Matrix Collection [5] ranging from $600K$ to $10M$ unknowns and requiring from 3.64 to 636 TFlops for the factorization.

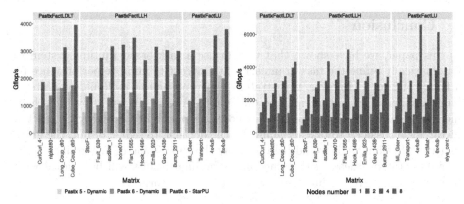

(a) Comparison of the versions studied on 4 nodes.

(b) Scalability study with the STARPU 2D/3D algorithm.

Fig. 3. Performance study of the factorization performance on the **bora** cluster with a set of 19 matrices.

Figure 3a compares the performance of the *Dynamic* scheduler in former and new releases of PASTIX with the proposed STARPU implementation. All versions use mixed strategies. While the new modular version of PASTIX slightly improves the performance, the proposed STARPU strategy largely increases the performance, especially in distributed, thanks to the extra level of parallelism exposed. This result is also illustrated by the scalability of the STARPU version shown in Fig. 3b that reaches an almost perfect speedup of 2.01 to 3.94 on 4 nodes, while keeping a very high scalability on 8 nodes despite the rather small problem sizes targeted.

5 Related Work

Other sparse direct solvers have also tried to solve the granularity vs. task size problem with their own solutions. In [9], they work on the CHOLMOD solver to propose an approach similar to the one proposed in this paper to create more or less parallelism. However, this solver relies on a left-looking approach that

---

[2] https://gitlab.inria.fr/solverstack/pastix.

focuses on parallelizing dot-product operations, while we have a right-looking algorithm that parallelizes an outer-product operation. SYMPACK [4] is the closest work as it uses a similar 2D/3D task scheme with an internally developed UPC++ scheduler targeting high performance communication for distributed systems. However, it focuses only on symmetric problems. In [1], they study a similar strategy on QR sparse factorization to partition the larger tasks and introduce parallelism in the QR kernels. This work was a precursor to automatic partitioning in STARPU and used manual data partitioning.

6   Conclusion

In this paper, we have shown that we can use a task-based runtime system to automatically refine the task granularity at low cost to improve performance by a factor of 2 to 4. However, this strategy, when pushed to its limit, generates a large number of tasks that may be difficult to process efficiently by the scheduler. In a future work, we plan to explore the possibility given by STARPU's hierarchical tasks [7] to take dynamically the decision to refine, or not, the granularity. Additionally, it would help to delay the submission of fine-grained tasks to reduce the overhead of the scheduler. The final results will be studied with respect to other sparse direct solvers and algorithm variants.

References

1. Agullo, E., Buttari, A., Guermouche, A., Lopez, F.: Multifrontal QR factorization for multicore architectures over runtime systems. In: Wolf, F., Mohr, B., an Mey, D. (eds.) Euro-Par 2013. LNCS, vol. 8097, pp. 521–532. Springer, Heidelberg (2013). https://doi.org/10.1007/978-3-642-40047-6_53
2. Augonnet, C., Thibault, S., Namyst, R., Wacrenier, P.A.: StarPU: a unified platform for task scheduling on heterogeneous multicore architectures. Concurr. Comput.: Pract. Exp. **23**(2), 187–198 (2011)
3. Ayguade, E., et al.: The design of OpenMP tasks. IEEE Trans. Parallel Distrib. Syst. **20**(3), 404–418 (2009). https://doi.org/10.1109/TPDS.2008.105
4. Bellavita, J., Jacquelin, M., Ng, E.G., Bonachea, D., Corbino, J., Hargrove, P.H.: symPACK: a GPU-capable fan-out sparse Cholesky solver. In: Proceedings of the SC 2023 Workshops, New York, NY, USA, pp. 1171–1184 (2023)
5. Davis, T.A., Hu, Y.: The University of Florida sparse matrix collection. ACM Trans. Math. Softw. **38**(1), 1:1–1:25 (2011). https://doi.org/10.1145/2049662.2049663
6. Dongarra, J., Croz, J.D., Hammarling, S., Duff, I.S.: A set of level 3 basic linear algebra subprograms. ACM Trans. Math. Softw. **16**(1), 1–17 (1990)
7. Faverge, M., et al.: Programming heterogeneous architectures using hierarchical tasks. Concurr. Comput.: Pract. Exp. **35**(25) (2023). https://doi.org/10.1002/cpe.7811, https://hal.science/hal-04088833
8. Hoque, R., Herault, T., Bosilca, G., Dongarra, J.: Dynamic task discovery in PaRSEC: a data-flow task-based runtime. In: Proceedings of the 8th Workshop on Latest Advances in Scalable Algorithms for Large-Scale Systems, ScalA 2017 (2017)
9. Le Fèvre, V., Usui, T., Casas, M.: A selective nesting approach for the sparse multi-threaded Cholesky factorization. In: 2022 IEEE/ACM 7th International Workshop ESPM2, pp. 1–9 (2022)

Experiences Porting Shared and Distributed Applications to Asynchronous Tasks: A Multidimensional FFT Case-Study

Alexander Strack[1]([✉]) [iD], Christopher Taylor[2] [iD], Patrick Diehl[3] [iD],
and Dirk Pflüger[1] [iD]

[1] Institute of Parallel and Distributed Systems, University of Stuttgart,
70569 Stuttgart, Germany
{alexander.strack,dirk.pflueger}@ipvs.uni-stuttgart.de
[2] Tactical Computing Labs LLC, 1001 Pecan St., Lindsay, TX, USA
ctaylor@tactcomplabs.com
[3] Center of Computation and Technology, Louisiana State University,
Baton Rouge, USA
patrickdiehl@lsu.edu

Abstract. Parallel algorithms relying on synchronous parallelization libraries often experience adverse performance due to global synchronization barriers. Asynchronous many-task runtimes offer task futurization capabilities that minimize or remove the need for global synchronization barriers. This paper conducts a case study of the multidimensional Fast Fourier Transform to identify which applications will benefit from the asynchronous many-task model. Our basis is the popular FFTW library [7]. We use the asynchronous many-task model HPX and a one-dimensional FFTW backend to implement multiple versions using different HPX features and highlight overheads and pitfalls during migration. Furthermore, we add an HPX threading backend to FFTW. The case study analyzes shared memory scaling properties between our HPX-based parallelization and FFTW with its pthreads, OpenMP, and HPX backends. The case study also compares FFTW's *MPI+X* backend to a purely HPX-based distributed implementation. The FFT application does not profit from asynchronous task execution. In contrast, enforcing task synchronization results in better cache performance and thus better runtime. Nonetheless, the HPX backend for FFTW is competitive with existing backends. Our distributed HPX implementation based on HPX collectives using MPI parcelport has similar performance to FFTW's *MPI+OpenMP*. However, the LCI parcelport of HPX accelerated communication up to factor 5.

1 Introduction

Asynchronous many-task runtimes, supporting global address spaces, are a promising alternative to message-based parallelization libraries like Open MPI

© The Author(s), under exclusive license to Springer Nature Switzerland AG 2024
P. Diehl et al. (Eds.): WAMTA 2024, LNCS 14626, pp. 111–122, 2024.
https://doi.org/10.1007/978-3-031-61763-8_11

[8]. Synchronous parallelization libraries often require algorithms to use global synchronization barriers. However, applying global synchronization barriers can cause an algorithm to experience adverse performance. Task futurization features provided by asynchronous many-task runtimes can remove or minimize the use of global synchronization barriers.

Applications ported to asynchronous tasks, *e.g.*, using HPX [10], can result in notable performance gains. There is no free lunch meaning some applications are better suited than others for migration to an asynchronous task model. Applications solving inhomogeneous problems with few global synchronization barriers and no significant data exchange between different nodes can experience the introduction of undesirable overheads, *e.g.*, by a global address space model and performance degradation.

We chose the multidimensional Fast Fourier Transform (FFT) as a case study to characterize applications better suited for migration to an asynchronous task model. Many applications take advantage of the FFT, ranging from image compression [16] to scientific applications like molecular dynamics [6] and convolutional neural networks [11]. Discrete two-dimensional FFT is an excellent application for identifying overheads in a port to future-based, asynchronous tasks. The two-dimensional signal data is dense. A parallel algorithm partitions the data in a homogeneous and equal manner, which does not play to the strengths of HPX. The combination of global synchronization barriers and load imbalances will therefore make the task scheduler's ability to hide latency with work-stealing difficult.

The algorithm requires the exchange of data partitions between compute hosts, which are known in advance. The data partitions exchanged are homogeneous on all nodes and require node-level synchronization. The data transfer percentage is more extensive than in other applications, *e.g.*, simulations in which small ghost layers must be communicated across neighboring nodes. Section 3 provides a more detailed explanation of the required synchronization and communication steps.

Our main contributions in this work include:

- First distributed FFT proof-of-concept that solely relies on the HPX runtime model for distributed and shared memory parallelization
- Evaluation of the scaling properties of several implementation variants to identify overheads and highlight pitfalls when porting applications to futurized, asynchronous tasks
- Comparison against the de-facto standard, the FFTW library and its built-in parallelization backends
- Implementation and performance comparison of an HPX backend for FFTW threading

The remainder of this work is structured as follows. Section 2 discusses related work considering FFT libraries and HPX. Section 3 introduces the discrete Fourier transform and a task-level parallelization approach for two-dimensional FFT. In Sect. 4, we provide additional information about the software framework. Section 5 presents our benchmark results on shared memory and distributed systems. In Sect. 6, we conclude and give an outlook on future work.

2   Related Work

To the best of our knowledge, all state-of-the-art distributed multidimensional FFT implementations rely on explicit message passing with MPI. A recent performance comparison can be found in [1]. The authors compare multiple FFT libraries including a handful of libraries with distributed GPU computing support. Most of the FFT libraries use FFTW [7] as a backend. We want to include two notable mentions. First, P3DFFT [14] uses FFTW as a backend. P3DFFT is one of the first libraries supporting a pencil-based domain decomposition for three-dimensional FFTs. In contrast, plain FFTW only supports slab decomposition, which is an expansion to three dimensions of the decomposition discussed in this work. The main advantage of pencil-based decomposition is that synchronization is exclusive to row or column-wise communicators. Second, we want to highlight AccFFT [9]. AccFFT has a cuFFT backend supporting distributed GPU computing. In [1], it is the best-performing library on CPU nodes and dominates the GPU benchmarks on Summit's Volta 100 accelerators. An overview of different asynchronous many-task systems is given in [15]. We focus on HPX because of its conformity with the C++ standard [10]. HPX can target various hardware via different executor backends [5]. Furthermore, HPX supports multiple parcelports that enable distributed computing. A recent addition is the Lightweight Communication Interface (LCI) parcelport [18]. Regarding tasking overheads, HPX, Charm++, and *MPI+OpenMP* were quantified in [17]. HPX currently lacks a versatile application portfolio. However, the stellar science simulation code Octo-Tiger is based on HPX [12] and can be considered the flagship application. Octo-Tiger implements a fast multipole method based on octrees.

3   Methods

This section introduces basic Fourier transform theory and discusses how the multidimensional FFT algorithm can be parallelized. The last subsection presents different implementation variants to determine performance differences and overheads within HPX. Furthermore, we state the benchmark hardware. We specifically focus on real-to-complex FFT in this work. There are other complex-to-complex or real-to-real transformations. However, only the basis function used by the FFT backend differs, while other aspects, such as synchronization and communication, are equivalent.

3.1   Fast Fourier Transform

The Fourier transform of a one-dimensional real-valued discrete signal $f = [f_0, ..., f_{N-1}]$ is given by

$$\hat{f}_k = \sum_{n=0}^{N-1} f_n \cdot \phi_k(n) \tag{1}$$

for $k = 0, ..., \frac{N}{2}$ with $\phi_k(n) = \exp(-2\pi i \cdot \frac{n \cdot k}{N})$ and imaginary unit $i = \sqrt{-1}$. A naive algorithm can compute $\hat{f}$ in $\mathcal{O}(N^2)$. Cooley and Tukey proposed a divide and conquer algorithm to compute the transform in $\mathcal{O}(N \cdot \log(N))$ for signal lengths to the power of two [4]. Over time, the FFT algorithm was improved, *e.g.*, by using different radices [2]. The amount of multiplications is reduced at the cost of more additions and larger intermediate storage. We refer to [2] for a detailed comparison of different algorithms.

The Fourier transform can be easily expanded to multiple dimensions. In practice, $\hat{F}$ can be computed by subsequent FFTs along each dimension. Note that the FFTs along the first dimension transform the signal into a complex signal. As a result, the second dimension requires complex-to-complex FFTs.

3.2 Parallelization

We first consider shared-memory parallelism. For task futurization, it is essential to determine the dependencies of tasks. Here, we define different tasks in the two-dimensional FFT algorithm. Furthermore, we show how they depend on each other and optimize synchronization. We assume a signal matrix of size $N \times M$ stored in row-major format. To ensure that the data for the one-dimensional FFTs is contiguous in memory, a basic algorithm consists of four computation steps:

- Real-to-complex one-dimensional FFTs in the first dimension
- Transpose matrix for the second dimension to be contiguous in memory
- Complex-to-complex one-dimensional FFTs in the second dimension
- Transpose matrix back to the original data layout

One-Dimensional FFT. As we use a backend to compute the one-dimensional FFTs, the smallest task size is given by the computation of one FFT. The task size can be enlarged by packing multiple FFTs that are contiguous in memory. For small matrices, one FFT can be too small to hide the launch overhead of the task. Here, an adjustable task size can improve performance.

Transpose. With a sequential algorithm, there are two approaches to compute the one-dimensional FFTs in the second dimension. First, it is possible to keep the data layout with the first dimension contiguous in memory and use a strided access scheme. Therefore, the next element is offset with N. This approach requires less memory and performs better than an explicit transpose of a small matrix. Nevertheless, transposing becomes more performant when the matrix rows no longer fit in the cache.

Defining the smallest task size is related to the FFT task size. After an FFT task is completed, a transpose task can, independent of the progress of other FFT tasks, insert row elements into the non-contiguous columns of the transposed matrix. All transpose tasks must finish for the second dimension FFT tasks to start. A global synchronization barrier is required. While this approach is intuitive, its performance is sub-optimal. Shifting the global synchronization barrier before the transpose tasks makes it possible to define tasks that do not read but write elements into contiguous memory. The impact on the algorithm performance is crucial for large matrices, as described in Sect. 5. Note that the performance is optimized not by softening or removing the synchronization barrier. Instead, we choose the task dependencies in a more memory-oriented fashion.

In the distributed two-dimensional FFT algorithm, data transfer between compute hosts or, in HPX terms, localities is necessary at two points. Once between the FFTs in the first and second dimension and once after the FFTs in the second dimension to get back to the original data layout on all N_{locs} localities. This adds more steps to the algorithm compared to the shared memory version. One is the communication step, and the other is a data layout rearrangement step. The question is whether to transpose before or after the communication steps. Since the communication step requires a global barrier beforehand, we do the transpose afterward.

Communicate. The communication scheme for distributed two-dimensional FFT is straightforward. Only $\frac{1}{N_{locs}}$ of the partial data remains on its current locality while the rest is sent to all other localities. Many distributed FFT implementations simplify communication by relying on MPI collectives. In contrast to message-based communication libraries, *e.g.*, Open MPI, where the idea is to send data to nodes to do the work, HPX aims to schedule tasks to the localities that hold the data to minimize data transfer. While this approach is rather elegant, it is not ideal for multidimensional FFT and applications with high data transfer. We know beforehand that $(1 - \frac{1}{N_{locs}})$ of the data has to be transferred to other localities. Relying on the implicit communication HPX allows, with its active global address space (AGAS), does not make sense. Instead, we use the HPX equivalents of the MPI collective operations to transfer the data explicitly.

Rearrange. The rearrange tasks perform the same amount of memory copies independent from when data is transposed. The tasks either split the local matrix into equally sized N_{locs} parts or concatenate the N_{locs} parts collected from other localities.

3.3 Different Implementations

We designed several implementations of the same two-dimensional real-to-complex FFT algorithm to evaluate potential overheads within HPX:

- *HPX future naive*: Intuitive future-based implementation that defines tasks to postpone or remove synchronization points.
- *HPX future opt*: Future-based implementation with optimized transpose.
- *HPX future sync*: Future-based implementation with synchronization after each algorithmic step.

- *HPX future agas*: Future-based implementation with (redundant) AGAS.
- *HPX for_loop*: Implementation using a synchronizing HPX feature called hpx::experimental::for_loop.
- *HPX future agas dist*: Future-based distributed implementation with AGAS and scatter or all_to_all collectives.
- *HPX for_loop dist*: Distributed implementation using the synchronizing HPX feature hpx::experimental::for_loop, scatter,and all_to_all collectives.

Two hardware system setups are used in this work. The distributed benchmark is computed on a 16-node cluster with homogeneous nodes. Each node contains a dual-socket AMD EPYC 7352[1] with 48 physical cores and a total of 256 MB of L3 cache. For our shared memory comparisons, we switch to a dual-socket AMD EPYC 7742[2] machine with 128 physical cores and a combined L3 cache of 512 MB to examine more scaling beyond 100 cores.

4   Software Framework

The two principal software tools we use are the C++ standard library for parallelism and concurrency HPX [10] and the FFT library FFTW [7].

4.1   HPX

HPX is an asynchronous, many-task runtime system implementing the ISO C++ language's support for data parallelism. HPX offers fine-grained parallelism and lightweight synchronization using futures and local control objects (latches, barriers, etc.). The features provided in HPX promote task-based algorithm decomposition. In addition, HPX implements an AGAS, allowing users to construct distributed data types and structures. Users can deploy functions and methods on the distributed data types all by using the future and local control objects to manage parallelism and concurrency. With the parcelport concept, HPX separates communication from a specific standard. Several parcelports are supported, ranging from TCP and MPI to the recently added LCI parcelport [18].

HPX contains several high-level parallelization features. We use the hpx::experimental::for_loop in this work. The syntax is similar to a classic C++ loop. However, it allows for the specification of a parallel execution policy similar to std::for_each. To optimize performance, the iterations are bundled into tasks. At the end of the loop, all tasks are synchronized.

4.2   FFTW

Since 20 years, the de-facto standard has been the Fastest Fourier Transform in the West (FFTW) library [7]. To date, FFTW is a very performant FFT library, which still serves as a backend for many state-of-the-art libraries. The secret of

[1] https://www.amd.com/de/products/cpu/amd-epyc-7352 (visited on 01/15/2024).
[2] https://www.amd.com/de/products/cpu/amd-epyc-7742 (visited on 01/15/2024).

FFTW's performance lies in planning. Each FFT requires a plan. Depending on the available resources, several planning options can be set. Estimated planning minimizes a heuristic cost function based on FLOPS and memory accesses. In contrast, patient planning uses dynamic programming to find an efficient algorithm from a set of plan combinations. A middle ground is measured (formerly impatient) planning that works with a reduced algorithm set. FFTW requires runtime initialization, a function to distribute work to the runtime system's workload manager, and runtime finalization. FFTW supports parallelization by offering several backends. Distributed FFTs are supported via an MPI backend. For shared memory parallelization, FFTW has a threads interface that supports pthreads [13] and OpenMP [3] out of the box. We add an HPX backend to FFTW. The HPX backend supports all functional requirements of the FFTW threads interface. A more detailed explanation of the process can be found in Subsect. 5.2.

Furthermore, we use FFTW as the one-dimensional backend for our HPX-based parallelization. All tasks can reuse FFTW plans as planning is only tied to the FFT length. Bringing multiple one-dimensional FFTs contiguous in memory is possible in one plan.

5   Results

We divide the results section into three parts. First, we consider a shared memory benchmark to compare our HPX-based implementations and expose overheads induced by code structure and HPX features. Second, we benchmark our best implementation against FFTW's backends, including the new HPX backend. The benchmark takes into consideration the impact of planning time. Third, we turn our attention to a distributed benchmark and compare the *MPI+X* approach of FFTW to purely HPX-based implementations based on collective operations. We use synthetic data and a problem size of $2^{14} \times 2^{14}$. For all runtimes, we take the median out of 50 runs and visualize error bars related to the best and worst runs. For additional information about the reproducibility of our results, we refer to the supplementary material.

5.1   Overheads

We use the shared memory system described in Sect. 3.3 to compare our different implementations. The strong scaling results on up to 128 cores are illustrated in Fig. 1. For the one-dimensional FFTs, we use estimated planning within the FFTW backend, resulting in neglectable planning time. To interpret the result correctly, it is essential to consider the system's hardware architecture. It contains two sockets with 64-core CPUs based on a chiplet design. Each CPU contains eight CCDs connected via AMD Infinity Fabric over an IO die.

First, observe the naive (orange) and optimized (brown) variants. Shifting the synchronization barrier such that cache performance is optimized has a visible impact on performance. Moreover, the completely synchronized future-based implementation (pink) performs better than its asynchronous counter-parts. Computing all transpose tasks at the same time further optimizes cache usage. These results perfectly visualize a common pitfall when applications are ported to asynchronous tasks. Reducing task dependencies and removing global synchronization barriers does not necessarily improve performance. When defining task dependencies, not only the algorithm but also other critical performance indicators, *e.g.*, cache performance, must be considered. The variant that accesses actions through the AGAS (dark blue) is plotted to visualize the induced overhead. The task size is too small to hide the overhead. The implementation based on the hpx::experimental::for_loop (pine) performs better than all future-based variants. It enforces task synchronization after the loop, making it the perfect choice for the FFT application. The redundant communication overhead of distributed implementations is visualized with dashed lines.

Figure 2 shows the runtime decomposition for selected synchronized versions. Compared to the hpx::experimental::for_loop variants, the future-based variant has more extensive runtimes across the board. These results further highlight the efficiency of the hpx::experimental::for_loop. The communication overhead is constant as a collective operation simplifies to a concatenation of move operations.

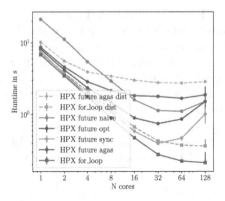
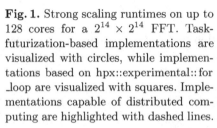

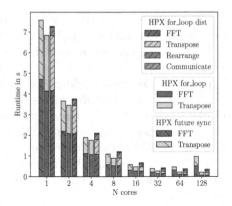

Fig. 1. Strong scaling runtimes on up to 128 cores for a $2^{14} \times 2^{14}$ FFT. Task-futurization-based implementations are visualized with circles, while implementations based on hpx::experimental::for_loop are visualized with squares. Implementations capable of distributed computing are highlighted with dashed lines.

Fig. 2. Selected strong scaling runtime distributions on up to 128 cores for a $2^{14} \times 2^{14}$ FFT (compare Fig. 1). The partial runtimes correspond to the computation steps in Sect. 3.2.

5.2   FFTW Backend

Apart from analyzing overheads within HPX, providing an HPX backend for FFTW is a major contribution to this work[3]. The HPX backend implements the existing threading interface provided by FFTW. The HPX backend is an optional compile-time target for FFTW. To start an initial HPX thread, the HPX backend uses hpx::threads::run_as_hpx_thread. The initial HPX thread segments the dataset and starts the asynchronous execution of threads on each segment using hpx::async. One of the challenges the HPX backend faced was the proper forwarding of runtime system arguments. The HPX backend solves this challenge by adding an environment variable, FFTW_HPX_NTHREADS. The new environment variable allows users to set the number of OS-level threads HPX creates during program and runtime system initialization. Without the environment variable, HPX will create a number of OS-level threads equal to the number of available cores returned by *hwloc*. The HPX default thread creation behavior is appropriate as a general solution, the new environment variable makes the performance analysis in this paper possible.

Figure 3 shows the HPX backend's performance compared to existing FFTW backends using estimated and measured planning. The runtime of our own HPX parallelization is added for scale. The HPX backend performs consistently worse than the other backends with FFTW's estimated planning. The runtimes skyrocket for all three threading backends, while the runtime of the MPI backend does not. According to our investigation, this is related to FFTW planning. Overall, our HPX-based parallelization has the best performance and scaling.

We switch to measured planning to increase the threading backends' performance for more than 16 cores. While the MPI backend does only marginally profit, the effect on the threading backends is enormous. The HPX backend now rivals the performance of the existing backends. In addition, our hpx::experimental::for_loop implementation also marginally profits from measured planning.

The corresponding planning times can be observed in Fig. 4. Since our parallelization only requires two one-dimensional plans, the planning time is not dependent on the core count. Two-dimensional planning is more complicated, requiring strided memory access or data transposition. Thus, the planning time is over factor 50 slower averaged over all FFTW backends. The OpenMP and pthreads backends require nearly the same amount of planning time. In contrast, FFTW with the HPX backend requires more time to create a plan. This is likely caused by HPX being poorly suited for some plans in the planning set, *e.g.*, plans similar to the estimated plan.

5.3   Distributed

We benchmark our distributed implementations based on the HPX collective operations and compare them against FFTW's parallelization based on *MPI+X*

---

[3] https://github.com/FFTW/fftw3/pull/341 (visited on 02/04/2024).

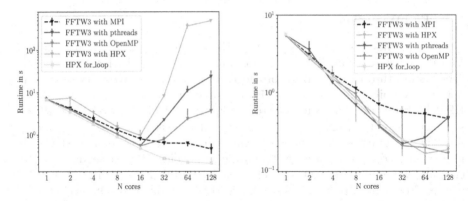

Fig. 3. Strong scaling runtimes on up to 128 cores for a $2^{14} \times 2^{14}$ FFT. The different FFTW's backends are visualized with triangles. FFTW's ESTIMATE planning (**left**) is compared to MEASURE planning (**right**). The runtimes of the hpx::experimental::for_loop implementation using the respective planning are also included.

(see Fig. 5). We set the number of threads of the shared memory parallelization to 48. Note that while the problem size is small for a cluster, it allows highlighting the communication overheads of the MPI and LCI parcelports. The results on one compute host match the result from Sect. 5.1 and 5.2. All implementations perform worse in a distributed setting due to the extensive communication overhead. The HPX collectives using the MPI parcelport can compete with FFTW's *MPI+OpenMP* but get outperformed by *MPI+pthreads*. Nonetheless, our pure HPX implementations taking advantage of the LCI parcelport have the best performance. Compared to the MPI parcelport we observe a communication speed-up of factor 4 to 5. In comparison to FFTW with *MPI+pthreads*, we observe a speed-up of factor 1.5 to 2. As a threading backend, FFTW currently supports OpenMP and pthreads. Providing an *MPI+HPX* backend is challenging since MPI would run on the OS system threads and HPX on its lightweight threads. The different threads interfere with each other. For that reason, the HPX backend for FFTW does not support MPI+HPX.

6   Conclusion and Outlook

In the scope of this work, we presented several different parallel implementations of a multidimensional FFT. We quantified overheads and revealed common misconceptions when porting code to asynchronous tasks. Asynchronous algorithms are not more efficient by default and can even perform worse. Cache performance is crucial when designing task graphs of parallel algorithms. For multidimensional FFT, the hpx::experimental::for_loop proved the most effective HPX tool. It yielded the fastest runtimes and the best scaling.

Furthermore, we implemented a shared memory backend for FFTW that uses HPX threading. A performance evaluation of the new FFTW HPX backend,

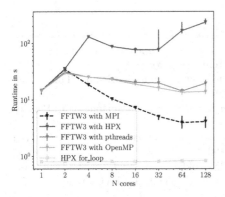

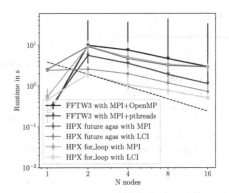

Fig. 4. Measured planing time for FFTW backend strong scaling (see Fig. 3). The different FFTW's backends are visualized with triangles. The plan times of the hpx::experimental::for_loop implementation are included for comparison.

Fig. 5. Distributed strong scaling on a 16-node cluster with 48-core nodes for a $2^{14} \times 2^{14}$ matrix. The FFTW backends are visualized with triangles, while our HPX implementations are visualized using circles and squares (compare Fig. 1).

compared to the existing FFTW backends, is made. Although FFTW's parallelization is not optimized for asynchronous runtime systems, the HPX backend performance is competitive with the OpenMP backend. Both show excellent scaling if FFTW uses measured planning. However, the HPX backend requires nearly ten times as much planning time. This can become an issue if plans are computed online and only executed a few times. Our parallelization using the hpx::experimental::for_loop is competitive with all FFTW backends while requiring significantly shorter planning time. Furthermore, we highlighted the communication overhead and compared FFTW's *MPI+X* to HPX collectives regarding distributed performance. While FFTW's *MPI+OpenMP* performed comparably to the HPX collectives using the MPI parcelport, the LCI parcelport resulted in a speed-up of up to factor 5 on our benchmark cluster.

Considering future work, we plan to expand our distributed testing and evaluate distributed HPX support for FFTW. In addition, we plan to run benchmarks on more hardware architectures, e.g., ARM or RISC-V, focusing on the power efficiency and performance portability of the different FFTW backends and our HPX parallelization.

Supplementary Materials

The source code and benchmark scripts are available at DaRUS[4]. The respective software and compiler versions are stated in the README.md of the source code.

---

[4] https://doi.org/10.18419/darus-4094 (visited on 13/03/2024).

References

1. Ayala, A., et. al.: FFT benchmark performance experimentson systems targeting exascale. Technical report, University of Tennessee (2022)
2. Burrus, C.S., Parks, T.W.: DFT/FFT and Convolution Algorithms: Theory and Implementation, 1st edn. Wiley, USA (1991)
3. Chandra, R., Dagum, L., Kohr, D., Menon, R., Maydan, D., McDonald, J.: Parallel Programming in OpenMP. Morgan Kaufmann (2001)
4. Cooley, J., Tukey, J.: An algorithm for the machine calculation of complex Fourier series. Math. Comput. **19**(90), 297–301 (1965)
5. Daiß, G., et. al.: Stellar mergers with HPX-Kokkos and SYCL: methods of using an asynchronous many-task runtime system with SYCL. In: IWOCL 2023. ACM, New York (2023)
6. Deserno, M., Holm, C.: How to mesh up Ewald sums. I. A theoretical and numerical comparison of various particle mesh routines. J. Chem. Phys. **109**(18), 7678–7693 (1998)
7. Frigo, M., Johnson, S.: The design and implementation of FFTW3. Proc. IEEE **93**(2), 216–231 (2005)
8. Gabriel, E., et al.: Open MPI: goals, concept, and design of a next generation MPI implementation. In: Kranzlmüller, D., Kacsuk, P., Dongarra, J. (eds.) EuroPVM/MPI 2004. LNCS, vol. 3241, pp. 97–104. Springer, Heidelberg (2004). https://doi.org/10.1007/978-3-540-30218-6_19
9. Gholami, A., et. al.: AccFFT: a library for distributed-memory FFT on CPU and GPU architectures. CoRR (2015)
10. Kaiser, H., et al.: HPX - the C++ standard library for parallelism and concurrency. J. Open Sour. Softw. **5**(53), 2352 (2020)
11. Lavin, A., Gray, S.: Fast algorithms for convolutional neural networks. In: CVPR, pp. 4013–4021 (June 2016)
12. Marcello, D.C., et al.: Octo-tiger: a new, 3D hydrodynamic code for stellar mergers that uses HPX parallelization. MNRAS **504**(4), 5345–5382 (2021)
13. Nichols, B., Buttlar, D., Farrell, J.P.: Pthreads Programming. O'Reilly & Associates Inc., USA (1996)
14. Pekurovsky, D.: P3DFFT: a framework for parallel computations of Fourier transforms in three dimensions. SISC **34**(4), C192–C209 (2012)
15. Thoman, P., et al.: A taxonomy of task-based parallel programming technologies for high-performance computing. J. Supercomput. **74**(4), 1422–1434 (2018)
16. Wallace, G.K.: The JPEG still picture compression standard. Commun. ACM **34**(4), 30–44 (1991)
17. Wu, N., et al.: Quantifying overheads in charm++ and HPX using task bench. In: Singer, J., Elkhatib, Y., Blanco Heras, D., Diehl, P., Brown, N., Ilic, A. (eds.) Euro-Par 2022. LNCS, vol. 13835, pp. 5–16. Springer, Cham (2022). https://doi.org/10.1007/978-3-031-31209-0_1
18. Yan, J., Kaiser, H., Snir, M.: Design and analysis of the network software stack of an asynchronous many-task system – the LCI parcelport of HPX. In: Proceedings of the SC 2023 Workshops, pp. 1151–1161. ACM, New York (2023)

An Abstraction for Distributed Stencil Computations Using Charm++

Aditya Bhosale[(✉)], Zane Fink, and Laxmikant Kale

University of Illinois Urbana-Champaign, Champaign, USA
{adityapb,zanef2,kale}@illinois.edu

Abstract. Python has emerged as a popular programming language for scientific computing in recent years, thanks to libraries like Numpy and SciPy. Numpy, in particular, is widely utilized for prototyping numerical solvers using methods such as finite difference, finite volume, and multigrid. However, Numpy's performance is confined to a single node, compelling programmers to resort to a lower-level language for running large-scale simulations. In this paper, we introduce CharmStencil, a high-level abstraction featuring a Numpy-like Python frontend and a highly efficient Charm++ backend. Employing a client-server model, CharmStencil maintains productivity with tools like Jupyter notebooks on the frontend while utilizing a high-performance Charm++ library on the backend for computation. We demonstrate that CharmStencil achieves orders of magnitude better single-threaded performance compared to Numpy and can scale to thousands of CPU cores. Additionally, we showcase superior performance compared to cuNumeric and Numba, popular Python libraries for parallel array computations.

Keywords: Python · Stencil · Distributed · Numpy · Charm++

1 Introduction

In recent years, Python has witnessed significant adoption in various domains, including machine learning, scientific computing, and data analytics. The expressiveness and productivity provided by tools like Jupyter notebooks, along with composable high-performance libraries built on top of foundations such as Numpy [6] and SciPy [11], have made it possible to implement sophisticated algorithms with relatively low programming effort and decent performance.

As a result, traditionally HPC-oriented domains like scientific computing have seen a rise in the popularity of Python. The interactivity and simplicity of Python tools and libraries has made it possible to prototype complex physical systems with relative ease. In particular, Numpy has simplified expressing computations on structured grids used for numerical methods in scientific computing, such as finite difference, finite volume, and multigrid methods. The highly regular nature of these computations has static and locally contained dependence patterns and can be succinctly expressed using slicing notations commonly used

© The Author(s), under exclusive license to Springer Nature Switzerland AG 2024
P. Diehl et al. (Eds.): WAMTA 2024, LNCS 14626, pp. 123–134, 2024.
https://doi.org/10.1007/978-3-031-61763-8_12

in Numpy. Figure 1 shows a single iteration of a 2D Laplace equation solver using Numpy.

While Numpy exhibits good single-threaded performance, leveraging efficient C implementations for common array operations, its parallel capabilities are restricted to a single node, relying on multi-threaded BLAS libraries for specific built-in operations. Moreover, for an arbitrary sequence of operations, Numpy suffers from high Python overheads and the creation of temporary arrays. As a result, domain scientists are forced to reimplement their applications using a lower-level programming model to run on a larger scale.

To address these challenges, we developed CharmTyles, a framework for implementing high-performance scalable abstractions on elastic parallel machines while maintaining the productivity offered by Python, along with tools like Jupyter notebooks. CharmTyles uses a client-server architecture with a Python client on the frontend and a parallel Charm++ server on the backend. In this paper, we present CharmStencil, a high-level stencil abstraction developed using the CharmTyles framework with a Python frontend and a Charm++ back-end that can execute arbitrary operations on a structured grid on distributed memory machines with minimal modifications to the Numpy code.

To create the stencil abstraction, we developed a frontend library that dynamically constructs an Abstract Syntax Tree (AST) using operations on the fields of the structured grid (Sect. 3.1). Subsequently, this frontend library asynchronously sends the AST to the backend. On the backend, we implemented a code generator that dynamically generates, compiles, and loads the local computation function. Additionally, the backend manages the necessary data movement for the local computation and invokes the local computation function (Sect. 3.2). Finally, we demonstrate the effectiveness of our asynchronous client-server model in overlapping Python overhead from the frontend with useful computation on the backend.

We further compare our abstraction with two state-of-the-art libraries - cuNumeric [1], a drop-in replacement library for Numpy based on the Legion runtime system, and Numba [8], a compiler for a subset of Python, showcasing superior performance. Additionally, we benchmark CharmStencil against a hand-written Charm++ benchmark, showing minimal Python overhead on up to 1024 cores (Sect. 4).

```
u[1:-1, 1:-1] = (u[2:, 1:-1] + u[:-2, 1:-1] + u[1:-1, 2:] + u[1:-1,:-2]) / 4
```

Fig. 1. 2D Laplace solver iteration using Numpy

2   Background

Charm++ [7] is an asynchronous message-driven parallel programming language. Users express their computation in terms of objects that interact with each other via asynchronous messages. These objects may belong to collections, called chare arrays; each chare array has its index structure, such as a 2D dense array, and supports collective communication operations over its members. The runtime system handles the mapping of these objects to processors. Each Processing Element (PE) has a scheduler and several message queues. When a message is to be sent to an object, the runtime system looks up the location of that object in a distributed location manager and directs the message to the corresponding PE where it is enqueued in one of the message queues. The scheduler picks messages out of the message queues and delivers them to the appropriate object.

The separation of computation from physical processors allows users to write parallel applications with runtime adaptivity without additional programming effort. For example, Charm++ can automatically balance the load every few iterations of an iterative application by migrating objects among processors. Moreover, if the parallel computation is over-decomposed, Charm++ can help facilitate computation-communication overlap.

This runtime adaptivity makes Charm++ an ideal choice for a programming model in applications with dynamic load imbalance and for execution on heterogeneous machines. The support for the migratability of objects also facilitates resource elasticity, making it a strong candidate for developing scalable applications in cloud environments.

3 Methodology

CharmTyles is a framework for developing abstractions based on a client-server model with a Python frontend running in a Jupyter Notebook on the user's machine and a Charm++ backend server running on a parallel machine. The backend has multiple collections of tiles, distributed across an elastic parallel machine such as in the cloud, a cluster, or a supercomputer, orchestrated from the frontend. Figure 2 shows the client-server architecture of CharmTyles.

The Python frontend and the Charm++ backend communicate using the Converse Client-Server (CCS) interface. CCS allows external programs to inject messages into Charm++ message queues. These messages are then picked up by the scheduler and passed to the corresponding handler. In our architecture, we send messages from the Python frontend to PE 0 of the Charm++ backend server. PE 0 then processes the message and sends a broadcast to all PEs specifying the computation.

The communication between the frontend and the backend is asynchronous. The frontend Python execution, i.e. the Python overhead, can thus be overlapped with useful computation on the backend. The frequency of messages from the frontend to the backend is a user-configurable parameter and results in different levels of pipelining as shown in Fig. 3. A smaller frequency of messages between the frontend and the backend results in a lower cost of broadcast on the backend, but will also have a smaller overlap as seen in Fig. 3a. On the other hand, a larger frequency of messages will result in a larger overlap, but will also incur a higher cost of broadcasting on the backend as shown in Fig. 3c.

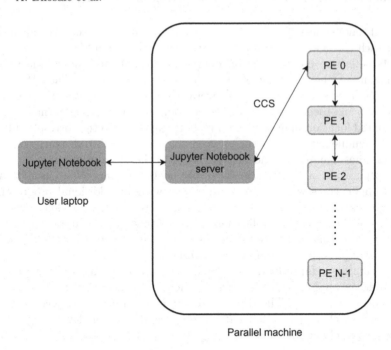

Fig. 2. CharmTyles client-server architecture

CharmStencil is an abstraction for stencil computations written using the CharmTyles framework. The frontend has a Numpy-like interface that expresses the stencil code. The computational grid is decomposed into equally sized tiles on the backend distributed across the parallel machine running the server. The following sections describe the frontend and backend of CharmStencil in more detail.

3.1 Frontend

Figure 4 shows a 2D Laplace equation solver written using CharmStencil. Users create a subclass using the provided Stencil class and overload the iterate method to express their computation. The users also specify the over-decomposition factor, which determines the number of tiles the domain is decomposed into, the ghost depth for each field, the size of the grid, and the number of fields to create. The call to initialize sends a message to the backend to create the stencil with the requested specifications. When solve is called on the object of this class, the iterate function is called in a loop until it returns true. The exchange_ghosts function is called in iterate to initiate the exchange of ghost data for the fields passed as arguments to the call. The backend_freq option sets the number of iterations after which a message is sent to the backend.

The frontend builds an AST for every call to iterate. It keeps track of all unique ASTs and a list of which AST needs to be executed for each iteration.

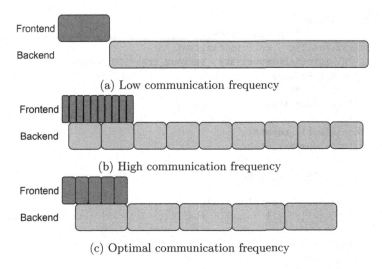

(a) Low communication frequency

(b) High communication frequency

(c) Optimal communication frequency

Fig. 3. Pipelined execution between frontend and backend helps hide Python overheads from the frontend

When the number of iterations reaches the maximum threshold specified by the user, the unique ASTs and the list of ASTs to execute at each iteration are serialized and sent to the backend. Figure 5 shows the AST generated for a 2D Laplace equation solver.

3.2   Backend

When the backend receives the creation message, it generates a chare array, with each element corresponding to a tile in the grid decomposition. The size of the chare array is determined by the over-decomposition factor provided by the user and the number of PEs on which the server is running. Each element of the chare array then allocates the requested size for its local data, along with buffers for communicating ghost data.

The backend handler on PE 0 generates C++ code for each unique AST received from the frontend and compiles it to a shared object identified by a 32-bit hash of the AST. The handler on PE 0 then broadcasts the list of the 32-bit hash values of each unique AST, the list of ASTs that need to be executed at each iteration, and the fields that need ghost exchanges at each iteration to all PEs. The compute function corresponding to each hash value is dynamically loaded from the file system on each logical node and cached locally on every PE. Every chare does its ghost exchanges, if any, at each iteration and then calls the compute function.

```
class Jacobi2D(Stencil):
    def __init__(self, n, interface):
        self.x, self.y = self.initialize(
            n, interface=interface, backend_freq=100, odf=2,
            num_fields=2)
        self.itercount = 0
        self.boundary_iter = True

    def iterate(self, nsteps):
        if self.boundary_iter:
            self.boundary(100.)
            self.boundary_iter = False
            return True
        self.exchange_ghosts(self.x)
        self.y[1:-1, 1:-1] = 0.25 * (self.x[:-2, 1:-1] + self.x[2:, 1:-1] +
                                     self.x[1:-1, :-2] + self.x[1:-1, 2:])
        self.x, self.y = self.y, self.x
        self.itercount += 1
        return self.itercount != nsteps

    def boundary(self, bc):
        self.x[0, :] = self.y[0, :] = bc
        self.x[-1, :] = self.y[-1, :] = bc
        self.x[:, 0] = self.y[:, 0] = bc
        self.x[:, -1] = self.y[:, -1] = bc

grid = Jacobi2D(n, interface)
grid.solve(1000)
```

Fig. 4. 2D Laplace equation solver example using CharmStencil

4   Performance Results

The following experiments were run on the NCSA Delta machine. Each node
of Delta has 2 sockets with an AMD EPYC 7763 64-Core processor on each
socket with HPE Slingshot 11 interconnect. We use the non-SMP Charm++
MPI build with OpenMPI 4.1.2. We compare the performance of CharmStencil
with cuNumeric, Numba, Charm++, and sequential Numpy. Because of issues
in building the multi-node version on Delta, we show comparisons with only the
single-node build of cuNumeric.

Figure 6 shows the effect of pipelined execution on a 3D Laplace equation
solver on 16 million grid points for 1024 iterations. A smaller backend_freq
results in more frequent communication between the frontend and the backend
resulting in greater overlap but also large communication cost and a higher
Python overhead due to the cost of serialization of the AST. Whereas, a larger
backend_freq results in low communication cost but also low overlap. We can
hide almost all of the Python overhead for a range of choices of backend_freq
between the 2 extremes.

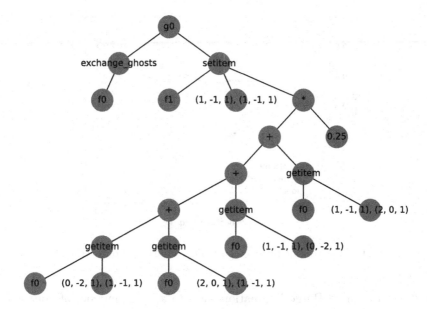

Fig. 5. AST generated by the frontend for a 2D Laplace equation solver

Figure 7 shows the scaling performance for a 2D Laplace equation solver for 128 iterations. The number of cores varies from 1 to 4096 (32 nodes). We see that Numpy cannot parallelize the operations and incurs significant overheads from creating temporary arrays for each operation. cuNumeric performs better than Numpy as the number of cores are scaled up, but still shows significant overhead. Numba exhibits decent scaling performance on a single node but requires users to indicate which loops to parallelize, similar to OpenMP, explicitly. Consequently, without explicit loop tiling from the programmer, Numba shows poor cache performance, resulting in worse strong and weak scaling than CharmStencil and Charm++ as we see in this case. CharmStencil can hide most of the Python overheads and match the Charm++ strong scaling performance until 1024 cores. Beyond the grain size of 3 ms per iteration, the Python overhead and communication costs between the frontend and the backend affect the strong scaling performance.

Figure 8 shows the scaling performance for a 2D Burger's equation which solves the following set of coupled PDEs,

$$
\begin{aligned}
\frac{\partial u}{\partial t} + u\frac{\partial u}{\partial x} + v\frac{\partial u}{\partial y} &= \nu\left(\frac{\partial^2 u}{\partial x^2} + \frac{\partial^2 u}{\partial y^2}\right) \\
\frac{\partial v}{\partial t} + u\frac{\partial v}{\partial x} + v\frac{\partial v}{\partial y} &= \nu\left(\frac{\partial^2 v}{\partial x^2} + \frac{\partial^2 v}{\partial y^2}\right)
\end{aligned}
\tag{1}
$$

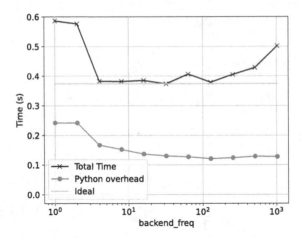

Fig. 6. Effect of pipelined execution on hiding Python overhead

The discretization of Burger's equation leads to a larger number of operations per iteration than the Laplace equation. As a result, the performance difference between Numpy and CharmStencil widens since the latter avoids the creation of intermediate arrays for each operation.

5   Related Work

There have been several projects aimed at parallelizing array computations while maintaining the productivity offered by Python. These projects span from parallel languages that can interoperate with Python to high-level libraries that invoke an underlying parallel implementation of a set of algorithms.

Cython [2] is a compiled language that serves as a superset of Python, enabling users to write Python code that interoperates with C/C++. Cython code is compiled to C using the Python-C API for Python objects, and it also supports parallel programming using OpenMP.

Numba [8] is an LLVM-based JIT compiler that translates a subset of Python into machine code. Numba generates parallel code for multicore CPUs and supports execution on GPUs. However, Numba cannot auto-parallelize sequential code; users need to express parallelism in their code using primitives defined by Numba.

JAX [3] is an XLA-based compiler for array computations on CPUs, GPUs, and TPUs, primarily targeted towards machine learning applications. Similar to Numba, users need to express parallelism in their code for JAX to run on parallel machines.

Dask [10] is a task-based runtime system supporting distributed execution with an array API almost identical to that of Numpy. However, the centralized

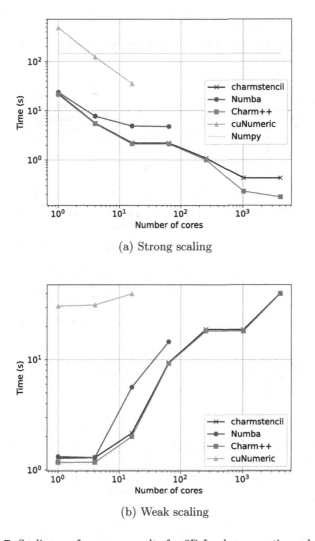

(a) Strong scaling

(b) Weak scaling

Fig. 7. Scaling performance results for 2D Laplace equation solver

dynamic task scheduler in Dask does not scale well on large machines. Moreover, local array operations in Dask are handled by Numpy, thus suffering from the same overheads as Numpy.

cuNumeric [1], as mentioned earlier, is another drop-in replacement library for Numpy built on top of the Legion runtime system. cuNumeric exhibits impressive scaling performance on multiple GPUs, but at least in the current implementations, our CPU performance is better.

Arkouda [9] is a Python library with Numpy-like arrays and Pandas-like dataframes designed for exploratory data analytics. Arkouda also utilizes a client-server model with a Python frontend and a Chapel server on the backend.

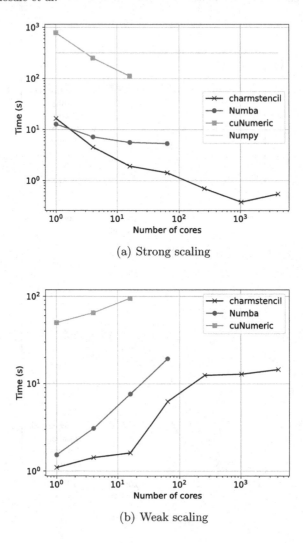

(a) Strong scaling

(b) Weak scaling

Fig. 8. Scaling performance results for 2D Burger's equation solver

Apart from these, there also exist low-level libraries for distributed programming such as MPI4Py [4] and Charm4Py [5] that provide a thin Python wrapper around MPI and Charm++. These libraries follow the semantics of the corresponding C libraries and demand considerable programming effort to implement parallel applications.

6 Future Work

There are several planned improvements for CharmStencil aimed at enhancing both the usability and performance of the abstraction. By allocating boundary layers separately from the internal grid, we can avoid copying boundaries into a contiguous memory buffer to send ghost data at every iteration, thus reducing the message packing cost incurred in each iteration.

While we demonstrate weak scaling performance comparable to a hand-written Charm++ implementation, strong scaling performance can still be enhanced by reducing the Python overhead and communication cost between the frontend and the backend. This can be achieved by introducing a loop construct in the AST, avoiding time-stepping iterations on the frontend. Instead, the outer loop can be encoded in the AST, sent to the backend only once, with minimal overhead on the frontend.

A departure from Numpy in our current implementation is the necessity of the `exchange_ghosts` call. Inferring ghost exchanges from array access patterns in the generated AST would significantly improve the abstraction's usability.

In addition to these optimizations, we plan to add the ability to check for convergence on the backend. We also plan to use the same frontend AST to generate CUDA code on the backend and leverage Charm++ HAPI to support execution on multiple GPUs.

7   Conclusion

Numpy has been extensively utilized for prototyping scientific computing applications. However, parallelizing these applications demands significant programming effort. While drop-in Numpy replacements exist to run the same applications on parallel machines, these alternatives often suffer from high overheads or necessitate a substantial rewrite of the source code. In this project, we introduced a highly scalable library designed for stencil computations on distributed memory machines using a Python frontend and a Charm++ backend, requiring users to make minimal changes to their sequential Numpy code. Our implementation was compared to two state-of-the-art Numpy alternatives, showcasing superior scaling performance.

References

1. Bauer, M., Garland, M.: Legate NumPy: accelerated and distributed array computing. In: Proceedings of the International Conference for High Performance Computing, Networking, Storage and Analysis, SC 2019. Association for Computing Machinery, New York (2019)
2. Behnel, S., Bradshaw, R., Citro, C., Dalcin, L., Seljebotn, D.S., Smith, K.: Cython: the best of both worlds. Comput. Sci. Eng. **13**(2), 31–39 (2011)
3. Bradbury, J., et al.: JAX: composable transformations of Python+NumPy programs (2018)
4. Dalcín, L., Paz, R., Storti, M.: MPI for Python. J. Parallel Distrib. Comput. **65**(9), 1108–1115 (2005)
5. Galvez, J.J. Senthil, K., Kale, L.: CharmPy: a Python parallel programming model. In: 2018 IEEE International Conference on Cluster Computing (CLUSTER), pp. 423–433 (2018)

6. Harris, C.R., et al.: Array programming with NumPy. Nature **585**(7825), 357–362 (2020)
7. Kalé, L.V., Krishnan, S.: CHARM++: a portable concurrent object oriented system based on C++. In: Paepcke, A. (ed.) Proceedings of OOPSLA 1993, pp. 91–108. ACM Press (1993)
8. Lam, S.K., Pitrou, A., Seibert, S.: Numba: a LLVM-based python JIT compiler. In: Proceedings of the Second Workshop on the LLVM Compiler Infrastructure in HPC, pp. 1–6 (2015)
9. Merrill, M., Reus, W., Neumann, T.: Arkouda: interactive data exploration backed by chapel. In: Proceedings of the ACM SIGPLAN 6th on Chapel Implementers and Users Workshop, CHIUW 2019, p. 28. Association for Computing Machinery, New York (2019)
10. Rocklin, M.: Dask: parallel computation with blocked algorithms and task scheduling. In: SciPy (2015)
11. Virtanen, P., et al.: SciPy 1.0: fundamental algorithms for scientific computing in python. Nat. Methods **17**, 261–272 (2020)

DLA-Future: A Task-Based Linear Algebra Library Which Provides a GPU-Enabled Distributed Eigensolver

Raffaele Solcà$^{(\boxtimes)}$ ⓘ, Mikael Simberg ⓘ, Rocco Meli ⓘ, Alberto Invernizzi ⓘ, Auriane Reverdell ⓘ, and John Biddiscombe ⓘ

Swiss National Supercomputing Center, ETH Zurich, Zürich, Switzerland
{raffaele.solca,mikael.simberg,rocco.meli,alberto.invernizzi,
auriane.reverdell,biddisco}@cscs.ch

Abstract. DLA-Future implements an efficient GPU-enabled distributed eigenvalue solver using a software architecture based on the C++ `std::execution` concurrency proposal. The state-of-the-art linear algebra implementations LAPACK and ScaLAPACK were designed for legacy systems and employ fork-join parallelism, which can perform inefficiently on modern architectures. The benefits of task-based linear algebra implementations are significant. The reduction of synchronization points and the ease of overlapping computation with communication are two of the main benefits that lead to improved performance. In specific cases, the ability to schedule multiple algorithms concurrently yields a noticeable reduction of time-to-solution.

We present the implementation of DLA-Future and the results on different types of systems starting from Piz Daint multicore and GPU partitions, moving to more recent architectures available in ALPS.

The benchmark results are divided into two categories. The first contains a comparison of DLA-Future against widely used eigensolver implementations. The second category showcases the performance of the eigensolver in real applications. We present results generated with CP2K, where DLA-Future support was easily added thanks to the provided C API, which is compatible with the ScaLAPACK interface.

Keywords: eigenvalue solver · generalized eigenvalue solver · task-based linear algebra · distributed linear algebra · std::execution · ScaLAPACK drop-in

1 Introduction

The time to solution of many scientific applications depends highly on dense linear algebra operations. A typical example can be found in materials science where the computational time is dominated by linear algebra tasks such as Hermitian eigenvalue problems. In many cases, the size of the operands involved is so large that it is necessary to operate over multiple computing nodes.

© The Author(s), under exclusive license to Springer Nature Switzerland AG 2024
P. Diehl et al. (Eds.): WAMTA 2024, LNCS 14626, pp. 135–141, 2024.
https://doi.org/10.1007/978-3-031-61763-8_13

ScaLAPACK [2] is the de facto standard implementation of linear algebra for distributed memory. It was designed for legacy systems, where nodes provided few cores and no accelerators were available. It employs fork-join parallelism which is inefficient on modern architectures. A more optimized distributed eigensolver is provided by ELPA [1,8], which includes a one-stage and a two-stage tridiagonalization approach and supports CUDA-capable GPUs.

SLATE [5], a task-based distributed linear algebra library based on OpenMP, has been developed within the Exascale Computing Project. Starting from release `2023.06.00` it provides a Hermitian eigenvalue solver. However, the implementation is still limited to square process grids.

In the present contribution we describe the DLA-Future library [11] and its eigensolver implementation. We give an overview of the challenges of a task-based implementation and how they have been solved.

2   DLA-Future

The main goal of DLA-Future is to provide an eigenvalue solver and a generalized eigenvalue solver for symmetric and Hermitian matrices, mainly focusing on use-cases from the materials science community. In particular, to simplify the use in existing applications, the aim is to provide a ScaLAPACK-like drop-in replacement. The integration of DLA-Future in CP2K [7] proved the effectiveness of the API.

During the design phase of DLA-Future it was clear that the implementation could benefit from a task-based programming model. Independent algorithms can be scheduled and executed concurrently leading to better resource usage. However, the main advantage is the possibility of introducing fine-grained task dependencies, which allow overlapping the execution of two subsequent algorithms working on the same matrix. DLA-Future uses the proposed C++ model for asynchronous execution `std::execution` [4], relying on pika [9] (a fork of HPX [6]) for the implementation. This allows seamlessly integrating dependencies between CPU, GPU, and communication tasks.

For communication, we chose the MPI library, with its asynchronous communication functions. It is a natural choice as it is used in many scientific applications and allows us to provide a ScaLAPACK-like replacement.

2.1   Eigensolver Implementation Description

A two-stage tridiagonalization approach was chosen for the eigensolver implementation. The algorithm presented in [10] has been modified to be suitable for matrix tile-driven dependencies. The eigensolver algorithm can be summarized in the following steps. The first stage consists of the application of a sequence of Householder transformations which reduce the dense Hermitian matrix to band form. The Hermitian band matrix is then further reduced to a real symmetric tridiagonal form using another set of Householder transformations generated by the bulge chasing technique. Then, Cuppen's divide and conquer algorithm [3] is used to compute the eigenvalues and eigenvectors of the tridiagonal matrix. Finally, the eigenvectors of the original problem are computed applying the Householder transformations generated in the first two stages to the eigenvectors of the tridiagonal matrix in the correct order.

A Hermitian generalized eigenvalue solver, which solves $Ax = \lambda Bx$ where B is positive definite, is also available. It combines the use of the Cholesky factorization and triangular solvers to transform the problem is a standard eigenproblem and back-transform the eigenvectors.

2.2 Implementation Challenges

During an initial implementation of Cholesky decomposition with C++ task parallelism, it became evident that there are challenges when writing maintainable linear algebra code with matrices decomposed into tiles. Some operations consume a given tile in a *read-only* manner (and contribute to the writing of a different tile), whilst other operations may modify a tile *in place*. Multiple operations concurrently working on tiles must carefully coordinate their access via tile senders [4], handles to asynchronous tiles.

Two subsequent *read-only* (hereafter `ro`) tile operations should run concurrently (subject to adequate available compute resources), but any *read-write* (hereafter `rw`) operation should not be scheduled until *all* previous operations on that tile are completed.

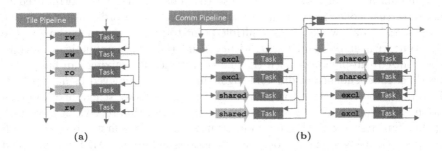

(a)   (b)

Fig. 1. Sender pipeline examples: (a) Tile and (b) Communicator. Blue arrows represent task scheduling and access type. Red arrows represent run time task/communication dependencies. Green arrows indicate pipeline flow. In (b) two algorithms running concurrently are synchronized by the communicator pipeline. (Color figure online)

We therefore introduced the concept of a tile pipeline which provides a unique (ownership) tile sender for `rw` operations and a shared (ownership) tile sender with `const` access semantics for `read` operations. Dependencies are triggered on destruction of each tile. Tiles are references to a region of matrix memory, which may have an arbitrary layout and location on any resource. Figure 1a shows a representation of the scheduling and execution of the tile pipeline flow.

Choosing the correct task size is another problem. In the pika runtime context switching, queue handling, and stack creation all contribute around 1 to 10 μs overhead per task. Therefore, with very small tasks (runtime less than 1 ms), overheads become noticeable and performance drops measurably. Conversely, coarse tasks limit the achievable parallelism and thus the optimal utilization of the system. In the Cholesky decomposition algorithm, all tasks involve either BLAS Level 3 operations on tiles, or a Cholesky decomposition of diagonal tiles. Assuming square tile sizes of $n_b \times n_b$, the complexity of each task is $O(n_b^3)$, i.e. they all complete in a similar amount of time. Therefore, the task size is fully determined by the tile size. For more complex algorithms, combining many small tasks into single tasks can reduce the impact of the task execution overhead.

A further challenge is memory management, in particular temporary tile buffers, such as those needed for communication. The simple solution of allocating space *on demand* is not ideal as memory usage quickly explodes when, for example, most receive operations have no dependencies on the receive side, and many can be scheduled immediately as the task graph is traversed. The solution chosen is to allocate some memory for each algorithm and reuse it multiple times. This introduces extra dependencies, but has the benefit of decreasing overall usage and reducing the number of pending receive tasks whose send counterparts still have unfulfilled dependencies.

To ensure correctness of algorithms, communication messages must be correctly matched: point to point communication may use unique MPI tags, whilst collective communications need to be ordered within a given communicator. A communicator pipeline, similar to the tile pipeline, has been introduced to guarantee that collective communications are executed in order using exclusive senders, and to allow executing multiple point-to-point communications at the same time with shared senders. Algorithms using the same communicator receive synchronized sub-pipelines, such that no communication mixing can happen at any time. Independence of different algorithms can be achieved using pipelines of clones of the respective communicator. Figure 1b shows scheduling and execution of the communicator pipeline, where each algorithm receives its own sub-pipeline (green arrows). All the communication tasks of the first sub-pipeline will be scheduled using asynchronous MPI functions before any MPI call is issued from the second algorithm, ensuring message matching even if the same MPI tag is used in two or more different algorithms.

3   Results

3.1   Eigensolver

Figure 2a presents the results of the eigensolver from Piz Daint-MC, a Cray XC40 system with Intel Broadwell CPUs (dual socket Intel E5-2695 v4).

The performance of DLA-Future with a small number of nodes is similar to the performance of the Intel MKL implementation of ScaLAPACK. On a larger number of nodes DLA-Future scaling is less optimal, and can be attributed to the need to use larger block-sizes to control the task size. Figure 2b contains the

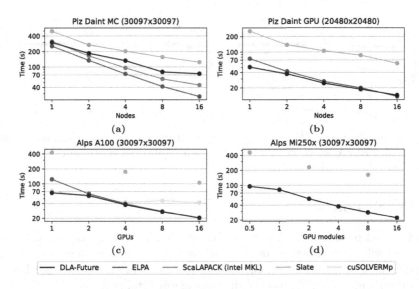

Fig. 2. Eigensolver strong scaling on different architectures. The best performing configuration is used for each library (block-size and MPI ranks per node). For A100 and MI250x one rank per GPU is used. For ELPA, two-stage performed better on multicore systems and one-stage on GPU.

results from Piz Daint-GPU, a Cray XC50 system whose nodes are equipped with an Intel Haswell E5-2690 v3 CPU and a NVIDIA P100 GPU. DLA-Future is in this case the best performing library among all the competitors.

Figure 2c, 2d contain the results from ALPS, a HPE Cray EX system equipped with different types of nodes. Figure 2c shows the results for nodes equipped with an AMD EPYC 7713 and four 80GB NVIDIA A100 GPUs (as Perlmutter GPU at NERSC). DLA-Future always equals or outperforms other libraries. Figure 2c shows the results for nodes equipped with an AMD EPYC 7A53 and four AMD MI250x (8 GPUs in total) (as LUMI-G at CSC). DLA-Future also performs well on AMD GPUs. Some points are missing in SLATE's results as the current eigensolver implementation constrains the execution to square process grids.

3.2 Integration in CP2K

DLA-Future is integrated in CP2K, using DLA-Future's ScaLAPACK-like C API. The C API allows to use DLA-Future as a ScaLAPACK replacement in existing applications.

Figure 3 shows the eigensolver and CP2K (v2024.1) runtime for a total energy calculation of a system of 512 water molecules, corresponding to an eigenvalue problem of size $20\,480 \times 20\,480$. Each calculation consists in 15 solutions of the eigenvalue problem, for iterative convergence of the total energy.

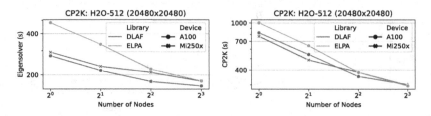

Fig. 3. Eigensolver and CP2K strong scaling on ALPS. DLA-Future is compared with the two-stage ELPA solver. BLAS, LAPACK, and ScaLAPACK are provided by Intel MKL. One rank per GPU is used.

4   Conclusion

We presented results of DLA-Future. The development of the library will continue and will cover different areas including C++ API improvements, performance focused implementation changes, introduction of GPU-direct MPI communication, and the exploration of different algorithms.

Acknowledgments. This work was supported by the Swiss Platform for Advanced Scientific Computing (PASC) project Abinitio (funding period 2021–2024) and partly supported by The Partnership for Advanced Computing in Europe (PRACE). The Implementation Phase of PRACE receives funding from the EU's Horizon 2020 Research and Innovation Programme (2014–2020) under grant agreement 823767. For more information, see www.prace-ri.eu.

Disclosure of Interests. The authors have no competing interests to declare that are relevant to the content of this article.

References

1. Auckenthaler, T., Blum, V., Bungartz, H.J., et al.: Parallel solution of partial symmetric eigenvalue problems from electronic structure calculations. In: Parallel Computing, pp. 783–794. Berg Univ Wuppertal, Fachbereich C, Wuppertal (2011)
2. Blackford, L.S., Choi, J., Cleary, A., et al.: ScaLAPACK Users' Guide. Society for Industrial and Applied Mathematics, Philadelphia (1997)
3. Cuppen, J.J.M.: A divide and conquer method for the symmetric tridiagonal eigenproblem. Numer. Math. **36**(2), 177–195 (1980)
4. Dominiak, M., Evtushenko, G., Baker, L., et al.: P2300 std::execution (2023). https://www.open-std.org/jtc1/sc22/wg21/docs/papers/2023/p2300r7.html
5. Gates, M., Charara, A., Kurzak, J., et al.: Slate users' guide. SLATE Working Notes 10, ICL-UT-19-01 (2020)
6. Kaiser, H., Diehl, P., Lemoine, A.S., et al.: HPX - the C++ standard library for parallelism and concurrency. J. Open Sour. Softw. **5**(53), 2352 (2020). https://doi.org/10.21105/joss.02352 https://doi.org/10.21105/joss.02352
7. Kühne, T.D., Iannuzzi, M., Del Ben, M., et al.: CP2K: an electronic structure and molecular dynamics software package - quickstep: efficient and accurate electronic structure calculations. J. Chem. Phys. **152**(19), 194103 (2020). https://doi.org/10.1063/5.0007045

8. Marek, A., Blum, V., Johanni, R., et al.: The ELPA library: scalable parallel eigenvalue solutions for electronic structure theory and computational science. J. Phys.: Condens. Matt. **26**(21), 213201 (2014)
9. Simberg, M., Reverdell, A., Biddiscombe, J., et al.: pika 0.22.1 (2024).https://doi.org/10.5281/zenodo.10579225
10. Solcà, R., Kozhevnikov, A., Haidar, A., et al.: Efficient implementation of quantum materials simulations on distributed CPU-GPU systems. In: SC 2015, pp. 1–12 (2015) https://doi.org/10.1145/2807591.2807654
11. Solcà, R., Invernizzi, A., Reverdell, A., et al.: DLA-future 0.4.0 (2024). https://doi.org/10.5281/zenodo.10518289

ALPI: Enhancing Portability and Interoperability of Task-Aware Libraries

Kevin Sala$^{(\boxtimes)}$, David Álvarez , Raúl Peñacoba , Rodrigo Arias Mallo ,
Antoni Navarro , Aleix Roca , and Vicenç Beltran

Barcelona Supercomputing Center (BSC), Plaça Eusebi Güell,
1-3, 08034 Barcelona, Spain
{kevin.sala,david.alvarez,raul.penacoba,rodrigo.arias,
antoni.navarro,aleix.roca,vbeltran}@bsc.es

Abstract. Task-based programming models are a promising approach to exploiting complex distributed and heterogeneous systems. However, integrating different communication, offloading, and storage APIs within tasks poses performance and deadlock risks. Several Task-Aware libraries, such as TAMPI, TASIO, and TACUDA, have been developed to integrate blocking and non-blocking APIs within task-based programming models efficiently. In this paper, we introduce the Asynchronous Low-level Programming Interface (ALPI) to enable the interoperability and portability of Task-Aware libraries across various programming models and runtime systems. We have implemented ALPI in the Nanos6 and nOS-V runtimes, enhancing the integration of Task-Aware libraries with the OmpSs-2 and OpenMP programming models. This work is a step towards improving the composability of parallel programming models by supporting Task-Aware libraries across different runtime systems.

Keywords: Task-based programming models · Runtime systems · OpenMP · OmpSs-2 · Portability · Interoperability

1 Introduction

Improvements in the manufacturing process of transistors have already slowed down, and soon, it will not be affordable to mass-produce chips with a higher density. To overcome these limitations, recent computing systems rely on large multi-core systems with multiple accelerators to increase performance and energy efficiency. At the same time, most parallel applications already struggle to exploit larger distributed multi-core systems because it is challenging to expose enough parallelism to feed all system cores. Upcoming highly heterogeneous systems will be even more complex and challenging to exploit.

Task-based programming models are a promising approach to dealing with complex distributed and heterogeneous systems. In task-based programming models, parallelism is expressed through tasks, which are managed and executed

© The Author(s), under exclusive license to Springer Nature Switzerland AG 2024
P. Diehl et al. (Eds.): WAMTA 2024, LNCS 14626, pp. 142–153, 2024.
https://doi.org/10.1007/978-3-031-61763-8_14

by a runtime system. The goal of the runtime system is to exploit the underlying hardware resources by dynamically scheduling ready tasks to idle worker threads while avoiding oversubscription issues.

Developing large applications on distributed and heterogeneous systems is a complex process, as different communication, offloading, and storage APIs must be combined carefully. Directly using such APIs inside tasks can lead to performance and programmability issues. Firstly, blocking interfaces like basic MPI functions (e.g., `MPI_Recv`) or `read`/`write` OS operations will block the CPU waiting for completion; no other task can reuse those CPUs meanwhile. Moreover, a deadlock may occur when re-ordering MPI communications [8]. Using non-blocking interfaces instead can help mitigate those issues. Network fabrics, accelerators, and storage devices have adopted high-performance interfaces based on non-blocking APIs and polling (i.e., busy-waiting). For instance, MPI, CUDA, and Intel SPDK expose such interfaces. Some even bypass the OS and enable a single thread to issue multiple I/O operations, significantly improving performance and decreasing latency. However, these APIs are low-level, so combining them with parallel programming models is challenging. Their non-blocking nature requires changing the applications' natural control flow and carefully synchronizing operations issued by different tasks or threads.

To overcome these drawbacks, we recently developed several Task-Aware libraries (TA-X), such as TAMPI [8], TASIO [6], and TACUDA, which efficiently integrate communication and offloading models with task-based programming models. These libraries are designed to support blocking and non-blocking API calls from inside tasks naturally and efficiently. Such libraries work over the model's library (e.g., an MPI library) and the underlying task-based runtime system. Currently, integrating these libraries with a task-based runtime requires the Task-Aware libraries to support the specific tasking services of that runtime. Thus, each Task-Aware library implements a different backend for each task-based runtime supported. This approach does not scale and introduces unnecessary complexity to the Task-Aware libraries. To overcome this problem, we propose the Asynchronous Low-level Programming Interface (ALPI), which enables all Task-Aware libraries to run seamlessly on any runtime system implementing it. Additionally, ALPI ensures the interoperability between Task-Aware libraries, making their combination safe and straightforward.

2   Background

There are many task-based programming models such as OpenMP [5], Parsec [4], StarPU [2], and Cilk [3], among others [9]. This paper uses the OpenMP and OmpSs-2 [7] programming models to demonstrate our ALPI proposal, which can also be applied to other runtime systems. OmpSs-2 is a task-based parallel programming model based on directives with a powerful data-flow execution model developed at the Barcelona Supercomputing Center. It is mainly used as a research platform to conceive, implement, and test new ideas and provide feedback to the OpenMP committee. The OmpSs-2 programming model is composed of an LLVM-based compiler, the Nanos6 runtime system, and the ovni instrumentation. An alternative OmpSs-2 runtime implementation is based on the nOS-V [10] tasking library. All these software projects are open-source.[1] In this section, we first describe how task-based runtime systems work, using as an example Nanos6 and nOS-V. Then, we describe the runtime services required to support the Task-Aware libraries (TA-X).

2.1   Task-Based Runtime Systems

The main goal of task-based runtime systems is to schedule tasks over all available resources. The four main components of a runtime system are the CPU manager, the thread manager, the dependency system, and the task scheduler. The first two components turn cores on and off based on the available ready tasks and control the pause/resume of worker threads, the dependency system orchestrates the fine synchronizations between tasks based on their data dependencies, and the task scheduler assigns ready tasks to idle workers following a scheduling policy. Some runtimes may merge the CPU and thread manager; others may not include a dependency system. Nonetheless, all runtime systems provide a tasking API to create and submit tasks.

Nanos6 is the default OmpSs-2 runtime system and includes the four components mentioned above and depicted in Fig. 1. The Nanos6 CPU manager turns cores on or off based on the number of ready tasks and the underlying scheduling policy (e.g., idle, busy, or hybrid). The Nanos6 dependency system implements the rich OmpSs-2 data-flow model, supporting advanced dependencies and reductions with a highly scalable wait-free implementation [1]. The Nanos6 runtime features a centralized task scheduler based on an efficient delegation lock [1] that scales to a high number of cores. This design allows implementing complex scheduling polices that consider task priorities and data locality.

The Nanos6 thread manager maintains a pool of worker threads, which are the ones that run on cores and execute tasks. Once scheduled, a ready task is assigned a worker thread to run the whole task body. The worker that runs a task has exclusive access to the assigned core. A worker becomes idle when it finishes running the assigned task, and then, the thread manager can reuse it to execute other ready tasks. Nanos6 supports tasks that block at any point, e.g., in *taskwaits* or through an API to pause tasks. When a task is paused, the worker thread executing it is also paused, and the thread manager starts another worker on the core that becomes idle. This way, tasks can be blocked at any point without blocking the underlying core. When a task is unblocked, it is re-submitted to the scheduler and eventually resumed on an idle core. Resuming a task involves resuming the thread that was running it. The runtime also supports pausing a task for a specific amount of time (i.e., like an OS `sleep` call). When a task completes the execution of its associated code (with no pending external events), it releases its dependencies, which might trigger other tasks in the dependency system to become ready.

---

[1] https://github.com/bsc-pm/ompss-2-releases.

NODES[2] is an alternative OmpSs-2 runtime system based on nOS-V [10]. nOS-V is a low-level threading and tasking library that exposes a tasking interface and implements the CPU and thread managers, and a generic task scheduler. The design and features of these three components are similar to the one provided by Nanos6 and depicted in Fig. 1. However, the nOS-V components are more flexible and generic because they have been designed to be used by other runtime systems. Then, LLVM/OpenMP-V[3] (libompv) is an OpenMP runtime ported to nOS-V. Both NODES and libompv leverage the thread manager, CPU manager, and task scheduler of nOS-V. Additionally, NODES implements the dependency system necessary to support the OmpSs-2 tasking model, whereas libompv implements the OpenMP dependency system and a task scheduler on top of the one provided by nOS-V (i.e., stacked schedulers).

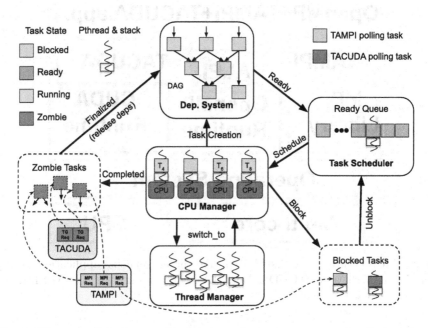

Fig. 1. Diagram of the interaction between the main components of a task-based runtime system. (Color figure online)

2.2 Task-Aware Libraries

Task-Aware libraries (TA-X)[4] aim to combine blocking and non-blocking APIs with task-based programming models. All TA-X libraries have a similar design

---

[2] https://github.com/bsc-pm/nodes.

[3] https://github.com/bsc-pm/llvm/tree/master/openmp.

[4] Available at https://github.com/bsc-pm/ta-x.

and architecture, implementing the corresponding native APIs and leveraging some tasking services of the task-based runtime system. Originally, the TA-X libraries implemented a different backend for each task-based runtime supported, increasing the libraries' complexity. By leveraging the ALPI interface described in Sect. 3, we have simplified the TA-X libraries and unified their support for task-based runtime systems. Figure 2 shows the components of a distributed and heterogeneous application combining OpenMP with the updated Task-Aware MPI (TAMPI) [8] and Task-Aware CUDA (TACUDA) libraries. Notice that TAMPI and TACUDA rely on an MPI library and CUDA runtime, respectively, and they use the ALPI interface to communicate with the OpenMP runtime.

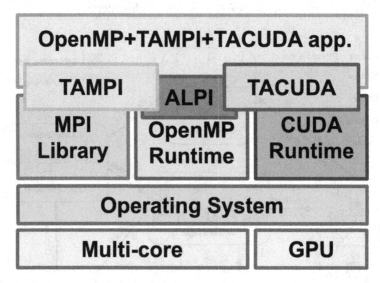

Fig. 2. Architecture of a distributed and heterogeneous application using OpenMP, TAMPI, and TACUDA. Both TA-X libraries use the new ALPI interface.

This section uses the TAMPI library to illustrate how TA-X libraries can support blocking and non-blocking API calls within tasks. TAMPI extends the functionality of standard MPI libraries by providing new mechanisms to improve the interoperability between task-based programming models and MPI communications. This library allows application's tasks to safely and efficiently issue MPI operations in parallel. By following the MPI Standard, programmers must carefully avoid deadlocks that may occur in hybrid applications (e.g., MPI+OpenMP) where MPI calls take place within tasks. The out-of-order execution of tasks can alter the execution order of the enclosed MPI calls and disturb how MPI operations are matched. The TAMPI library ensures a deadlock-free execution of such hybrid applications by implementing a cooperation mechanism between the MPI library and the task-based runtime system.

```
1   if (rank == 0) {
2     #pragma oss task in(data[0;n])  label("T0")
3     {
4       MPI_Send(data, n, MPI_INT, 1, tag, MPI_COMM_WORLD);
5       // Data buffer can be reused by the app.
6     }
7   } else if (rank == 1) {
8     #pragma oss task out(data[0;n]) label("T1")
9     {
10      MPI_Recv(data, n, MPI_INT, 0, tag, MPI_COMM_WORLD, MPI_STATUS_IGNORE);
11      // Data buffer can be read by the app.
12    }
13  }
14  #pragma oss taskwait
```

Listing 1. Example of using blocking MPI primitives inside OmpSs-2 tasks.

Supporting Blocking APIs. The blocking mode of TAMPI targets the safe and efficient execution of blocking MPI operations (e.g., MPI_Recv) from inside tasks. Listing 1 shows a code fragment with two OmpSs-2 tasks (lines 2 and 8) that call the MPI_Send and MPI_Recv blocking primitives, respectively. When any of these tasks call a blocking operation that is not completed immediately, the task (and the thread running it) is paused, and the core is re-used to execute other ready tasks. Figure 1 shows one task (bottom-right) that has been blocked together with the thread running it. We can also see the TAMPI polling services (the yellow task running on one core) that periodically checks all in-flight MPI requests. Once an MPI operation is completed, the TAMPI polling service will resume the paused task associated with this MPI request. This task will be added again to the queue of ready tasks so that an idle core will eventually execute it. All this is done transparently to the user, meaning all blocking MPI functions maintain the blocking semantics described in the MPI Standard. This approach prevents applications from blocking all cores inside MPI (i.e., waiting to complete some operations), which could result in a deadlock due to the lack of progress. Thus, programmers can instantiate multiple communication tasks (that call blocking MPI functions) without serializing them with artificial dependencies, which is usually necessary if TAMPI is not used. This way, communication tasks can run in parallel, and even re-ordered by the task scheduler. Notice that supporting the blocking mode of a TA-X library requires that the underlying native API provides equivalent non-blocking primitives, as is the case in MPI.

Supporting Non-blocking APIs. One approach to support non-blocking operations inside tasks is to call one or more non-blocking operations and then block the current task, as shown in lines 4–6 of Listing 2. This way, we can ensure that the task data dependencies are respected; dependencies are not released until all non-blocking operations are completed. The blocking mode presented

```
1   if (rank == 0) {
2     #pragma oss task in(data[0;n])  label("T0")
3     {
4       MPI_Request request;
5       MPI_Isend(data, n, MPI_INT, 1, tag, MPI_COMM_WORLD, &request);
6       MPI_Wait(&request, MPI_STATUS_IGNORE);
7       // Data buffer can be reused by the app.
8     }
9   } else if (rank == 1) {
10    #pragma oss task out(data[0;n]) label("T1")
11    {
12      MPI_Request request;
13      MPI_Irecv(data, n, MPI_INT, 0, tag, MPI_COMM_WORLD, &request);
14      TAMPI_Iwait(&request, MPI_STATUS_IGNORE);
15      // Data buffer can NOT be read inside this task
16    }
17  }
18  #pragma oss taskwait
```

Listing 2. Example of using blocking MPI_Wait and non-blocking TAMPI_Iwait calls inside OmpSs-2 tasks.

previously supports this approach but has some drawbacks. We are pausing the execution of a task at the very end to only prevent the release of dependencies until all non-blocking operations have been completed. In Nanos6 and nOS-V, this requires pausing a thread and starting a new one. Moreover, when the non-blocking operations are complete, the paused task becomes ready again and is inserted into the scheduler's ready queue. Eventually, an idle worker thread will try to resume this task, which already has a worker assigned and blocked, and thus, it will require another context switch. Finally, the task will resume, finish immediately (because the MPI_Wait in line 6 of Listing 2 was the last statement in the task body) and release the dependencies associated with this task. As we can see, this approach requires two thread context switches and additional latency (one round-trip to the scheduler) between the actual completion of the non-blocking operations and the release of its dependencies. It also forces the runtime system to keep an OS thread and its stack alive (e.g., 8MB of stack size), and increases the scheduling overhead. That problem is exacerbated when combining non-blocking operations from different APIs (e.g., MPI and CUDA) in the same task, as we have to wait for the operations of each API one after the other, requiring a full pause and resume cycle each time.

To avoid those performance problems, TAMPI provides the non-blocking TAMPI_Iwait primitive, which has the same parameters as the blocking MPI_Wait. When a task calls this function, like in line 14 in Listing 2, the task binds its completion to the MPI request passed as parameter by incrementing its pending event counter by one. When the task finishes the execution of its body, it becomes *zombie*, as shown in Fig. 1. A zombie task only completes and releases its dependencies when its event counter becomes zero.

Since `TAMPI_Iwait` is non-blocking, the user cannot know if the corresponding operations have already finished inside the task. For this reason, the communication buffers related to those requests should not be consumed or reused inside that task. The proper way is to correctly annotate the communication and computation tasks with the dependencies on the corresponding communication buffers. In this way, the tasks that consume these buffers will become ready once the data buffers are safe to be accessed (i.e., once the MPI communications have been completed). Thus, defining the correct dependencies of tasks is essential to guarantee a correct execution order.

It is worth noting that both TAMPI's blocking and non-blocking modes are compatible and can be combined in the same task.

3   The ALPI Interface

This section describes the primary services provided by ALPI that a task-based programming model has to implement to support Task-Aware libraries. The complete API definition is available online.[5]

ALPI functions can be grouped into four categories: helper functions, creation of polling tasks, pause and resume tasks, and management of task's events counter. There are several helper functions, but the most important one is used to get the handler of the running task. The `alpi_task_self` function checks whether the current thread runs within a task and retrieves the task's handle, a parameter required in most other functions.

The `alpi_task_spawn` call is used to create independent tasks that will execute the polling services of the Task-Aware libraries. Tasks that run polling services (polling tasks) are expected to run in short bursts and then block for some time before checking for new events. In order to block until a timeout elapses, these tasks must call `alpi_task_waitfor_ns`, which allow other tasks to be scheduled on the current core in the meantime. With this function, Task-Aware libraries can easily control the execution frequency of their polling services.

The `alpi_task_block` function blocks the execution of the calling task, which will be unblocked with a matching call to `alpi_task_unblock` and eventually resumed by the runtime system on an idle core.

Each task has a counter of in-flight external events. The counters are managed through the `alpi_task_events_increase` and `alpi_task_events_decrease` functions, which increase and decrease the number of external events of a task, respectively. Only the task during its execution can increase its event counter. In contrast, the event counter of a task may be decreased by any thread. When a task finishes the execution of its body, it will transition to a *Zombie* state (see Fig. 1), in which it will remain until all its external events are fulfilled (i.e., the event counter becomes zero).

---

[5] https://gitlab.bsc.es/alpi/alpi/-/blob/master/alpi.h.

We have implemented ALPI on the Nanos6[6] and nOS-V[7] runtime systems. The ALPI support in Nanos6 and nOS-V enables the development of applications using the TA-X libraries with OmpSs-2 and LLVM/OpenMP-V. In fact, the ALPI implementation in nOS-V can be leveraged by any runtime ported on top of nOS-V to support all TA-X libraries.

4   Implementing TAMPI Using the ALPI Interface

This section describes how the TAMPI library is implemented using the ALPI interface described in the previous section. We show the implementation for the blocking and non-blocking modes of TAMPI.

To implement the blocking mode, TAMPI transparently intercepts all the blocking MPI calls performed by an application. Listing 3 shows the code executed when an application performs an `MPI_Recv` call from inside a task. The blocking call is transformed into its non-blocking counterpart, an `MPI_Irecv` (line 3). The code then checks if the operation is immediately completed by calling to `MPI_Test` (line 4). If so, the function returns without blocking the task, as the MPI operation has already been completed. Otherwise, a ticket object is created and filled with the information about the ongoing MPI operation and the current task (line 8). Next, the ticket is registered inside the Task-Aware library (line 9), and the task is paused (lines 10). The polling service will periodically check the completion of the MPI operation, and it will resume the task when the operation completes. All other blocking MPI functions, including collective operations, are intercepted and managed similarly.

The non-blocking mode is implemented by the non-blocking `TAMPI_Iwait` primitive, which binds the release of the calling task's dependencies with the completion of the MPI request passed as parameter. The function leverages the task external events described in Sect. 3. Listing 3 shows the code executed when an application calls `TAMPI_Iwait` inside a task. Such a task has usually issued a standard non-blocking MPI operation before calling to `TAMPI_Iwait`, as shown in Listing 2. Firstly, the task checks if the MPI request passed as a parameter is immediately completed (line 16) and returns directly if so. Otherwise, a ticket object is allocated and filled with the required information (line 20), and an external event is registered to the calling task (line 21). Unlike the blocking mode, the ticket object cannot reside in the task's stack since the function always returns immediately.

Listing 4 shows the code of the polling service (lines 3–18), which is spawned as an independent task when TAMPI is initialized (line 1). This task periodically checks all in-flight MPI requests (line 5). When an operation completes, the ticket is removed (line 9), and the task is either resumed if the task was paused (line 11) or its event counter decreased (line 13). Finally, once all MPI requests have been checked, the task sleeps for 100 μs (line 16).

---

[6] https://github.com/bsc-pm/nanos6.

[7] https://github.com/bsc-pm/nos-v.

```
1   int MPI_Recv(void *buf, ..., MPI_Status *status) {
2     MPI_Request request;
3     int completed, err = MPI_Irecv(buf, ..., &request);
4     MPI_Test(&request, &completed, status);
5     if (!completed) {
6       struct alpi_task *task;
7       alpi_task_self(&task);
8       Ticket ticket(&request, status, task, /* blocking */ true);
9       pendingTickets.add(ticket);
10      alpi_task_block(task);
11    }
12    return err;
13  }
14
15  int TAMPI_Iwait(MPI_Request *request, MPI_Status *status) {
16    int completed, err = MPI_Test(request, &completed, status);
17    if (!completed) {
18      struct alpi_task *task;
19      alpi_task_self(&task);
20      Ticket *ticket = new Ticket(request, status, task, /* non-blk */ false);
21      alpi_task_events_increase(task, 1);
22      pendingTickets.add(ticket);
23    }
24    return err;
25  }
```

Listing 3. Pseudo-code of the MPI_Recv and TAMPI_Iwait in TAMPI.

```
1   alpi_task_spawn(&tampi_poll, 0, 0, 0, "TAMPI polling service", 0);
2   /* ... */
3   void tampi_poll(void *args) {
4     while (!tampi_shutdown) {
5       for (Ticket &ticket : pendingTickets) {
6         int completed = 0;
7         MPI_Test(ticket._request, &completed, ticket._status);
8         if (completed) {
9           pendingTickets.remove(ticket);
10          if (ticket.blocked)
11            alpi_task_unblock(ticket.task);
12          else
13            alpi_task_events_decrease(ticket.task, 1);
14        }
15      }
16      alpi_task_waitfor_ns(1e5 /* 100 us */ , 0);
17    }
18  }
```

Listing 4. Pseudo-code of the TAMPI polling service.

5   Interoperability Between TA-X Libraries

Our proposal enables all the TA-X libraries on any runtime system that implements our interface and allows combining TA-X libraries efficiently and naturally. All the blocking interfaces provided by TA-X libraries can be trivially combined inside the same task without restrictions, as each function retains its sequential semantics; only one pause-resume cycle can be active for a task at any point.

Similarly, all the non-blocking interfaces provided by TA-X libraries can also easily be combined within a task since all TA-X libraries use the same task event counter. A task will only be completed once its code has been executed and all its events are fulfilled (i.e., the event counter becomes zero).

Then, `alpi_spawn_task` enables creating one or more polling services for each TA-X library, which are managed by the underlying runtime systems like any other task (i.e., avoiding oversubscription).

Thus, combining TA-X libraries is straightforward, and the OpenMP and OmpSs-2 data flow models can be used to orchestrate the whole program, including computations, network I/O, disk I/O, and offloading, to name a few. TA-X libraries can also work with fork-join models, including blocking APIs, where worker threads of a parallel section pause while waiting for the completion of an event, and non-blocking APIs, in which a barrier in a parallel section waits for all workers to reach it and all event counters associated with the workers to become zero.

6   Conclusions

Task-based programming models are a promising approach to tackling the complexity of highly heterogeneous systems. However, combining task-based systems with blocking and non-blocking APIs is not trivial. Several Task-Aware libraries (TA-X) have been developed to solve this interoperability issue elegantly. However, supporting a TA-X library on N different runtimes requires the development of N backends, which is not sustainable. In this paper, we have proposed the Asynchronous Low-level Programming Interface (ALPI), which defines the runtime services required by all TA-X libraries to overcome this problem. Moreover, ALPI enables the interoperability of multiple TA-X libraries, which can be easily combined, even inside the same task. This approach enables any TA-X library to run out of the box on any runtime system directly implementing ALPI or running on top of the nOS-V threading and tasking library. The ALPI interface will help increase the adoption of task-based runtime systems and TA-X libraries.

Acknowledgements. This work was supported by the Spanish Ministry of Science and Innovation (grant PID2019-107255GB) and the Severo Ochoa Program (grant CEX2021-001148-S), both funded by MCIN/AEI/10.13039/501100011033. The Generalitat de Catalunya also supported this work via grant 2021-SGR-01007.

Disclosure of Interests. The authors have no competing interests to declare that are relevant to the content of this article.

References

1. Álvarez, D., Sala, K., Maroñas, M., Roca, A., Beltran, V.: Advanced synchronization techniques for task-based runtime systems. In: Lee, J., Petrank, E. (eds.) PPoPP 2021: 26th ACM SIGPLAN Symposium on Principles and Practice of Parallel Programming, Virtual Event, Republic of Korea, 27 February–3 March 2021, pp. 334–347. ACM (2021). https://doi.org/10.1145/3437801.3441601
2. Augonnet, C., Thibault, S., Namyst, R., Wacrenier, P.A.: StarPU: a unified platform for task scheduling on heterogeneous multicore architectures. CCPE - Concurrency and Computation: Practice and Experience, Special Issue: Euro-Par **2009**(23), 187–198 (2011)
3. Blumofe, R.D., Joerg, C.F., Kuszmaul, B.C., Leiserson, C.E., Randall, K.H., Zhou, Y.: Cilk: an efficient multithreaded runtime system. In: Proceedings of the Fifth ACM SIGPLAN Symposium on Principles and Practice of Parallel Programming, PPOPP 1995, pp. 207-216. Association for Computing Machinery, New York (1995). https://doi.org/10.1145/209936.209958
4. Bosilca, G., Bouteiller, A., Danalis, A., Herault, T., Luszczek, P., Dongarra, J.: Dense linear algebra on distributed heterogeneous hardware with a symbolic DAG approach. Scalable Computing and Communications: Theory and Practice, pp. 699–735 (2013)
5. Dagum, L., Menon, R.: OpenMP: an industry standard API for shared-memory programming. IEEE Comput. Sci. Eng. **5**(1), 46–55 (1998). https://doi.org/10.1109/99.660313
6. Roca Nonell, A., Beltran Querol, V., Mateo Bellido, S.: Introducing the task-aware storage I/O (TASIO) library. In: Fan, X., de Supinski, B.R., Sinnen, O., Giacaman, N. (eds.) IWOMP 2019. LNCS, vol. 11718, pp. 274–288. Springer, Cham (2019). https://doi.org/10.1007/978-3-030-28596-8_19
7. Perez, J.M., Beltran, V., Labarta, J., Ayguadé, E.: Improving the integration of task nesting and dependencies in OpenMP. In: IEEE International Parallel and Distributed Processing Symposium (IPDPS), pp. 809–818 (2017). https://doi.org/10.1109/IPDPS.2017.69
8. Sala, K., Teruel, X., Pérez, J.M., Peña, A.J., Beltran, V., Labarta, J.: Integrating blocking and non-blocking MPI primitives with task-based programming models. Parallel Comput. **85**, 153–166 (2019). https://doi.org/10.1016/J.PARCO.2018.12.008
9. Thoman, P., et al.: A taxonomy of task-based parallel programming technologies for high-performance computing. J. Supercomput. **74**(4), 1422–1434 (2018). https://doi.org/10.1007/s11227-018-2238-4
10. Álvarez, D., Sala, K., Beltran, V.: nOS-V: co-executing HPC applications using system-wide task scheduling. In: IEEE International Parallel and Distributed Processing Symposium, IPDPS 2024, San Francisco, CA, USA, 27–31 May 2024 (2024). https://doi.org/10.48550/arXiv.2204.10768

Evolving APGAS Programs: Automatic and Transparent Resource Adjustments at Runtime

Jonas Posner[1]([✉])(ID), Raoul Goebel[1], and Patrick Finnerty[2](ID)

[1] University of Kassel, Kassel, Germany
jonas.posner@uni-kassel.de, uk000330@student.uni-kassel.de
[2] Kobe University, Kobe, Japan
finnerty.patrick@fine.cs.kobe-u.ac.jp

Abstract. In the rapidly evolving field of High-Performance Computing (HPC), the need for resource elasticity is paramount, particularly in addressing the dynamic nature of irregular computational workloads. A key area of elasticity lies within programming models that typically offer limited support.

Fully elastic programs are both *malleable*—capable of dynamically adjusting resources in response to external job scheduler requests—and *evolving*—autonomously deciding when and how to adjust resources, e.g., through automated decision-making. Previous elasticity approaches typically relied on iterative workloads and required complex code modifications.

Asynchronous Many-Task (AMT) programming is emerging as a powerful alternative. In AMT, computations are split into fine-grained *tasks*, allowing transparent task relocation by the runtime system and unlocking significant potential for efficient elasticity.

This work-in-progress proposes an extension to the existing AMT *APGAS* that recently incorporated malleability. Our extension adds evolving capabilities providing automatic and transparent resource adjustments to meet changing computational workloads at runtime. Our easy-to-use abstractions require only minimal code additions; adjustments such as process initialization and termination are managed automatically. Our extension is validated via a load-balancing library for irregular workloads.

We propose two heuristics for automatic computational load detection: one that uses CPU loads provided by the operating system, and another that exploits detailed insights into task loads. We evaluate our approach using a novel synthetic benchmark that starts with a single task evolving into two irregular trees connected by a long sequential branch. Preliminary results are promising, indicating that both the CPU-based heuristic and the task-based heuristic showing similar efficiency.

Keywords: Resource Elasticity · Evolving Programs · Asynchronous Many-Task

P. Diehl et al. (Eds.): WAMTA 2024, LNCS 14626, pp. 154–165, 2024.
https://doi.org/10.1007/978-3-031-61763-8_15

1   Introduction

The field of High-Performance Computing (HPC) is characterized by the relentless pursuit of efficiency and performance, requiring continuous advancements in both hardware and software paradigms. As the complexity and diversity of supercomputing hardware resources continue to grow, so too does the nature of application workloads, leading to an increasing prevalence of *dynamic* and *irregular* computational workloads. These workloads are characterized by their variable computational demands and unpredictable behavior, creating significant challenges. Combined with the traditional practice of *static* resource allocation on supercomputers, this results in inefficient resource utilization and a consequent decline in overall system performance.

While static applications retain their resource allocations throughout their execution, even when some application phases require fewer resources, *resource elasticity* allows applications to dynamically adjust their resource allocation at runtime. Resource elasticity manifests in several forms [7], including *malleable*—the job scheduler initiates resource changes and applications respond accordingly—and *evolving*—the applications themselves decide when to change their resource allocation. These decisions can be programmed by the developer using constructs provided by the programming system, or they can be made automatically by a runtime system. This flexibility is particularly relevant in contexts such as adaptive mesh refinement [17] or multiscale analysis [16], where resource requirements may vary unpredictably at runtime.

Moreover, elastic applications bring numerous benefits to supercomputers. For example, they can *shrink* their current resource allocations to allow other applications to start earlier. Conversely, by *growing* their resource allocation, they can accelerate their completion. Consequently, elasticity holds the promise of significantly improving resource utilization, increasing job throughput, and optimizing overall performance [19].

However, developing elastic applications is significantly more complex than their rigid counterparts. In addition, support for elasticity in job schedulers and established inter-node programming models such as MPI is currently rudimentary. Numerous approaches have been proposed to address these issues, but they often require extensive and complicated modifications to the application code. Predominantly, these approaches are designed for iterative computations, naturally offering convenient synchronization points for adjusting resources [14].

The *Asynchronous Many-Task (AMT)* programming model presents a viable approach for facilitating programmer productivity, managing dynamic and irregular workloads, and enabling elasticity with only minor adjustments to the application code. AMT programmers break large computations into numerous fine-grained execution units, called *tasks*. The AMT runtime system dynamically assigns these tasks to processing units, called *workers*. This intrinsic transparent management of resources holds great promise for providing flexible and efficient approaches to resource elasticity. However, there is a notable lack in the current availability of AMT systems that efficiently and easily support such elastic capabilities.

This work-in-progress aims to address this shortcoming by introducing evolving capabilities as an extension to an AMT library—the open-source *APGAS of Java* [22] (*APGAS* for short). *APGAS* extends the well-known *Partitioned Global Address Space* (PGAS) programming model by adding asynchronous task capabilities [21]. A recent extension of *APGAS* has introduced malleability capabilities that include automatic process management and easy-to-use abstractions [9,10]. This research builds on the recent malleable *APGAS* and proposes evolving capabilities, making the following major contributions:

- We propose an innovative evolving technique and implement it as an extension to *APGAS* [9,22]. Our extension is designed to allow programmers to integrate evolving capabilities into their applications with minimal code changes, thanks to our well-defined abstractions. It makes resource adjustments in response to dynamic computational workloads encountered at runtime automatic and transparent. Runtime adjustments such as process initiation and termination are managed without programmer intervention.
- We demonstrate the practical usability of our evolving *APGAS* through its integration with the *Lifeline-Based Global Load Balancing (GLB)* library [8,23].
- We propose two heuristics for automatic detection of computational loads: the $Heur_{CPU}$ heuristic, which uses CPU data from the operating system, and the $Heur_{Task}$ heuristic, which uses detailed insight into task loads from *GLB*.
- We develop a new configurable benchmark designed specifically to evaluate performance under dynamically changing workloads, called *EvoTree*.
- Our experimental studies investigate the effectiveness of our evolving technique using combined *GLB* and *APGAS*. Preliminary results are promising, indicating that both $Heur_{CPU}$ and $Heur_{Task}$ perform efficiently and similarly.

The rest of this article is organized as follows. Section 2 starts by providing background on *APGAS*. We then present our evolving extension to *APGAS* in Sect. 3. Section 4 describes our experimental evaluations and the lessons learned. Then, Sect. 5 gives an overview of related work. The article concludes with Sect. 6, which summarizes our findings and contributions.

2   Background

This section gives a brief overview of the parallel programming system *APGAS of Java* [22], which we extend with evolving capabilities in Sect. 3.

APGAS integrates the parallel programming concepts from IBM's X10 [5] into Java. It allows programmers to create lightweight asynchronous tasks that encapsulate computations on local (with `async`) or remote (with `asyncAt`) *places*—i.e., a fraction of memory plus computational resources. Typically, one place is started on each node of a cluster. While *APGAS* automatically schedules tasks within each place among all worker threads, the mapping of tasks to places is left to programmers. Similarly, programmers are responsible for distributing data to places. The `finish` construct enables global synchronization by waiting for the completion of all spawned tasks, including those that have been spawned recursively and remotely.

3   Evolving APGAS Programs

Making an *APGAS* application *evolving* requires multiple components to interact gracefully with each other. First, the program needs to be able to communicate and negotiate with the job scheduler. While releasing nodes currently in use is a one-sided decision by the evolving program, acquiring additional nodes requires the approval of the job scheduler. This part is beyond the limited scope of this work and is left as future work.

Secondly, it is necessary to define the operations required to transition from running with a certain number of nodes to a different number. These operations are application-specific and should be defined by programmers, see Subsect. 3.2.

Finally, a monitoring and decision-making mechanism is required to gain insight into the behavior of the distributed program and to determine whether an adjustment in node allocation is appropriate. We propose two heuristics for automatic computational load detection in Subsect. 3.3.

Each component is presented into more details in the following subsections, after the general lifecycle of an evolving program is explained in Subsect. 3.1. Lastly, in Subsect. 3.4, we briefly illustrate how *GLB* was adapted to become an evolving application. The source code of both evolving *APGAS*[1] and *GLB*[2] are publicly available on GitHub.

3.1   Lifecycle

An application can be made *evolving* by programmers calling the **define-EvolvingHandler** construct and implementing some abstractions, see Subsect. 3.2. Once enabled, a so-called *MgmtThread* is started on process 0, which autonomously manages decision-making and resource adjustments, i.e., starting and releasing processes. The *MgmtThread* continues to run until the programmer calls **disableEvolvingHandler**, i.e., the application is no longer evolving and will no longer adjust its resources. The decision to allocate the *MgmtThread* on process 0 derives from the *APGAS* implementation where process 0 has a special role in the runtime and may never be removed.

In addition, a thread is started on each process that runs a heuristic, see Subsect. 3.3, at a definable interval (every second by default) to measure the computational load. These threads send a value between 0 and 100 to process 0, where the *MgmtThread* evaluates the overall system load. If the overall system load exceeds the **high** program parameter, a process is started; if it falls below the **low** program parameter, the process with the lowest load is released. In

---

[1] https://github.com/ProjectWagomu/APGAS/releases/tag/v0.0.3
https://doi.org/10.5281/zenodo.10730889.

[2] https://github.com/ProjectWagomu/LifelineGLB/releases/tag/v0.0.3
https://doi.org/10.5281/zenodo.10731946.

addition, if a heuristic sends a value of 0 the corresponding process is released, regardless of the overall system load. All this is performed automatically and autonomously by the runtime system.

3.2 Programmer Abstractions

Since both malleable and evolving programs need to adapt to resource changes, we adapted the programmer abstractions from malleable *APGAS* [9]. Programmers must implement the following methods to describe the actions to perform before and after a node addition or removal:

- `List<Place> preShrink(List<Place> placesToRemove)`
- `void postShrink(int nbPlaces, List<Place> removedPlaces)`
- `void preGrow(int nbPlaces)`
- `void postGrow(int nbPlaces, List<Place> continuedPlaces,`
            `List<Place> newPlaces)`

3.3 Heuristics

We propose two heuristics for automatic detection of computational load, where each process periodically sends a value between 0 and 100 to proces 0.

$Heur_{CPU}$ uses CPU load data provided by the operating system. Over the course of a second, it reads the CPU status 20 times at 50 ms intervals. An average of these readings is then calculated to indicate the CPU load for that particular second, helping to smooth out any rapid fluctuations in load levels. If this load is below 1, a timestamp is additionally stored. This timestamp will be referenced later in subsequent intervals to determine whether the load has stayed below 1 for a specified amount of time (10 s by default). If so, 0 is sent to process 0, resulting in the release of that process.

$Heur_{Task}$ takes advantage of the task load knowledge of *GLB*, see Subsect. 3.4. Since *GLB* uses multiple worker threads per process, $Heur_{Task}$ calculates the number of tasks per worker. If this value is greater than 0, it is multiplied by the number of workers (up to a maximum of 100) and sent to process 0.

If the value is 0, a timestamp is additionally stored, similar to $Heur_{CPU}$. This timestamp is used on the next interval call to check if the process has had 0 tasks for a specified amount of time (10 s by default). This approach takes into account that under *GLB*'s load balancing scheme, any process could theoretically receive new tasks at any time. Within the specified amount of time, a value of 0.01 is sent to process 0, but after that, a value of 0 is sent to process 0, resulting in the release of that process.

These two simplistic heuristics are intended as example implementations. For implementations tailored to a specific application, only a provided interface needs to be implemented. The desired heuristic can then be passed as a parameter at program start.

3.4   Example: GLB Library

Since malleable *APGAS* [9] was evaluated using the *Global Load Balancing (GLB)* library and we adopted the programmer abstractions for our new evolving capabilities, we were able to easily adapt *GLB* to be evolving.

In short, *GLB* employs cooperative work stealing to provide automatic load balancing for irregular workloads at runtime. Specifically, a process with no tasks sends a steal request to another process, which either transfers some of its tasks or rejects the request. In addition, *GLB* organizes processes into a small-diameter graph for both work-stealing victim selection and termination detection. To enable evolving capabilities, the abstractions from Subsect. 3.2 are implemented as follows:

- preShrink: disconnect the processes to remove from the graph and reassign their tasks and intermediate results to a continuing process
- postShrink: no operation to perform
- preGrow: no operation to perform
- postGrow: initialize the new processes and make them join the graph

defineEvolvingHandler is called at the beginning of the computation, and the application remains evolving until completion. Our combination of *GLB* and *APGAS* allows evolving resource changes without interrupting the computation.

4   Evaluation

In this section, we experimentally evaluate our evolving *APGAS* and *GLB* implementations. We start by introducing a new benchmark in Subsect. 4.1, followed by evaluating the benefits of evolving capabilities in Subsect. 4.2.

4.1   EvoTree Benchmark

To evaluate the evolving capabilities of *APGAS* and *GLB* under dynamic and highly irregular workloads, we developed a synthetic benchmark based on [18] called *EvoTree*. *EvoTree* provides *smooth weak scaling*—i.e., the work increases with increasing number of (initial) processes—using placeholder computations and mimics situations where real-world evolving applications, e.g. [16,17], which require rapid resource addition or release.

Figure 1 illustrates a possible execution. *EvoTree* initiates with a single task (1), dynamically creating a perfect m-ary task tree during runtime. The rightmost task in the last level (2) generates a sequential branch of configurable length (3). The last task in this sequential branch then starts a second perfect m-ary task tree (4). This scenario challenges both *GLB*'s load balancing and *APGAS*'s evolving capabilities, resulting in numerous process adjustments.

Users of *EvoTree* specify a base computation time $\widehat{T}(p)$. The two perfect m-ary task trees take about $\widehat{T}(p)$ to complete (with p processes), while the sequential branch takes $2 \times \widehat{T}(p)$ (with one process). Consequently, a *fixed* execution

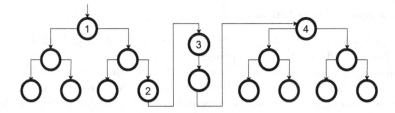

Fig. 1. *EvoTree* benchmark: Example run with two perfect m-ary task trees, each with two children and a depth of three, connected by a sequential branch of two.

takes roughly $T_{fixed}(p) = 4 \times \widehat{T}(p)$. Note that due to the smooth weak scaling of *EvoTree*, the running time for fixed executions remains constant for any number of initial processes. However, due to parallel computations, the sequential branch which starts from the rightmost task in the last level is not guaranteed to be the last computed task in the first tree. Thus, the first part of the sequential branch could be computed in parallel to some tasks of the first tree. In addition, there is some overhead due to load balancing.

EvoTree adeptly determines the most suitable configuration for the trees, encompassing the selection of m and an adjustment to the user-specified *tasks per worker* value. We configured a base computation time of $\widehat{T}(p) = 100s$, approximately 10 million tasks per worker, a task duration variation of 20%, and a sequential branch length of 5000 tasks.

4.2   Experiments

Experiments were conducted on the University of Kassel cluster [6], which provides Infiniband-connected nodes with two 24-core AMD EPYC 7443 CPUs and 256 GB main memory. We allocate one process per node with 48 worker threads each on up to 16 nodes. Java version 19.0.2 was used. We ran *EvoTree* (parameters from Subsect. 4.1), setting `low` to 0.1 and `high` to 0.9, in three configurations:

- *Fixed:* evolving capabilities are disabled, no resource adjustments is made
- $Heur_{CPU}$: evolving capabilities are enabled, $Heur_{CPU}$ is used as the heuristic
- $Heur_{Task}$: evolving capabilities are enables, $Heur_{Task}$ is used as the heuristic

In both $Heur_{CPU}$ and $Heur_{Task}$, the number of nodes used can be increased up to double the initial number of nodes during runtime. Note that this limit was set specifically for these experiments—theoretically, there is no upper limit. An evolving run *without* resource adjustments would therefore take approximately the same time as a fixed run with the same initial number of processes.

Figure 2 shows the average running times for the three configurations, based on 20 runs each. Recall that we set $\widehat{T}(p) = 100s$, which should lead to an estimated duration of about 400 s for *Fixed*. The measurements confirm this, as the running times for *Fixed*, over 1 to 8 initial numbers of nodes (due to smooth

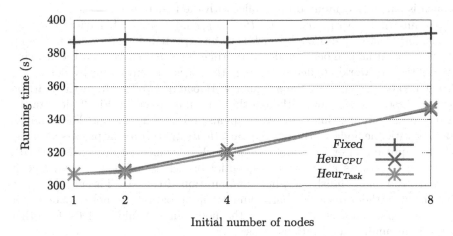

Fig. 2. Running times of *EvoTree* (base computation time $\widehat{T}(p) = 100s$) executed with *Fixed*, *Heur$_{CPU}$*, and *Heur$_{Task}$*. The initial number of nodes/processes is scaled from 1 to 8. For both *Heur$_{CPU}$* and *Heur$_{Task}$*, the maximum number of nodes at runtime can be up to double the initial number.

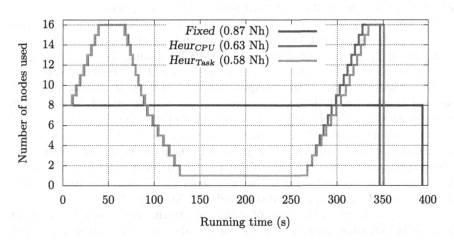

Fig. 3. Time course of resource allocations of *EvoTree* (base computation time $\widehat{T}(p) = 100s$) executed with *Fixed*, *Heur$_{CPU}$*, and *Heur$_{Task}$*. The initial number/processes of nodes is set to 8. For both *Heur$_{CPU}$* and *Heur$_{Task}$*, the maximum number of nodes/processes at runtime can be up to double the initial number. While *Fixed* consumed 0.87 Nh (node-hours, i.e., total node usage), *Heur$_{CPU}$* and *Heur$_{Task}$* consumed 0.63 and 0.58 Nh, respectively.

weak scaling), are about 390 s. The slight difference arises because the sequential branch is partially computed in parallel with the first tree.

We find that both $Heur_{CPU}$ and $Heur_{Task}$ exhibit similar behavior. They are consistently faster than *Fixed*, which is to be expected since they can utilize up to twice the initial number of nodes at runtime. This also shows that the evolving capabilities are working effectively, as both heuristics automatically detect the task generations caused by the irregular workload of *EvoTree* to justify starting new processes. In addition, although this does not appear in Fig. 2, despite the faster overall running times, processes are also released at runtime. For example, starting with one node, both $Heur_{CPU}$ and $Heur_{Task}$ start a new process after 4 s, release a process after 58 s (first tree is finished, sequential branch is started), start a new process after 254 s (sequential branch is finished, second tree is started), and finally finish the whole computation after 303 s. This clearly shows that in this rather obvious scenario, an evolving program can not only be faster by about 80 s, but can also free up the nodes in the middle 200 s for other potentially running applications to use.

Figure 3 illustrates the resource allocation over time for all configurations, starting with eight nodes/processes. Both $Heur_{CPU}$ and $Heur_{Task}$ initially increase the number of processes to 16 as new tasks are generated by the first tree. This increase is stepwise, as currently only one process is started at a time, never multiple at the same time. In addition, starting a process incurs costs for process management and integration into the work-stealing graph. The costs are similar to those in the malleable *APGAS* [9], with about 3 s for *APGAS* process management and about 0.1 s for *GLB* work-stealing integration.

Releasing processes by both $Heur_{CPU}$ and $Heur_{Task}$ starts off similarly. Upon computing the sequential branch, processes are released stepwise. Shrinking incurs similar costs as with malleable *APGAS* [9], taking about 2.7 s for process management and about 0.4 s for moving tasks and intermediate results.

After the midpoint of the computation, the pattern of adding processes between $Heur_{CPU}$ and $Heur_{Task}$ is quite similar, though slightly staggered in time, resulting in a slight shift in the completion of the computation.

Even in this more complex scenario, automatic shrinking and growing are intuitively effective, launching new processes when the workload is large and releasing processes when the workload is insufficient to keep all processes busy. As a result, *Fixed* consumed 0.87 Nh (node-hours, i.e., total node usage), while $Heur_{CPU}$ and $Heur_{Task}$ consumed 0.63 and 0.58 Nh, respectively.

Stepwise scaling and the costs of shrinking/growing contribute to the slight increase in run time with the number of initial nodes for both heuristics, as observed in Fig. 2. Both heuristics need just one node mid-computation, enabling parallel execution of other applications.

Further evaluation is needed to determine the extent to which these heuristics can be used to seamlessly adjust the number of nodes/processes. This could potentially lead to even greater benefits in terms of runtime efficiency and resource utilization. Additionally, advancements like PMIx [12] may drastically lower *APGAS*'s process management overhead to milliseconds.

5   Related Work

A recent comprehensive study on the use of MPI in open-source HPC applications revealed that the process management feature of MPI, involving the creation and communication of new MPI processes, is rarely used [15]. The study attributes this to the syntactical complexity and cumbersomeness involved, including the need to merge multiple intercommunicators. In contrast, this work, along with previous work on malleable *APGAS* [9], introduces easy-to-use programming constructs aimed at facilitating malleable and evolving capabilities, which is considered essential for promoting the wider adoption of resource elasticity.

Although resource elasticity is not yet widespread in supercomputing practice, recent years have witnessed a surge in research interest in this area, leading to the proposal of various resource elasticity techniques and research-based prototypes across different approaches and directions [2, 11].

While programming systems that support user-level resource elasticity remain rare, examples such as ULFM [3], X10 [5,13], and Charm++ [1] stand out. ULFM is primarily designed to handle crashed processes and involves procedures for managing communicators, providing a basic foundation for fault-tolerant libraries. In contrast, Charm++ closely aligns with our approach, enabling elasticity of their independent objects, *chares*, while requiring only some code adjustments [20]. Since *APGAS* is derived from X10, they initially shared commonalities, including basic support for place changes. The malleable *APGAS* extension [9] significantly improves elasticity and usability, while this work introduces novel capabilities for automatic computational load detection, resulting in decisions about when to perform place changes from the perspective of the application.

Research on elastic algorithms has largely centered on iterative workloads, naturally offering convenient synchronization points for adjusting resources [14]. While our evolving *APGAS* requires minimal code additions, it is not limited to iterative workloads, but rather is well suited for dynamic and irregular workloads.

Some research extended existing job schedulers such as Torque [20] and Slurm [14], typically in the form of prototypes tailored to specific combinations of runtime systems and job schedulers. In contrast, while malleable *APGAS* has been evaluated with a job scheduler prototype, this work lacks an evaluation of evolving *APGAS* with a job scheduler. Addressing this gap requires the development of a new "evolving protocol" to enable communication between the job scheduler and evolving jobs. Many complex challenges arise with a fully elastic supercomputer, such as dealing with scenarios where an application requires additional nodes to continue, but no additional nodes are available because all are already assigned to jobs. Not only is this future work, this also emphasizes the importance of a generic elasticity protocol that can ideally be supported by all production job schedulers and runtime systems.

The potential of resource elasticity in AMT programming systems has yet to be fully explored. Previous research allowed the addition of new workers to an X10 *GLB* variant at runtime but lacked the ability to remove them [4]. However, a newer *APGAS GLB* variant supports both addition and removal of places [18] and has seen recent improvements [9]. In this work, we leveraged the latter *GLB* to showcase the ease-of-use of our evolving *APGAS*. Importantly, our proposed evolving capabilities extend beyond *GLB* and can be applied to all *APGAS* applications. To the best of our knowledge, this represents the first easy-to-use AMT providing both malleable and evolving capabilities.

6   Conclusion

In this work, we proposed evolving *APGAS* that allows automatic and transparent resource adjustments in response to changing computational loads at runtime. Our user-friendly abstractions were demonstrated using *GLB*.

For automatic computational load detection, we proposed two heuristics: one using CPU load metrics and the other using task metrics from the considered application. Experiments with a new benchmark showed that both the CPU-based and the task-based heuristic performed well in terms of effectiveness, without a clear winner. Crucially, both heuristics demonstrated their ability to both add processes to speed up the computation, and release nodes in a way that is conducive to their use by other jobs in a supercomputing environment.

Future work will focus on coupling evolving *APGAS* with a job scheduler to allow a comprehensive evaluation of supercomputing metrics such as job throughput and overall efficiency. Additionally, we will expand the evaluations to include more heuristics and real-world applications on a larger number of nodes.

References

1. Acun, B., et al.: Parallel programming with migratable objects: CHARM++ in practice. In: International Conference for High Performance Computing, Networking, Storage and Analysis (SC), pp. 647–658. IEEE (2014). https://doi.org/10.1109/SC.2014.58
2. Aliaga, J.I., Castillo, M., Iserte, S., Martín-Álvarez, I., Mayo, R.: A survey on malleability solutions for high-performance distributed computing. Appl. Sci. **12**(10) (2022). https://doi.org/10.3390/app12105231
3. Bland, W., Bouteiller, A., Herault, T., Bosilca, G., Dongarra, J.: Post-failure recovery of MPI communication capability: design and rationale. Int. J. High Perform. Comput. Appl. **27**(3), 244–254 (2013). https://doi.org/10.1177/1094342013488238
4. Bungart, M., Fohry, C.: A malleable and fault-tolerant task pool framework for X10. In: Proceedings International Conference on Cluster Computing. IEEE (2017). https://doi.org/10.1109/cluster.2017.27
5. Charles, P., et al.: X10: an object-oriented approach to non-uniform cluster computing. SIGPLAN Not. **40**(10), 519–538 (2005). https://doi.org/10.1145/1103845.1094852
6. Competence Center for High Performance Computing in Hessen (HKHLR): Linux Cluster Kassel (2024). https://www.hkhlr.de/en/clusters/linux-cluster-kassel
7. Feitelson, D.G., Rudolph, L.: Toward convergence in job schedulers for parallel supercomputers. In: Feitelson, D.G., Rudolph, L. (eds.) JSSPP 1996. LNCS, vol. 1162, pp. 1–26. Springer, Heidelberg (1996). https://doi.org/10.1007/bfb0022284

8. Finnerty, P., Kamada, T., Ohta, C.: A self-adjusting task granularity mechanism for the Java lifeline-based global load balancer library on many-core clusters. Concurr. Comput. Pract. Experience **34**(2) (2021). https://doi.org/10.1002/cpe.6224

9. Finnerty, P., Posner, J., Bürger, J., Takaoka, L., Kanzaki, T.: On the performance of malleable APGAS programs and batch job schedulers. SN Comput. Sci. (2024). https://doi.org/10.1007/s42979-024-02641-7

10. Finnerty, P., Takaoka, L., Kanzaki, T., Posner, J.: Malleable APGAS programs and their support in batch job schedulers. In: Zeinalipour, D., et al. (eds.) Euro-Par 2023. LNCS, vol. 14352, pp. 89–101. Springer, Cham (2024). https://doi.org/10.1007/978-3-031-48803-0_8

11. Galante, G., da Rosa Righi, R.: Adaptive parallel applications: from shared memory architectures to fog computing. Clust. Comput. **25**(6), 4439–4461 (2022). https://doi.org/10.1007/s10586-022-03692-2

12. Huber, D., Streubel, M., Comprés, I., Schulz, M., Schreiber, M., Pritchard, H.: Towards dynamic resource management with MPI sessions and PMIx. In: European MPI Users' Group Meeting. ACM (2022). https://doi.org/10.1145/3555819.3555856

13. IBM: Elastic X10 (2014). http://x10-lang.org/documentation/practical-x10-programming/elastic-x10.html

14. Iserte, S., Mayo, R., Quintana-Ortí, E.S., Peña, A.J.: DMRlib: easy-coding and efficient resource management for job malleability. Trans. Comput. **70**(9), 1443–1457 (2021). https://doi.org/10.1109/tc.2020.3022933

15. Laguna, I., Marshall, R., Mohror, K., Ruefenacht, M., Skjellum, A., Sultana, N.: A large-scale study of MPI usage in open-source HPC applications. In: International Conference for High Performance Computing, Networking, Storage and Analysis (SC). ACM (2019). https://doi.org/10.1145/3295500.3356176

16. Müller, S., Müller, S.: Adaptive Multiscale Schemes for Conservation Laws (2003). https://doi.org/10.1007/978-3-642-18164-1

17. Plewa, T., Linde, T., Weirs, G.: Adaptive Mesh Refinement - Theory and Applications (2008). https://doi.org/10.1007/b138538

18. Posner, J., Fohry, C.: Transparent resource elasticity for task-based cluster environments with work stealing. In: International Conference on Parallel Processing Workshop, pp. 1–10. ACM (2021). https://doi.org/10.1145/3458744.3473361

19. Posner, J., Hupfeld, F., Finnerty, P.: Enhancing supercomputer performance with malleable job scheduling strategies. In: Zeinalipour, D., et al. (eds.) Euro-Par 2023. LNCS, vol. 14352, pp. 180–192. Springer, Cham (2024). https://doi.org/10.1007/978-3-031-48803-0_14

20. Prabhakaran, S., Neumann, M., Rinke, S., Wolf, F., Gupta, A., Kale, L.V.: A batch system with efficient adaptive scheduling for malleable and evolving applications. In: Proceedings International Parallel and Distributed Processing Symposium (IPDPS), pp. 429–438 (2015). https://doi.org/10.1109/IPDPS.2015.34

21. Saraswat, V., et al.: The asynchronous partitioned global address space model. In: Proceedings SIGPLAN Workshop on Advances in Message Passing (AMP). ACM (2010)

22. Tardieu, O.: The APGAS library: resilient parallel and distributed programming in Java 8. In: Proceedings of the ACM SIGPLAN Workshop on X10, pp. 25–26. ACM (2015). https://doi.org/10.1145/2771774.2771780

23. Zhang, W., et al.: GLB: Lifeline-based global load balancing library in X10. In: Proceedings Workshop on Parallel Programming for Analytics Applications (PPAA), pp. 31–40. ACM (2014). https://doi.org/10.1145/2567634.2567639

Optimizing Parallel System Efficiency: Dynamic Task Graph Adaptation with Recursive Tasks

Nathalie Furmento, Abdou Guermouche, Gwenolé Lucas, Thomas Morin[(✉)],
Samuel Thibault, and Pierre-André Wacrenier

CNRS, Inria, LaBRI, Université de Bordeaux, Bordeaux, France
`thomas.morin@u-bordeaux.fr`

Abstract. Task-based programming models significantly improve the efficiency of parallel systems. The Sequential Task Flow (STF) model focuses on static task sizes within task graphs, but determining optimal granularity during graph submission is tedious. To overcome this, we extend StarPU's STF recursive tasks model, enabling dynamic transformation of tasks into subgraphs. Early evaluations on homogeneous shared memory reveal that this just-in-time adaptation enhances performance.

Keywords: Task-based programming · Granularity · Runtime System

1 Introduction

Heterogeneous architectures play a crucial role in the development of high-performance computers. The effective utilisation and capability to achieve portable performance relies on Runtime Systems (RS). Most of them use task-based parallelism. With this model, the application is represented as a graph of small units of work called tasks. A widely used task-based paradigm is the Sequential Task Flow (STF) model as seen in frameworks like OpenMP, StarPU or StarSs. However, the STF model has some limitations, notably its reliance on sequential task submission. This constraint can pose challenges in dynamically adjusting task granularity during execution. To overcome these issues, we extend the STF model by using recursive task parallelism. A recursive task can either undergo normal execution or be split, transforming into a subgraph of tasks during execution. This extension prompts two critical questions: firstly, the technical implementation of recursive tasks in a Runtime System; and secondly, the determination of which tasks should be split.

The first question has been previously addressed in [3]. In this paper, we focus on addressing the second question by using the recursive tasks of StarPU [1]. Therefore, our contributions in this paper are as follows:

- Introduction of a novel decision-tool, referred to as the splitter, designed to decide which tasks should be split.
- Presentation of a preliminary experimental evaluation that illustrates the potential efficiency of our approach.

P. Diehl et al. (Eds.): WAMTA 2024, LNCS 14626, pp. 166–172, 2024.
https://doi.org/10.1007/978-3-031-61763-8_16

By exploring these aspects, we aim to enhance the understanding of recursive task parallelism within the context of STF models, paving the way for improved adaptability and performance in heterogeneous computing environments.

2 Granularity Challenges Within the STF Model

The STF model relies on sequential consistency to automatically infer dependencies between tasks through the analysis of data accesses. Its capability to streamline the utilisation of heterogeneous machines, combined with its seemingly straightforward design, positions it as a model attracting increased attention. However, it is important to note that this model comes with inherent limitations. Firstly, the submission of large DAGs presents challenges: submitting tasks well before their execution can result in unnecessary system congestion. Attempting to regulate submissions by periodically suspending them is not without risks, as suboptimal submission order may lead to idle periods. Secondly, the utilisation of different types of processing units (PUs) poses challenges, as a one-size-fits-all approach becomes not applicable. GPUs excel with coarse-grained parallelism, while CPUs require finer-grained parallelism to effectively utilise all cores. Thirdly, even with homogeneous computing units, accommodating varying granularities is essential. Large tasks are generally the most efficient, yet transforming such tasks into subgraphs may increase parallelism. Thus, optimising the overall application completion time may entail considering multiple granularities.

To tackle granularity issues, Runtime Systems (RS) can allow a task to be executed on multiple CPU cores, as shown in StarPU [2]. This makes CPUs competitive with GPUs on coarse-grained tasks, but this technique does not create different granularities. Programmers can also submit tasks with varying granularities. However, this manual approach is labour-intensive and does not adapt well to the dynamic nature of the graph, since the optimal granularity may not be known at submission time. Fortunately, RS provide features that enable tasks to become subgraphs at execution time. These contributions can be classified based on their approach to handle heterogeneity, their expression of dependencies, and their methods to manage data. OmpSs [5] introduces weak dependencies to establish fine-grained relationships between tasks and a subgraph. TaskFlow [4] introduces advanced tasking schemes to enable the dynamic generation of task subgraphs. Additionally, ParSEC allows hierarchical Directed Acyclic Graphs (DAGs) to achieve high performance on hybrid distributed systems [6].

Recursive tasks have recently been introduced in StarPU [3], where programmers describe a data hierarchy and submit tasks that can be transformed into DAGs that will work on sub-data. StarPU's key feature is an automatic data manager without spurious synchronisation in a heterogeneous context. In the case of task splitting, the data manager automatically introduces a task called *Partition Task* (PT) to partition the input data for sub-DAG tasks. Conversely, when a task is not split, and the data was previously partitioned, the data

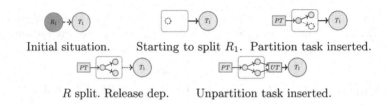

Fig. 1. Recursive task graph processing by StarPU's data manager.

manager automatically introduces an *Unpartition Task* (UT) to wait for output data from sub-DAG tasks and gather them, as illustrated in Fig. 1. On the one hand, we have the *normal* dependencies, related to the dependencies introduced by the sequential consistency. For a recursive task, these are released when the subgraph has been submitted. On the other hand, we have the *recursive* dependencies, which are introduced by *PT* and *UT*.

3   Just-in-Time Task Splitting in StarPU

This section presents the integration of a new component, the splitter, within StarPU's scheduling framework. The role of the splitter is to receive a potential recursive task as input and ascertain whether it evolves into a recursive form or remains a regular task. The submission of the subgraph is then done by a worker. Following this, we address three pivotal questions.

The first question concerns **which** task to split, by identifying the relevant criteria, aiming to optimise the system's overall efficiency. Striking a balance between task efficiency and parallelism is crucial, as coarse-grain parallelism tends to be more efficient but potentially less parallel. To make the decision to split a task, two criteria are considered: the efficiency of the splitting in terms of potential created parallelism and the need for parallelism, particularly when there are a limited number of tasks to complete.

Having determined the parameters that need to be taken into account, the second question focuses on **when** to split tasks. The timing significantly influences the quality of the information used for decision-making. Ensuring the alignment of the recursive task-splitting process with the progression of computations is essential. Splitting tasks too early may overload the system, while delayed decisions may lead to idle periods.

Task-splitting decisions can be made at various stages of the RS workflow, including the submission stage. While splitting at submission minimises overhead, it has two drawbacks: (1) it does not significantly reduce the number of tasks stored in the system, and (2) the decision to split a task could be made far in advance of its execution, lacking comprehensive knowledge of the machine's future state. Hence, it is advantageous to delay the decision-making process until a recursive task has fulfilled all its normal dependencies. However, exercising this precaution alone may not be entirely effective. Let us consider a sequence of recursive tasks denoted as $R_1 \rightarrow R_2 \cdots \rightarrow R_k$. Let us assume that all tasks

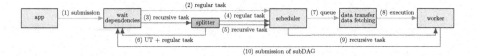

Fig. 2. Scheme of the insertion on existing architecture of our solution. Existing components and paths in orange, added in blue. (Color figure online)

preceding R_k are split. The decision to split R_k can be made before the execution of the subtasks generated by R_1. Without additional safeguards, the splitting decision might occur well before the computation progresses significantly.

Therefore, in order to harmonise the task splitting decision with the computation progress, we have developed a technique to postpone the release of outgoing normal dependencies of a recursive task. Instead of releasing these dependencies immediately after the submission of its subgraph, the release is deferred until the execution of one of its subtasks. Thus, the subgraph submission of a sequence of recursive tasks will occur gradually: a recursive task R_2 following a split recursive task R_1 will remain blocked until the execution of a R_1 subtask.

The third question is related to the design of the RS, specifically determining **where** to place the splitter within the workflow. We have already seen that the splitter component should be placed later than the submit phase. In addition, unlike regular tasks, the execution of a recursive task does not require any data transfer. Therefore, to avoid potentially redundant transfers, it is advisable to make the task splitting decision before the data prefetching stage.

As shown in Fig. 2, we position the splitter at the initial stage of the scheduler. The handling of a recursive task is as follows: upon submission by the application (1), the recursive task is given to the splitter (3) once its dependencies are satisfied. The splitter then takes its decision. If the task requires splitting, it is assigned directly to the scheduler (5), which then places it in the execution queue of a worker (9). The processing of this recursive task results in the submission of a sub-DAG (10). If the task is not split, the recursive task is transformed into a regular task. In the scenario where its data is not split, the regular task can be executed as usual (4). Alternatively, if its data is processed by subtasks at a lower recursive level, an unpartitioning task (6) is automatically submitted to maintain sequential consistency.

4 Study Case: Cholesky Factorisation

In this section, we illustrate our solution on homogeneous systems by making a performance study case with the Cholesky factorisation. The platform has two Intel(R) Xeon(R) Gold 6240 CPU @ 2.60 GHz, having 18 cores each. We compare three tile sizes: the coarse one (1120), the medium one (560) and the fine one (280). A task is split if the number of ready tasks is less than four times the number of cores, and the split efficiency is better than 50%. The locality-aware work-stealing scheduler (*lws*) from StarPU was used for all the experiments.

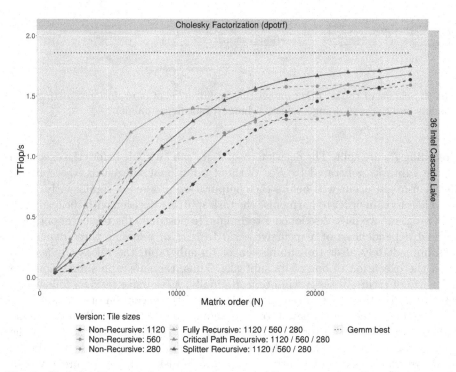

Fig. 3. Cholesky Factorisation performance according to matrix order, tile size and recursive version.

Figure 3 compares the non-recursive version using coarse, medium and fine tile sizes, with recursive versions which choose the granularity dynamically. Three recursive variants are considered : 1) the fully recursive variant where each task is split to the fine granularity (280), 2) the critical path variant where a task is split if it is on the Critical Path, 3) the splitter recursive version relies on the criteria presented above. We observe that our criteria allow a speed-up of approximately 10 % compared to the best non-recursive version (tile size 1120), and a speed-up of 5 % over the Critical Path recursive version. The fully recursive version is the fastest for small matrices because all tasks are split; and with recursive tasks, task submission is parallelised, thus reducing the submission bottleneck. Finally, when comparing small matrix sizes, the splitter-recursive version makes a good trade-off between efficiency and parallelism, and succeeds in obtaining performance close to the best.

Figure 4 shows the available number of floating operations all along the execution of a Cholesky factorisation for a matrix of order 26 880. The colours represent the level of the floating operations, *i.e.* in blue (resp. orange, green), we represent the available floating operations for coarse (resp. medium, fine) grain tasks. We observe that the splitter policy is able to react whenever the number of available operations drops, by creating smaller tasks.

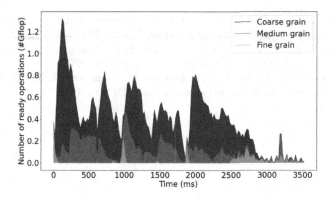

Fig. 4. Evolution of the number of flops during a Cholesky execution for a matrix of order 26 880 according to the task level. (Color figure online)

5   Conclusion

The increasing complexity of computing platforms has led to the development of advanced runtime systems that aim to separate problem expression from execution. Many of these systems use tasks, with some adopting the Sequential Task Flow paradigm. While powerful, this paradigm has limitations that we address by extending StarPU's recursive tasks. This extension allows StarPU to smartly select which tasks to split, and shows promising preliminary results.

Our ongoing efforts aim to extend these results to heterogeneous scenarios where tasks need to be differentiated for CPUs and GPUs. We are investigating three different plans: one optimised for efficiency when tasks are abundant, another that prioritises parallelism in the presence of a slowing-down task on the critical path, and a balanced approach to distribute work based on computational power. Additionally, we are exploring the extension of recursive tasks for a distributed context. We seek to minimise the impact of communication tasks on the runtime system and to dynamically adapt execution strategies.

References

1. Augonnet, C., Thibault, S., Namyst, R., Wacrenier, P.-A.: STARPU: a unified platform for task scheduling on heterogeneous multicore architectures. In: Sips, H., Epema, D., Lin, H.-X. (eds.) Euro-Par 2009. LNCS, vol. 5704, pp. 863–874. Springer, Heidelberg (2009). https://doi.org/10.1007/978-3-642-03869-3_80
2. Cojean, T., Guermouche, A., Hugo, A., Namyst, R., Wacrenier, P.A.: Resource aggregation for task-based Cholesky factorization on top of modern architectures. Parallel Comput. **83**, 73–92 (2019)
3. Faverge, M., et al.: Programming heterogeneous architectures using hierarchical tasks. Concurrency Comput. Pract. Experience **35**(25), e7811 (2023)

4. Huang, T.W., Lin, D.L., Lin, C.X., Lin, Y.: Taskflow: a lightweight parallel and heterogeneous task graph computing system. IEEE TPDS **33**(6) (2022)
5. Perez, J.M., Beltran, V., Labarta, J., Ayguadé, E.: Improving the integration of task nesting and dependencies in OpenMP. In: IPDPS (2017)
6. Wu, W., Bouteiller, A., Bosilca, G., Faverge, M., Dongarra, J.: Hierarchical DAG scheduling for hybrid distributed systems. In: IPDPS (2015)

HPX with Spack and Singularity Containers: Evaluating Overheads for HPX/Kokkos Using an Astrophysics Application

Patrick Diehl[1,2](✉) ⓘ, Steven R. Brandt[1], Gregor Daiß[3], and Hartmut Kaiser[1] ⓘ

[1] Center of Computation and Technology, Louisiana State University, Baton Rouge, USA
{pdiehl,sbrandt,hkaiser}@cct.lsu.edu
[2] Department of Physics and Astronomy, Louisiana State University, Baton Rouge, USA
[3] Institute for Parallel and Distributed Systems, University of Stuttgart, Stuttgart, Germany
Gregor.Daiss@ipvs.uni-stuttgart.de

Abstract. Cloud computing for high performance computing resources is an emerging topic. This service is of interest to researchers who care about reproducible computing, for software packages with complex installations, and for companies or researchers who need the compute resources only occasionally or do not want to run and maintain a supercomputer on their own. The connection between HPC and containers is exemplified by the fact that Microsoft Azure's Eagle cloud service machine is number three on the November 23 Top 500 list. For cloud services, the HPC application and dependencies are installed in containers, *e.g.* Docker, Singularity, or something else, and these containers are executed on the physical hardware. Although containerization leverages the existing Linux kernel and should not impose overheads on the computation, there is the possibility that machine-specific optimizations might be lost, particularly machine-specific installs of commonly used packages. In this paper, we will use an astrophysics application using HPX-Kokkos and measure overheads on homogeneous resources, e.g. Supercomputer Fugaku, using CPUs only and on heterogenous resources, *e.g.* LSU's hybrid CPU and GPU system. We will report on challenges in compiling, running, and using the containers as well as performance differences.

Keywords: C++ · HPX · AMT · Parallelism

1 Introduction

In recent years, cloud computing for high performance computing resources gained more interest. The most recent traction was that Microsoft's Aszure Eagle

P. Diehl et al. (Eds.): WAMTA 2024, LNCS 14626, pp. 173–184, 2024.
https://doi.org/10.1007/978-3-031-61763-8_17

cloud service machine is number three on November 23 Top 500 list. Another example was The Salishan 2023 conference where the gains and losses of HPC applications in the cloud and opportunities and challenges in adopting cloud software technologies for HPC were discussed. In this paper, we use cloud software technologies, like Singularity, to compile and run our astrophysics HPC application. We look into the potential gains of using containers for HPC applications. On the other side, we look into potential losses for using containerization. One common question for containerization is the performance difference compared to running on the host.

Before we can measure any performance differences, we must compile our HPC application. The original workflow was to SSH to the head node and use either module files to load compilers and dependencies and use a standard build system, *e.g.* Cmake or Make. Another option is the usage of Spack or Easy-Build as HPC packet managers (we do not wish to give the impression that the installation of a complex software application is ever easy). However, when using containers, our workflow is different. Our preferred option was to generate a Docker file and compiler Octo-Tiger using Spack. Since Docker requires root permission this step was outsourced to our local machines. The compiled image was converted using singularity build on the cluster.

One attractive property of containerization is that it offers better reproducibility [12]. To reproduce the results in a published paper many details, *e.g.* compiler version, software versions, and input files, must be carefully documented. The Supercomputing (SC) conference series introduced the reproducibility initiative, requiring detailed provenance and documentation on compiling, installing, and running the software [28]. However, sometimes compiler versions and libraries change, for example, due to updates of the supercomputer. If the container is archived, it can be later used to run the HPC application with the same compiler and library versions. Running on the same hardware is a different story if the supercomputer is decommissioned.

The paper is structured as follows: Sect. 2 discusses the related work. Section 3 introduces the software stack. Section 4 emphasizes the workflow to compile and run HPX applications within containers. Section 5 investigates the performance differences. Finally, Sect. 6 concludes the paper.

2 Related Work

There have been many studies of the impact of containers on HPC codes. The performance of Docker containers was studied in [8,29,32,34]. The usage of Docker in HPC applications was studied [2,10,11,22]. A comparison of virtualization and containers was done in [25]. Sarus, a container engine for HPC environments was presented in [6]. The integration of MPI with Docker containers is described in [3,5]. Production runs using containers in biological simulations were conducted in [31]. A representative study of state-of-the-art container solutions (Docker, Podman, Singularity, and Charliecloud) in HPC environments was presented in [1]. Overheads of computation and communication on Linux containers were documented in [30]. However, none of these investigated the overheads for asynchronous many-task runtime systems, like the C++ standard library for parallelism and concurrency (HPX). Other distributed many-task runtime systems that could be studied are Charm++ [24], Unitah [20], Chapel [9], PaRSEC [7], and Legion [4]. For a detailed comparison of these systems (independent of any containerization considerations), we refer to [35].

3   Software Stack

In this section, we give a brief overview of Octo-Tiger, its most important dependencies and the dependency management.

3.1   Notable Octo-Tiger Dependencies

HPX: HPX is an Asynchronous Many-Task Runtime System (AMT) [21]. With it, we can manage data and execution dependencies within Octo-Tiger with a task graph built by using C++ futures and continuations (`hpx::future`). HPX can easily handle millions of tasks, which are being processed by just a few (usually one per CPU core) HPX worker threads. Beyond futures, HPX implements the C++20 API for parallelism and concurrency, for example including functionality such as `hpx::mutex`. HPX also comes with distributed capabilities: We can asynchronously call methods on HPX components residing on other compute nodes, getting futures in return to integrate these calls into the task graph. HPX supports the same syntax and semantics for these remote function calls as for local function calls by using an Active Global Address Space (AGAS) underneath. HPX further offers multiple communication backends, based on either TCP, MPI or LCI. Furthermore, HPX offers tight integrations with CUDA, ROCm and, recently, also SYCL [15], allowing us to integrate asynchronous GPU kernels and CPU/GPU data-transfers into the task graph as well.

Kokkos and HPX-Kokkos: Kokkos is a framework for developing performance-portable compute kernels [37]. With it, we can write a compute kernel once and run it on different execution and memory spaces, depending on the target device. These spaces are available for all major platforms. For example, there are CUDA execution and memory spaces available to target NVIDIA GPUs. Notably, Kokkos also contains an HPX execution space, which allows Kokkos kernels to run on HPX worker threads, eliminating the need for conflicting thread pools (as we would encounter if we tried to use the OpenMP Kokkos execution space in an HPX application). Kokkos also includes SIMD types to allow for explicit SIMD vectorization. These use the appropriate SIMD instructions when instantiated on the CPU (for example AVX512), while keeping the kernel compatible with GPUs by using scalar operations there [33].

HPX-Kokkos is an additional, thin compatibility layer between HPX and Kokkos [14]. Unlike the aforementioned HPX Execution Space within Kokkos (meant for running Kokkos kernels on the HPX worker threads), HPX-Kokkos allows us to treat Kokkos kernels themselves as HPX tasks. This enables us to seamlessly integrate Kokkos kernels into the HPX task graph. This is extremely useful for scheduling asynchronous continuations for Kokkos kernels, post-processing or communicating their results automatically once the respective kernel is done.

By now, all major compute kernels in Octo-Tiger have been ported to Kokkos and support using explicit SIMD vectorization with the aforementioned SIMD types if necessary.

CPPuddle: CPPuddle is a utility library for task-based GPU programming, suited for use with HPX. It provides special allocators for GPU buffers (reusing previous allocations wherever possible) and executors for work aggregation (kernel fusion) which can fuse together similar GPU kernels on-the-fly [17]. Together, they help to avoid GPU device starvation when dealing with a multitude of small GPU kernels, making CPPuddle especially suited for adaptive, tree-based codes like Octo-Tiger.

Other Dependencies: In addition to the aforementioned dependencies, Octo-Tiger requires a number of other frameworks installed. We need hdf5 and silo to handle IO. We further use hwloc and jemalloc for efficiency, and we need Boost for its various utilities. Depending on the machine we target, we also need CUDA, ROCm, or OneAPI (for SYCL) installed. For each of the aforementioned dependencies we also need to handle their respective dependencies. Overall this set of dependencies often leads to us using slightly different dependency versions depending on what machine we run on as we have to work with the given modules and versions.

3.2   Octo-Tiger

Oct-Tiger is an astrophysics application for the simulation of stellar mergers, written in C++ [26]. It simulates binary star systems where a mass transfer between the two stars occurs. Depending on the conditions in these systems, this mass exchange can lead to a merger which in turn can yield various interesting outcomes, such as a Type Ia supernovae. Previously, Octo-Tiger has been used to study R Coronae Borealis stars and the merger of bipolytropic stars [23]. Earlier runs with Octo-Tiger were conducted on Piz Daint [13] and Cori. Currently we are testing the code on Perlmutter and Fugaku [18]. Octo-Tiger's need for computational resources also makes cloud computing, and by extension containers, interesting for us.

Octo-Tiger models stars as self-gravitating, inviscid fluids. Thus, we need two coupled solvers: We employ the Fast-Multipole-Method to get the gravitational field generated by the fluid, and we use finite volumes for the hydrodynamics solver. Octo-Tiger uses an adaptive octree as its data-structure, with the resolution focusing on the atmosphere between the two stars where the mass transfer is happening. For efficiency, each tree-node in Octo-Tiger contains an entire $8\times8\times8$ sub-grid (though this is configurable at compile time).

Octo-Tiger is completely built upon HPX, with each tree-node being an HPX component. HPX was an ideal choice here, as it makes distributed tree-traversals convenient from a developer's standpoint: For instance, we do not need to remember whether a tree child-node is located on the same compute node or not. We can invoke its functions all the same, with HPX taking care of communicating the call to the correct compute node, giving us a future in return. This allows for quickly and asynchronously building a task-graph for each tree-traversal, which crucially helps us to avoid resource starvation by making parallel work available as soon as possible in large, distributed runs.

Together with the performance-portability of the Kokkos kernels, these distributed HPX features allow Octo-Tiger to target both current GPU and CPU supercomputers efficiently.

3.3   Build and Dependendency Management

Legacy Buildscripts: To manage builds with Octo-Tiger and all its dependencies, we previously used a set of custom bash build scripts[1]. However, these build scripts became unwieldy over time as we targeted more machines and platforms, especially since this often meant adding more dependencies (for example, CUDA, ROCm, Kokkos, SYCL or explicit SIMD SVE types for Fugaku). This made the deployment on new Supercomputers possible but bothersome, as we usually had to manually adjust the build scripts yet again for each new machine while trying not to break any of the existing support for other platforms.

Ensuring the reproducibility of builds (and thus of the performance results) was challenging as well, as this involved manually fixing the build scripts to a certain commit, as well as outlining the exact way of invoking the scripts and listing all modules that have to be loaded. An example of this can be seen in the reproducibility appendix of [16].

This ultimately prompted us to look for alternatives, leading us to Spack and, later on, Singularity.

Spack: Spack [19] is a package manager to build and install multiple versions and configurations of software. Spack allows the installation of packages in the user space and is, therefore, widely adopted in the HPC community. Another solution worth mentioning here is *EasyBuild*. However, we decided on Spack due to the flexibility it provides.

Spack expresses a package's variants, dependencies, utilized compiler and target platforms all in one single string called Spack spec. When installing a package, the user provides a spec that allows them to extensively modify the package without having to change the package recipe itself. The Spack concretizer will turn this input spec into a complete, concretized spec (meaning it

---

[1] https://github.com/STEllAR-GROUP/OctoTigerBuildChain.

will discover a compatible set of dependencies that works with the given input spec according to the constraints within all involved packages). This concretized spec will then be built and installed together with its dependencies.

This makes Spack a powerful tool to adjust packages to each machine in question as it allows us to work around problems by, for example, easily switching dependency versions, variants, and compilers or by disabling certain features. For example, the input Spack spec used on Fugaku was:

Listing 1.1. Spack command to compile Octo-Tiger on Supercomputer Fugaku

```
spack -v  install -j 4 octotiger@0.10.0 +kokkos +
    kokkos_hpx_kernels simd_extension=SVE simd_library=
    STD build_type=Release %gcc@12.2.0 ^hpx malloc=
    jemalloc networking=none instrumentation=apex +
    generic_coroutines ^bzip2@1.0.6 ^git@2.39.1 ^silo~
    mpi
```

For brevity, we omit the concretized spec as it contains all dependencies, not just the ones we manually adjusted, and is thus extremely verbose.

Reproducibility is also streamlined with Spack (compared to our custom build scripts), too. We simply need to store the string with the concretized Spack spec for each machine, as well as the Spack version used. Even packages already provided on the system (by modules) will show up in this concretized Spack spec if they have been added as an external package to Spack previously.

One of the contributions of this paper is providing a Spack package for Octo-Tiger: Creating this Spack package for Octo-Tiger was eased by the fact that HPX, Kokkos, and HPX-Kokkos are already available as Spack packages. While we had to adapt those package recipes slightly (mainly to support our SYCL variant), the main chunk of work for this was to create the new CPPuddle and Octo-Tiger Spack package recipes, as they needed to support a multitude of versions and variants.

The new Octo-Tiger package and all our modifications to other Spack packages are available in our Spack repository on GitHub[2]. The Spack package is already in use by our developers both on our local development machines, our university servers and Supercomputers such as Perlmutter and Fugaku. We further integrated the Octo-Tiger Spack package in our CI pipeline as a Jenkins matrix job over a list of tuples, with each tuple consisting of a SLURM command and an associated Spack spec. This provides an easy way of testing all our relevant variants on different machines in a single Jenkins Pipeline.

Singularity: Docker images [27] are widely used as containers. However, most docker commands require root access to be executed. Root access is possible on local development machines but not on HPC resources, like supercomputers or the cloud. Singularity can convert Docker images, however, and already existing

---

[2] https://github.com/G-071/octotiger-spack.

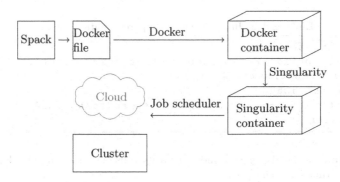

Fig. 1. Workflow to run in containers: A Docker file contains the information of the operating system and Spack instructions to compile Octo-Tiger. We use Docker to generate a Docker container using the Docker file. The Docker container is converted to a Singularity container on the cluster. With singularity, the container can be executed without root access. We use the cluster's job scheduler, *e.g.* slurm, to submit the job within the container.

ones can still be used. Unlike Docker, Singularity does not require root access which is essential for supercomputers or the cloud.

Spack provides experimental support for generating container files from its package recipes. These can be used with Docker and Singularity, which is something we were interested in trying out and will subsequently test in this work as well.

4 Workflow

The simplest way to obtain the singularity file would be to prepare a file `spack.yaml` and use `spack containerize > octotiger.def` to generate the instruction file `octotiger.def`. After that, the command `singularity build --fakeroot octotiger.sif octotiger.def` builds the singularity image. However, we encountered issues with the generated instruction file on Supercomputer Fugaku. One issue was that on Super Computer Fugaku CentOS 8 is required to import the RPM packages for the Fujitsu compiler provided by Riken. However, as of this writing, Spack supports only CentOS 7.[3]. We used the workflow in Fig. 1. First, we generate a Docker file where we specify the operating system of the Docker image and use our new Spack package to compile Octo-Tiger. We use singularity to convert the Dockerfile into a Singularity file. We use the job scheduler to run Octo-Tiger within the Singularity image. The same singularity image could be executed in the cloud or the HPC cluster. However, cloud resources were not the scope of this paper. Listing 1.2 shows the instructions to generate the singularity file from a Docker image and run Octo-Tiger in the image on Supercomputer Fugaku.

---

[3] https://spack.readthedocs.io/en/latest/containers.html.

Listing 1.2. Instructions on Supercomputer Fugaku

```
1 # Generating the image
2 singularity build -F /worktmp/wamta24.simg docker://
    stevenrbrandt/wamta24:arm64
3 # Running the image
4 singularity exec --bind /worktmp/ /worktmp/wamta24.simg bash
    octotiger
```

Table 1. Statistics for the regular and singularity runs on Supercomputer Fugaku. We executed ten runs for each option.

	Min Time	Median Time	Average Time	Max Time	Standard derivation
Singularity	267.5	277.3	277.1	286.8	6.2
Regular	214.1	215.2	221.1	237.6	9.8

4.1 Challenges in Compiling and Running Within Containers

We identified the following challenge on Supercomputer Fugaku. First, on Fugaku the Fusitju compiler and MPI wrapper are available. The user can not easily install these. Riken provides some Docker images and RPM packages to install these packages. However, we use the GCC compiler since the Fusitju compiler does not support C++ 17 which is required for Octo-Tiger and HPX. We have the same issue with compiling Octo-Tiger before and this issue is not related to containerization. So adding vendor-specific compilers, *e.g.* Cray Compiling Environment (CCE) or IBM's compiler for Power architecture, were not trivial tasks. Second, the Docker image needs to be generated on the host architecture. A challenge was here that we had no access to an A64FX machine with Docker to compile the image. We used Docker's buildx command with support for Linux/arm64 provided by Docker to generate an A64FX-based image. However, Docker's buildx uses cross-compilation for the A64FX-based image. According to the documentation[4] there is cross-compilation support in Spack. However, we encountered build issues and built Octo-Tiger without Kokkos support using CMake.

5   Performance Differences

There is no free lunch. To investigate the overheads introduced by Singularity images on HPC clusters, we compiled the same version of Octo-Tiger and all its dependencies using spack. The versions used on both supercomputers are documented in the supplementary materials using **spack concretize**. First, we compile Octo-Tiger without any container on the node. Second, we compile Octo-Tiger within Docker. After that, we run the rotating star example on the node directly and within the image.

---

[4] https://spack.readthedocs.io/en/latest/features.html.

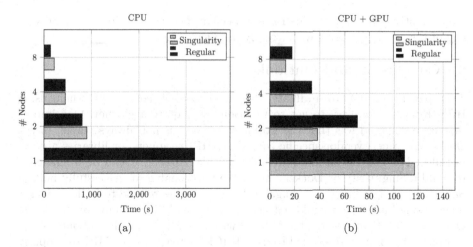

Fig. 2. Comparison of regular and singularity runs on DeepBayou using CPUs (a) and CPUs + GPUs (b).

5.1 Supercomputer Fugaku (A64FX)

On Supercomputer Fugaku, we only present single-node scaling. For the distributed runs additional effort was required to add Fusitju MPI with Tofu-D support to the Singularity container. Table 1 shows the statistics out of ten regular and ten singularity runs. We observed that the regular runs were on average 50 s faster. The standard derivation is slightly higher for the regular runs.

5.2 DeepBayou

Deep Bayou is a small GPU cluster hosted at LSU with two 24-core Intel Xeon Gold 6248R CPUs and two NVIDIA V100S GPUs per node. Here, we used spack to compile Octo-Tiger with Kokkos support for NVIDIA GPUs. Figure 2a shows the measurements using the CPUs without GPUs. For most runs, we observe that the computation time is comparable. Figure 2b shows the measurements on a single node up to eight nodes using the CPUs and GPUs. For the CPU runs both versions are on par, however, for the GPU runs the singularity runs were faster. This has been observed for other runs as well [36]. We are using the default performance parameters without further tuning them for the platform or GPU architecture. We note that it was far less challenging to get the code running on Deep Bayou as we were able to use Spack for both the image and the native build to compile.

The CPU-only runs with one node appear to be an anomaly: Here we are slower than expected, both for the regular run and for the singularity run. However, this does only happen in the CPU runs with one node, not in any of the other runs. The other CPU runs with two or more nodes running as expected (causing a super linear speedup when going from one node to two nodes). We are currently investigating this issue, especially because we do not see this on any of the other platforms we currently use Octo-Tiger.

6   Conclusion and Outlook

This paper set out to evaluate the overheads of containers when using HPX/Kokkos. However, to get to this point was quite a journey. One important lesson learned was that the workflow in Fig. 1 is not always viable. In the Docker container, vendor-specific compilers, MPI wrappers, or libraries are not installed. For nonconventional architecture, like A64FX, it can be a challenge to build a Singularity or Docker image. We were unable to successfully build a Singularity image directly on Fugaku, however, we were able to build a docker image using buildx (but could not get Spack to work in that environment). On Queen Bee 3 (qbc) we were able to build with Spack both inside and outside the container, but found we needed to use MPICH instead of OpenMPI to properly interface with LSU Slurm. After struggling with building, on the other hand, running the containers was a walk in the park. For the performance difference due to potential overheads, we observed that on Supercomputer Fugaku the regular runs were faster. On DeepBayou for CPU runs, there was not much difference. However, for CPU and GPU runs, we identified some differences on a single node, but all distributed runs in the container crashed.

We conclude that containers offer benefits for reproducibility, porting, and running HPC applications, but building in a container is not always easier. While performance on Fugaku did benefit from running outside the container, the gains in reproducibility and documentation of the build process probably outweigh them.

For future work, we would to get the Fusitju MPI to interface with the container and do distributed runs. For the runs with GPUs, more investigation into why we observe the performance difference is needed. In addition, we would expand our study to larger GPU-based supercomputers such as NERSC's Perlmutter.

Supplementary Materials

All scripts are available on GitHub (https://github.com/diehlpkpapers/dockerizeHPX).

Acknowledgments. Funded partly by NSF #229751: POSE: Phase 1: Constellation: A Pathway to Establish the STE——AR Open-Source Organization. Computational resources of the Supercomputer Fugaku provided by the RIKEN Center for Computational Science were used.

References

1. Abraham, S., et al.: On the use of containers in high performance computing environments. In: 2020 IEEE 13th International Conference on Cloud Computing, pp. 284–293 (2020)

2. Alles, G.R., et al.: Assessing the computation and communication overhead of Linux containers for HPC applications. In: 2018 Symposium on High Performance Computing Systems, pp. 116–123. IEEE (2018)

3. Azab, A.: Enabling docker containers for high-performance and many-task computing. In: 2017 IEEE International Conference on Cloud Engineering, pp. 279–285 (2017)

4. Bauer, M., et al.: Legion: expressing locality and independence with logical regions. In: SC2012: Proceedings of the International Conference on High Performance Computing, Networking, Storage and Analysis, pp. 1–11. IEEE (2012)

5. de Bayser, M., et al.: Integrating MPI with docker for HPC. In: 2017 IEEE International Conference on Cloud Engineering, pp. 259–265 (2017)

6. Benedicic, L., Cruz, F.A., Madonna, A., Mariotti, K.: Sarus: highly scalable docker containers for HPC systems. In: Weiland, M., Juckeland, G., Alam, S., Jagode, H. (eds.) ISC High Performance 2019. LNCS, vol. 11887, pp. 46–60. Springer, Cham (2019). https://doi.org/10.1007/978-3-030-34356-9_5

7. Bosilca, G., et al.: Parsec: exploiting heterogeneity to enhance scalability. Comput. Sci. Eng. **15**(6), 36–45 (2013)

8. Casalicchio, E., Perciballi, V.: Measuring docker performance: what a mess!!! In: Proceedings of the 8th ACM/SPEC on International Conference on Performance Engineering Companion, pp. 11–16 (2017)

9. Chamberlain, B.L., et al.: Parallel programmability and the chapel language. Int. J. High Perform. Comput. Appl. **21**(3), 291–312 (2007)

10. Chung, M.T., Quang-Hung, et al.: Using Docker in high performance computing applications. In: 2016 IEEE Sixth International Conference on Communications and Electronics, pp. 52–57 (2016)

11. Chung, M.T., et al.: Using docker in high performance computing applications. In: 2016 IEEE Sixth International Conference on Communications and Electronics, pp. 52–57. IEEE (2016)

12. Courtes, L.: Reproducibility and Performance: why choose? Comput. Sci. Eng. **24**(03), 77–80 (2022)

13. Daiß, G., et al.: From piz daint to the stars: simulation of stellar mergers using high-level abstractions. In: Proceedings of the International Conference for High Performance Computing, Networking, Storage and Analysis. SC 2019, ACM, New York, NY, USA (2019)

14. Daiß, G., et al.: Beyond fork-join: integration of performance portable Kokkos kernels with HPX. In: 2021 IEEE International Parallel and Distributed Processing Symposium Workshops, pp. 377–386. IEEE (2021)

15. Daiß, G., et al.: Stellar mergers with hpx-kokkos and SYCL: methods of using an asynchronous many-task runtime system with SYCL. In: Proceedings of the 2023 International Workshop on OpenCL. ACM, New York, NY, USA (2023)

16. Daiß, G., et al.: From merging frameworks to merging stars: experiences using HPX, Kokkos and SIMD types. In: 2022 IEEE/ACM 7th International Workshop on Extreme Scale Programming Models and Middleware, pp. 10–19. IEEE, Los Alamitos, CA, USA (2022)

17. Daiß, G., et al.: From task-based gpu work aggregation to stellar mergers: turning fine-grained CPU tasks into portable GPU kernels. In: 2022 IEEE/ACM International Workshop on Performance. Portability and Productivity in HPC, pp. 89–99. IEEE, Los Alamitos, CA, USA (2022)

18. Diehl, P., et al.: Simulating Stellar Merger using HPX/Kokkos on A64FX on Supercomputer Fugaku (2023)

19. Gamblin, T., et al.: The Spack package manager: bringing order to HPC software chaos. In: Proceedings of the International Conference for High Performance Computing, Networking, Storage and Analysis, pp. 1–12 (2015)
20. Germain, J.D.D.S., et al.: Uintah: a massively parallel problem solving environment. In: Proceedings the Ninth International Symposium on High-Performance Distributed Computing, pp. 33–41. IEEE (2000)
21. Hartmut, K., et al.: HPX-the C++ standard library for parallelism and concurrency. J. Open Source Softw. **5**(53), 2352 (2020)
22. Higgins, J., et al.: Orchestrating docker containers in the HPC environment. In: Kunkel, J.M., Ludwig, T. (eds.) ISC High Performance 2015. LNCS, pp. 506–513. Springer, Cham (2015). https://doi.org/10.1007/978-3-319-20119-1_36
23. Kadam, K., et al.: Numerical simulations of mass transfer in binaries with bipolytropic components. MNRAS **481**(3), 3683–3707 (2018)
24. Kale, L.V., Krishnan, S.: Charm++ a portable concurrent object oriented system based on C++. In: Proceedings of the Eighth Annual Conference on Object-Oriented Programming Systems, Languages, and Applications, pp. 91–108 (1993)
25. Li, Z., et al.: Performance overhead comparison between hypervisor and container based virtualization. In: 2017 IEEE 31st International Conference on Advanced Information Networking and Applications, pp. 955–962 (2017)
26. Marcello, D.C., et al.: Octo-Tiger: a new, 3D hydrodynamic code for stellar mergers that uses HPX parallelization. MNRAS **504**(4), 5345–5382 (2021)
27. Merkel, D., et al.: Docker: lightweight linux containers for consistent development and deployment. Linux j **239**(2), 2 (2014)
28. Plale, B.A., Malik, T., Pouchard, L.C.: Reproducibility practice in high-performance computing: community survey results. Comput. Sci. Eng. **23**(05), 55–60 (2021)
29. Rad, B.B., et al.: An introduction to docker and analysis of its performance. Int. J. Comput. Sci. Netw. Secur. **17**(3), 228 (2017)
30. Rezende Alles, G., et al.: Assessing the computation and communication overhead of Linux containers for HPC applications. In: 2018 Symposium on High Performance Computing Systems, pp. 116–123 (2018)
31. Rudyy, O., et al.: Containers in HPC: a scalability and portability study in production biological simulations. In: 2019 IEEE International Parallel and Distributed Processing Symposium, pp. 567–577 (2019)
32. Saha, P., et al.: Evaluation of Docker containers for scientific workloads in the cloud. In: Proceedings of the Practice and Experience on Advanced Research Computing. PEARC 2018, ACM, New York, NY, USA (2018)
33. Sahasrabudhe, D., Phipps, E.T., Rajamanickam, S., Berzins, M.: A portable SIMD primitive Using Kokkos for heterogeneous architectures. In: Wienke, S., Bhalachandra, S. (eds.) WACCPD 2019. LNCS, vol. 12017, pp. 140–163. Springer, Cham (2020). https://doi.org/10.1007/978-3-030-49943-3_7
34. Sparks, J.: Enabling docker for HPC. Concurrency Comput. Pract. Exp. **31**(16), e5018 (2019)
35. Thoman, P., et al.: A taxonomy of task-based parallel programming technologies for high-performance computing. J. Supercomput. **74**(4), 1422–1434 (2018)
36. Torrez, A., et al.: HPC container runtimes have minimal or no performance impact. In: 2019 IEEE/ACM International Workshop on Containers and New Orchestration Paradigms for Isolated Environments in HPC, pp. 37–42 (2019)
37. Trott, C.R., et al.: Kokkos 3: programming model extensions for the Exascale era. IEEE Trans. Parallel Distrib. Syst. **33**(4), 805–817 (2022)

Author Index

P. Diehl et al. (Eds.): WAMTA 2024, LNCS 14626, pp. 185–186, 2024.
https://doi.org/10.1007/978-3-031-61763-8

Printed in the United States
by Baker & Taylor Publisher Services